SEEDTIME
FOR FASCISM

FRANZ'JOSEPH'I

SEEDTIME
FOR FASCISM
THE DISINTEGRATION
OF AUSTRIAN POLITICAL
CULTURE, 1867-1918

GEORGE V. STRONG

M.E. Sharpe
Armonk, New York
London, England

Photo, p. ii: Portrait of Kaiser Franz Joseph I painted by Wilhelm List, 1904–06.
Courtesy of the Österreichische Postparkasse, Vienna.

Library of Congress Cataloging-in-Publication Data

Strong, George V., 1933–
Seedtime for fascism : the disintegration of Austrian political culture,
1867–1918 / George V. Strong.
p. cm.
Includes bibliographical references and index.
ISBN 0–7656–0189–3 (alk. paper). — ISBN 0–7656–0190–7 (pbk. : alk. paper)
1. Political culture—Austria. 2. Austria—Politics and government—1867–1918.
3. Nationalism—Austria. 4. Austria—Ethnic relations. 5. Socialism—Austria—
History—19th century. 6. Conservatism—Austria—History—19th century. I. Title.
JN2012.3.S85 1998
306.2'09436'09034—DC21
97–30245
CIP

Printed in the United States of America

The paper used in this publication meets the minimum requirements of
American National Standard for Information Sciences—
Permanence of Paper for Printed Library Materials,
ANSI Z 39.48-1984.

MV (c) 10 9 8 7 6 5 4 3 2 1
MV (p) 10 9 8 7 6 5 4 3 2 1

To Ellen,
the brightest light in my life

Contents

SEEDTIME
FOR FASCISM

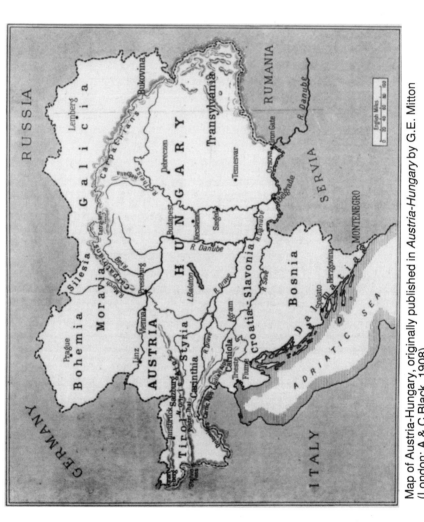

Map of Austria-Hungary, originally published in *Austria-Hungary* by G.E. Mitton (London: A & C Black, 1908).

✧ 1 ✧

A Framework of Reference

A study of the political culture that took hold in Austria-Hungary after 1850 has relevance for Americans today in that the history of the Dual Monarchy may be viewed as a failed experiment by a state that attempted to sustain itself by reconstructing itself on the basis of its newly discovered cultural diversity. It needs no saying that today cultural diversity is an issue all Americans face. What this issue will bring to Americans cannot be foreseen. But old Austria, for her part, never found a formula whereby her diversity might be accommodated; granting its disparate parts civil recognition within a popular and liberal political framework brought about a fatal balkanization of the state as a whole, and so the state ultimately disintegrated into various combinations of its components under circumstances that robbed old Austria's inhabitants of the fruits of her vibrant civilization.

There is yet another compelling reason why the workings of the Dual Monarchy during the era of Franz Joseph both fascinate and perplex historians. It would seem that almost every symptom of the societal ailments that bedeviled the European twentieth century (and indeed those who lived beyond Europe's shores) was to be found enmeshed in the glitter and decadence of Austrian culture. On the political plane, one sees the rise of the prototype of modern mass political parties, fused along ideological lines and thereby creating a turgid and turbulent atmosphere founded on the politics of victimization and loud demands for the blood of scapegoats.[1] One heard at the same time, often but not exclusively linked with this politicization of the masses, the sanguine rhetoric of prejudice on the basis of race and gender.[2] One also heard voices calling for rough-hewn dictatorship as a solution to the seeming disintegration of things.[3] It is not easy to overlook that the future führer of the Third Reich fabricated many of his preposterous views between the years 1907 and 1913 while walking the streets of Franz Joseph's imperial city.[4] Moreover, Benito Mussolini and both Lenin and Stalin knew Vienna before they made their dolorous appearances on Clio's stage. It was in Vienna that Sigmund Freud destroyed the older assumptions of the fundamental perfectibility of human nature with his ideas of our primeval drives motivated by an insufficiently repressed subconscious; at least in the view of some, this rendered the belief in forgiveness and resurrection irrelevant to life, even relegating it to the dustbin as the superstition of an outworn past. Further, Vienna's spheres of artistic creation, whether in drama, music, or art, witnessed challenges from experimental subgroups at least in part propelled by Freudian assumptions that, whatever their individual merits, generated immense antagonism and rippled through the many complex layers of Austrian society. And of course all this cacophony in the political, intellectual, and artistic spheres of activity was accompanied by social misery and individual degradation in both the agricultural and industrial sectors of Austrian life, generated by the impact of capital and technology as these destroyed the traditional ways of the old rooted communities. It would make a happy ending nonetheless if one could point to some signs of resolution out of these horrendous developments. But one cannot. The era of Franz Joseph ended in the most complete catastrophe: the outbreak of world war, in which young men once prized for being made in the image of God were transformed into common cannon fodder, and which led to the disintegration of the promises and potential not only of Austrian civilization but of Europe's as well.[5]

These losses, it might be added, were an unintended result of the activities of a diverse mix of political reformers and dreamers, extending from Austrian socialists such as Otto Bauer and Karl Renner to the American president Woodrow Wilson. But then too, the glittering civilization lost in 1918 itself was the unintended result of self-interested state-building activity by a diverse group of adventurers operating prior to the eighteenth century in the lands that came to be a part of the Habsburg realm. Indeed, the end results of historical causality are most often unintended, because of the complexity of the impact of causality on events. But this is not to say that nothing can be learned from history. And so the outcome of Austria's confrontation with her diversity should be a compelling reason why twenty-first-century Americans, being driven to embark on social experimentation of their own, might wish to read the history of Austria-Hungary.

Because of its unique evolution so as to include eleven different nations, the issue of multiculturalism in Austria-Hungary brings up the question of how a state might accommodate cultural nationalism. During the era of Emperor Franz Joseph I, this issue unfolded so as to underscore the inherent tension that inevitably exists not only between nations and the concept of modern parliamentary unitary states, but among nations themselves, living ad hoc under stately umbrellas created out of impersonal historical processes. But because Austria failed to contain the chauvinistic striving that was driving her nations toward cultural fulfillment, not only did this failure bring about the collapse of the state, but the historical processes involved played a primary role in the unleashing of the twentieth century's two great catastrophes: the First and Second World Wars. It requires no retelling that the first of these cataclysms was sparked by the assassination of the Austrian-Hungarian heir to the throne in the Bosnian capital, Sarajevo, by the Serb nationalist Gavrilo Princip. Neither does it require retelling that World War II was unleashed in great part because of the latent violence that continued to live within and among those nations that had shared in old Austria, long after the old state had departed from the world stage.

The following chapters must be understood within the framework of not only the general values of the era but also Austria-Hungary's stratagems as it played its role in the great power game and the impact of the prosperity emanating from the era of industry and capital on the experiences and perception of Franz Joseph's people. It is our understanding of our experience within the parameters of society's general values that generates perception. Perception thereby shapes general culture, including the political culture that drives politics.

The fabrication of the political culture of Austria-Hungary parallels the Dual Monarchy's political history, while at the same time it drove that history. But it propelled it in symbiotic fashion; that is, while culture drives politics, the end result of political developments, in turn, gives color to political culture. Hence, the ambience of a given political culture must be comprehended within the framework of political history for the Dual Monarchy, especially its international dimension.

Austria-Hungary, which strictly speaking was constituted only in 1867, has its genesis in the events that destroyed the German Confederation founded at the Congress of Vienna in 1815. This destruction resulted from Prussian actions during the years 1862–1866, and especially those inspired by its prime minister, Otto von Bismarck, which brought about the creation of the North German Confederation. Indeed, it was this Prussian-inspired German civil war, the Seven Weeks' War of 1866, that forced Austria to take her German territories (along with her rights as one of the confederation's sovereign powers) out of Germany, thereby destroying the German Confederation. This action left the bulk of the remaining German territories under Prussia's thumb, and hence fodder for the agenda set forth in the name of its Berlin resident dynasty, the House of Hohenzollern. It was out of the mostly Protestant territories among them that Prussian policy fashioned the North German Confederation, which stood until, in turn, it was replaced at the conclusion of the Franco-Prussian War in 1871 by the Protestant and Catholic German Second Reich.

In the meanwhile, the Austrian Empire, having been so proclaimed in 1806 under the press of defeat during the Napoleonic wars and sanctified in 1815 at the Congress of Vienna, underwent several permutations during the decades following 1815 in an unsuccessful search for her political equilibrium within the general European settlement to the wars of the French Revolution. It was the shattering of this elusive equilibrium that propelled the nineteen-year-old Franz Joseph to the throne in 1848, his elevation played out on December 2 in the somber and depressed ambience of Olmütz (today's Olomouc), where the imperial family had taken refuge from the rebellious Viennese. As Franz Joseph was a mere stripling, his youthful but shy self-confidence matched only by his inexperience, the real mover of events was Franz Joseph's first minister, Prince Felix Ludwig zu Schwarzenberg. The prince was unmoved by those liberal and popular aspirations that had been articulated in the politics of the revolutions of 1848. Moreover, Schwarzenberg was determined, if pragmatic, and comprehended completely what could be achieved through the ruthless use of political power. By 1850 the German Confederation with Austria at its center was back in place. Further, the return of the House of Habsburg to the tenets of absolutism had put an end to Austria's previous flirtation with popular political institutions. If the prince had not died suddenly in 1852, there is no telling what he might have achieved for his sovereign. But as it was, while really unready for the exercise of power, the twenty-two-year-old monarch determined that he would rule in his mentor's stead. And so the years 1852–1859 turned out to be ones of enervating political experimentation for Austria. For example, toward affairs abroad, Austrian neo-absolutism exhibited deplorable vacillation. The resultant loss of potential support from the Russian czar emboldened Prussian aspirations for hegemony in Germany; worse, the young Franz Joseph managed to enmesh Austria in a hopeless struggle in Italy against both the forces of nationalist Piedmont and the wily machinations of Louis Napoleon Bonaparte. The end result was Austria's loss of the rich province of Lombardy and the general weakening thereby of her position in Mitteleuropa. It was these circumstances that forced the shelving of neo-absolutism and the advent, albeit at first very limited, of constitutional monarchy through the handing down of two imperial rescripts (patents) in October of 1860 and February of 1861. It was while the state structure was in the process of assimilating these changes, and in the face of Vienna's insistence that Austria remain a unitary state (which angered her un-happy Magyar subjects in Hungary), that Otto von Bismarck drew Franz Joseph into what proved to be the disastrous Seven Weeks' War during June and July of 1866.[6] This humiliation at the hands of Berlin forced the government of Austria's Emperor Franz Joseph I to face up to a long-simmering dispute be-tween his government and his Magyar subjects concerning the House of Habsburg's sovereign pretensions over the ancient Kingdom of Hungary. The end result of negotiations between Vienna and Budapest was the *Ausgleich,* a constitutional compromise between the emperor in Vienna and the Magyar lead-ership in Budapest that yielded that cumbersome stately device known as Aus-tria-Hungary, generally referred to as the Dual Monarchy.[7]

The construction of the Dual Monarchy aimed at achieving several objectives that fundamentally were at odds with one another. It aimed to preserve the monarchical authority of the dynasty, the House of Habsburg-Lorraine, but framed that authority within a halfhearted liberal-style constitution and its conse-quent legal parameters. Nevertheless, it did permit a significant slice of Austria's haute bourgeoisie resident in these lands to participate, if in a limited manner, in the dual state's political decision-making processes. Further, this constitution was designed to buttress those traditional elements, their roots in the realm's variegated feudal past, that had most often supported the monarchy down through the centuries in both halves of the realm; that is, the magnates in Hung-ary and the aristocrats and gentry in Austria. But at the same time, mostly by means of weighted voter qualification, it thereby willy-nilly brought into its political processes those activist elements whose self-image and confidence rested on the Dual Monarchy's waxing industrial and capitalistic development. And although it divided the state so that there were two capitals and two ministries, it also sought to maintain the leverage of a single state, necessary if Austria-Hungary was to play a continuing great-power role in the international sphere. So the two halves were joined, not only through the powerful traditions surrounding the ruling Habsburg sovereign, but also on the basis of a joint ministry for finance, war, and foreign affairs and the possession of a common army in which German, albeit a kind of "pig German," was the sole language of command. In addition, there was a third, perhaps incipient legislative body, the House of Delegates, that met to represent the views of the parliaments belonging to the two parts of the whole. The *Ausgleich,* in addition, required a negotiated tariff and general financial settlement for the operation of the Dual Monarchy, a vexatious provision requiring renegotiation once every ten years.[8] Nevertheless, the divided realm was joined together by more than a personal union through the monarch and, at least in 1867, it was hoped that this incipient constitutional infrastructure would lead to more intricate development over the years that really would fuse Austria's parts together into a workable whole. These hopes did not entirely succeed, although neither was this cooperation a complete failure, especially when consideration is given to the fact that the *Ausgleich* was attempting to join together in cooperation two quite different peoples with quite different political experiences and hence perspectives; added to this, the two nations together were to hold sway over the other nine, less articulate nations residing in Austria.

The weakness of the *Ausgleich,* and perhaps its fatal flaw, was that it provided that only Austria's German and Magyar nations be the nations of state. That is, only the German and Magyar languages were to be the languages of civil discourse in their respective halves of the Dual Monarchy. It did not provide for the accommodation of the waxing chauvinistic instincts of the nine other nations residing in the dual state. This lack was not only because of the political ramifications of overweening Magyar (and to a lesser extent, German) chauvinism, but also simply because of the Vienna government's blind eye toward the sensitivities of these other nations.[9] At that time Europe in general was undergoing the growth and spread of nationalism, and it was this lack of accommodation that gave rise to the very fractious issue known as the nationality question.[10]

The Dual Monarchy added to the internal stresses and strains generated out of the *Ausgleich* because external political constellations drove it to continue Austria's role as a great-power player in Europe. To be sure, the power game as played by Vienna was far less aggressive than that of Great Britain, France, Germany, or even the Russian Empire.[11] This restraint, however, was less an expression of will than a reflection of Austria-Hungary's inherent lack of cohesion (because of the nationality question). But even though Vienna's game was defensive, in favor of the status quo, there were nevertheless sufficient difficulties in this stance to embroil the Dual Monarchy in the most dangerous of international political currents.[12]

Austria-Hungary was especially bedeviled by the ramifications of the loosening of the Ottoman Empire's hold over her Balkan lands in the course of the nineteenth century. The collapse of Istanbul's rule over these Slavic subjects, because it was accompanied on all sides by both the rhetoric and bloody deeds of chauvinism, gave an opening to the greatest of Europe's Slav powers, the Russian Empire, to herald St. Petersburg as protector of her weaker Slavic sisters from their enemies. Thereby too an opening was presented where Russia might occupy the Balkans—if not directly, at least in the sense of spheres of influence. This development overflowed into Austria's internal and external concerns due to the fact that many of her peoples were Slavic and not inured to the irredentist nationalist appeals generated by strife in the Balkans but packaged with the political interests of the self-appointed Russian standard bearer. These developments ultimately led both Vienna and Berlin to see that they had common interests vis-à-vis the Russian Empire; further, it caused the Dual Monarchy to swallow memories of the humiliation of Austrian arms by Prussia's at Königgrätz, where Berlin had sealed her victory over the German Confederation during the Seven Weeks' War in July of 1866. The result of this new modus vivendi between Berlin and Vienna was the famous 1879 Dual Alliance, whereby the German chancellor, Otto von Bismarck, sought to prop up Austria-Hungary in the face of Slavic resurgence with what was at bottom a kind of refabrication of the old German Confederation in the form of an Austrian-German axis. This cooperation continued to operate until the defeat and extinction of both powers in 1918 but, at least during the years between 1879 and 1903, in a way that gave Vienna to understand that she was the junior partner. The Austrians understood that they could relax in the face of the uneasiness generated by Russian-led pan-Slavism only because behind Austria stood the vaunted might of the German *Reich*.

A change in the nuances of the seemingly enduring Dual Alliance came after 1903, when a gory palace revolution in Belgrade brought the fall of the Serb Obrenović dynasty and the rise of the rival Karageorgević regime. With the Obrenovićs went a dynasty that was willing to live, albeit grudgingly, within the status quo with Austria-Hungary; in came a government that was both out-and-out Austrophobic and expansionist. It was the Karageorgević regime that articulated the greater Serb idea whereby south-central Europe's Croats, Slovenes, and Serbs would be fused, by hook or by crook, into a single Yugoslav monarchy under the Karageorgević scepter. Moreover, Belgrade insisted upon Russia's commitment to this agenda, thereby bringing to a boil that always simmering antipathy between St. Petersburg and Vienna as well as that between German and Slav in the south-central and east European living space. These changes in the Austrian-Serbian posture were concurrent with the period in which relations between Europe's preeminent powers, Great Britain and the German *Reich,* were in rapid deterioration due to their worldwide economic and imperial rivalries. Moreover, clumsily operated German foreign initiatives had resulted in Berlin's near diplomatic isolation by her clever British and French opponents. Further, the then evolving diplomatic constellation, the Triple Entente, highlighted by cooperation among the British, French, and Russians (to be completed by 1907), implicitly pitted its members against Austria and Germany and less so against the notoriously unreliable Italian kingdom, which had joined the Dual Alliance in 1882, making it the Triple Alliance. These circumstances, in turn, rendered Austria-Hungary as Berlin's only dependable ally among the great powers in Europe. Hence, whereas before 1903 one might have said that it was the German dog that wagged the Austrian tail, after 1903 the opposite became true, with the result that the Dual Monarchy's flaws, stemming from its nationality question, had become real liabilities for Germany's great-power position in the game of international politics.[13]

The transformation of attitudes defining the relations between the two partners in the Dual Alliance perhaps is best observed in Austria-Hungary's handling of her mandate over Bosnia-Herzegovina, which she exercised between the years 1878 and 1908. The wording in the Treaty of the Congress of Berlin, that assembly of the representatives of the European powers sponsored primarily by Otto von Bismarck and called together in 1878 in an effort to find a modus vivendi in the Balkans that would satisfy all the actors interested in the region, turned over the provinces to Austrian administration. Further, language in the treaty permitted the Dual Monarchy to transform its occupation and administration to outright sovereignty and possession, provided the other signatory great powers agreed. And so it was, amidst the murky swirling of the diplomacy of the moment, that Austria-Hungary announced the annexation of the territories in 1908. Thus was born the annexation crisis: Given the heating up of national and imperial rivalries during the preceding five years, both Russia and Serbia reacted with hot indignation, and Russia's partners in the entente roundly condemned the action, though they stopped short of demanding Austria's withdrawal. Nevertheless, the entire issue skirted dangerously close to being the outbreak of a general war and perhaps was avoided in the final analysis only by Germany's vigorous support of the Dual Monarchy. However, this support was couched in such bellicose and sanguine words that while Russia backed off, she did so burning with humiliation and the embarrassment of having to leave an unhappy Serbia in the lurch. To some observers looking backward from 1914, the annexation crisis seemed to have served as a dress rehearsal for the maneuvering that took place during July of 1914 following the assassination of the Austrian archduke and heir to the throne, Franz Ferdinand, at Sarajevo. But the latter event ended not in an unhappy peace but in world war. Did not, therefore, the actors during the summer of 1914 draw the wrong lesson from the dress rehearsal of 1908? Perhaps too many of these observers overlooked the flotsam that, following the

Russian-Serb denouement in 1908, led to the outbreak of a series of wars, first between the Ottoman Empire and Italy in 1911 and then among the Balkan states and Turkey in 1912 and again in 1913. In any event, by June of 1914, tensions between the two power blocs, to say nothing of those seething within the Balkan states, were at an all-time high. Little wonder, then, that these factors might finally spill over into world war during the summer of 1914.

Too often a focus on the turgid international politics that led to the catastrophe of world war in 1914 has pulled historians who would study the Dual Monarchy away from the assessment of the regime's real economic advances, at least in the standard measure of what passes for modernization in the usual Western canon defining progress. As a result, insufficient notice has been taken of the consequent elevation in the standard of living that many of Austria-Hungary's citizens gained from the industrialization that had taken place within the Habsburg realm concurrent with and parallel to the evolving international tragedy. While it is true that Austria-Hungary experienced no economic miracle as dramatic as that of the Hohenzollern *Reich,* its economic development, at least after the pan-European depression of 1873–1876, was both continuing and continuous. Moreover, this development often was impressive. For example, the true gross social product per head *(Bruttosozialprodukt),* where 100 percent equals that of the second Austrian Republic in 1976, stood at 86 percent in the Dual Monarchy in 1913 as against 65 percent in 1870. Hence, this growth averaged about 1.45 percent per year between 1870 and 1913, contrasting markedly with the .05 percent growth that took place within the realm of the Habsburgs between 1830 and 1870. One might therefore conclude that at the very least, the *Ausgleich* seemed to have expedited economic growth in the lands of the Habsburgs.[14]

The modern industrial and capitalistic nature of this economic growth is underscored if one confines an analysis of growth to the crown lands, that is, to the Austrian half of the Dual Monarchy during the years after 1870. So, for example, while the gross social product per head in the agricultural sector actually declined in Austria between 1870 and 1913 (as against Hungary), from 46.5 percent to 26.6 percent, the same measure shows industry to have grown from 34.8 percent to 50.5 percent, and commerce from 18.7 percent to 22.9 percent during these years. The same is not true for Hungary, however, where the agrarian sector of the economy remained primary right up to the outbreak of the First World War.[15]

The Dual Monarchy was, in terms of population and extent of territory, second only to the Russian Empire in Europe. Further, unlike Russia, a significant element of its population was highly literate, educated, and possessed of economic talent natural to a realm that invested in and possessed a variety of institutions for advanced learning. In addition, its lands contained a goodly supply of natural resources necessary for industrial development. These elements were bound together in a common whole by the rapid construction of railroads and waterways commencing in the 1880s. Before the advent of the railway, one could argue that a combination of Austria's physical geography and her ethnic diversity worked to pull her apart economically by connecting her rimlands with the states surrounding the monarchy; however, the reverse is true after the 1880s. Further, one sees that in an era of minimal nationalistic strife, the Habsburg realm was less economically cohesive, whereas in the era of intense nationalism-fueled centrifugal pull, the Dual Monarchy was economically cohesive. Therefore, at least on the economic plane, a combination of resources and technology had produced a happy result for those Austrians who, like their counterparts in western Europe in general, stood favorably poised before the juggernaut of industry and capital. For example, railroads made it possible to process the iron ore found in Styria by providing the steel mills there with coal or coke from Bohemia. Thus, to continue with this example, Bohemia and the southern German lands were tied together in mutual and happy dependency through the advent of railroads. By the same token, many of the blue-collar workers who found jobs in these industries found sufficient profit to move up and so join the ranks of the bourgeoisie.

Another measure of Austria-Hungary's economic success is the increase in the supply of capital and the associated growth and spread of sophisticated fiscal infrastructures; for example, the accumulation of pools of venture capital by banks in central Europe, whose chief function was to distribute capital in order to fund the growing industries that provided the modern vehicles for upward social mobility. The growth and spread of capital might be measured by the growth in the number of large banks founded in Vienna, which had become south-central Europe's financial capital in the years following 1870. Whereas between the years 1899 and 1909 forty-three such banks were founded in the imperial city, the number rose to sixty-seven in the years following 1909.[16] And of course this measure is reflected too in the growth of Austria's cities—which entailed both the spread of slums as well as the development of middle- and upper-class residences, along with cafes, department stores, and the like. But this story is not essentially different from that of the rest of industrial Europe, in which the impact of capital and industry transformed the socioeconomic world to create not only beneficiaries but losers as well. Historians are all too versed in the truth that modernism created a rootless and oppressed proletariat both on the land and in the cities. This was no less so for the Dual Monarchy. But certainly it was no more so. The perspective of the larger picture should not be lost because of a myopic focus on its parts.

Lastly, the development of steam-turbine-propelled steel ships played a rather ironic role in economically fusing Austria and Hungary into an economic whole. With this development, for example, the vast yields of grain from North America came to undercut the price of grain grown within the Dual Monarchy (particularly Hungary). For obvious political reasons, Vienna threw up a tariff wall against this imported grain to secure Austria's markets, especially those of the great cities of Vienna and Prague, for Hungary and Galicia. And while these policies did generate political problems of their own—for urban Austria disliked paying higher prices for food when it could be had cheaper—the farmers of Transleitha (and Galicia) became economically dependent on the populous crown lands. This economic dependence both belied and weakened the immediacy of the chauvinistic rhetoric that ran back and forth between Budapest and Vienna or between the Austrian capital and Cracow.[17] A similar dependence existed between the Dual Monarchy and Serbia, and this too became a means by which Vienna might dampen Austro-Serb irredentist sentiments by forcing Belgrade to cool the rhetoric it hurled at its neighbor.[18]

Political tension, as against growing economic interdependence—between Vienna and her Serbs, for example—was not, of course, the only arena in which potentially lethal nationality conflict took place. The former Austrian crown land of Bohemia, for example, had developed over the course of several centuries into a kingdom having two cultures: German and Czech. These cultures shared Bohemia more or less harmoniously until the modern era. But by the latter half of the nineteenth century, each culture, having become acutely conscious of its identity, demanded domination of the kingdom at the expense of the other. The Habsburg government tried a number of expedients in an attempt to preserve the cohesion of Bohemia as a whole within the Austrian state, but Vienna's effort was unsuccessful, and so the German-Czech struggle continued well into the twentieth century. Indeed, the German-Czech conflict over culture in Bohemia constituted one of the elements in the gathering political storm threatening the stability of Europe long before the outbreak of the First World War.[19]

That threat overtook European civilization in August of 1914. By the late fall of 1918, when the dust had settled, not only had old Austria disappeared, but Bohemia now was the nucleus of the newly created multinational Czechoslovakian state.[20] The issue of national diversity was now to be played out within the framework of Czechoslovakia. The controversy took a crucial turn in September of 1938 with the signing of the infamous Munich accords. The resultant breakup of the first Czech republic led directly to the eruption of the Second World War in 1939. It was only in the wake of Nazi Germany's overwhelming defeat and discredit that the German-Czech controversy finally was settled. However, this settlement came only at the expense of the blood of many German Bohemians, who fell victim to the Czech Bohemians in what today is called "ethnic cleansing." The shedding of so much blood on both sides makes it quite clear that neither the Czechs nor the Germans benefited from the cultural war that took place between them in Bohemia beginning in the middle of the nineteenth century. By the same token, the outcome whereby the Germans were driven from the Bohemian soil they had occupied for centuries demonstrates that these cultural wars, unrestrained by the rule of law (in this case that of old Austria), permit no compromise within the territory where the struggle has been carried on. It was only because of the general chaos at the end of the Second World War in what had once been civilized European living spaces that the ethnic cleansing of the German population of Bohemia passed more or less unnoticed in 1945.[21]

The year 1992, however, witnessed the outbreak of cultural war accompanied by brutal violence in parts of what once was Yugoslavia. Further, public opinion having grown accustomed since 1950 to both stability and human progress in Europe, it seems unbelievable that such brutality could take hold over a people that are taken to be among the prosperous and civilized. Indeed, less than a decade before these events, the capital of Bosnia, Sarajevo, had hosted the Winter Olympics. Consequently, her people, their lifestyle, and indeed, their general civilization received worldwide exposure through the ubiquity of television. World opinion was impressed with the apparently stable, reasonably progressive people hosting the games; moreover, one felt certain that Sarajevo must reflect the Yugoslav people as a whole. And while many in the West still were dubious about Yugoslavia being Communist, it was also true that the Cold War was fading under the apparent determination of the Soviet Union, then led by Mikhail Gorbachev, to bury past hostilities and seek genuine cooperation with the West. Hence, the Sarajevo Winter Olympics were suffused with a certain euphoria, as the threats of the recent past had evaporated, the future appeared bright, and the possibilities for constructive progress were thought to be endless. There seemed to be not the slightest reason for resurrecting old ghosts—for recalling, for example, that Sarajevo was where once a fuse had been lit that set Europe on the path to war and revolution for the better part of the twentieth century.

If history is any measure, our euphoria is always brought up short by unforeseen circumstance and, more especially, historical reality. Human beings, because of their imagination as well as their collective nature, are subject not only to those catastrophes brought about by physical phenomena but also to human storms generated, so to speak, by the abstract intellectual forces that shape human history. What, then, were the forces promoting the most recent debacle in what was the Yugoslav state? What were the perceptions causing Muslim and Christian, Croat and Serb, to brutally attack one another? Why did the Slovenes break loose from the rule of Belgrade? And why do Yugoslav Macedonians, Montenegrins, and Albanians cringe lest they also feel the too-hot breath of their former Serbian compatriots? At bottom, the answer to these questions is simple enough: The centripetal forces that held the Yugoslav state together were overwhelmed by the centrifugal forces that always had existed within it. The Yugoslav synthesis, first joined by the terms of the Pact of Corfu in the midst of the First World War during the spring of 1917, came apart. The component parts of what had been Yugoslavia could not agree on how to divide the Yugoslav heritage, and hence came to fight one another over what remained of the south Slav carcass. And so the present carnage.

A more fundamental approach to understanding the disintegration in the Balkans—which, at this writing, is threatening other parts of what had been the Soviet empire—is to put what we observe in some sort of historical perspective. And while, of course, such a perspective in no way justifies the bloody events taking place, it does provide a framework for the comprehension of those same events.

First, it is necessary to list and define the terms used to describe the historical processes that long have been at work underneath the cultural-political surface of south-central Europe. Further, because perception is a function of experience, the terms must be specifically defined as they apply to the experience of that region. It must be recalled, therefore, that within the parameters of central Europe, and in eastern Europe as well, the terms *state, nation,* and *nation-state* are used to distinguish political organization from cultural identity; that is, whereas *state* refers to a political organization through which a given territory is governed, *nation* is an ethno-cultural term applied to the peoples living within a political territory. A *nation-state* exists when a people perceive that the territory in which they live is exclusively occupied by them.

The nation-state is a perception probably having little reality in external terms. But, of course, history is as much driven, if not more so, by the *perception* of reality as by external reality. And so the perceived reality in the experience of central and eastern Europe is that one's proper ethno-cultural community, that is, one's nation, is reflected in language, and sometimes also by religion. One is Serb, for example, if one's first language is Serbian, or one is German if one speaks German as one's first language, and so on. In addition, at least in present-day Bosnia, evidently the present perception is that one cannot be both Serb and Muslim at the same time. A nation-state, then, is no more than a perception, but it is a powerful, driving one wherein a people in a given territory attend the same church because they speak the same language. Further, this linguistic and/or religious community demands that it be given tangibility by being governed by worthies speaking their language and/or attending their church.

Of course, all the difficulties related to the semantics of *state, nation,* and *nation-state* may be avoided by simply using the term *country.* However, whereas *country* can have a vague political dimension in the Anglo-American tradition, in the German tradition, for example, there is no equivalent. In German, *country* can be translated as *Land* or *Staat.* But in German *Land* and *Staat* are more specific than is their generic counterpart, *country,* in English. In the former Yugoslavia, to give another example, one's fatherland was Yugoslavia, whereas one's *Land* was Croatia or Slovenia, and so on. And further, as will be seen, this slice of political culture is an inheritance from the earlier political culture that suffused the region before there was a Yugoslavia.

Indeed, historically, central and eastern Europe, including the territory that once made up Yugoslavia, had been dominated by states: the czarist Russian Empire, the Ottoman Empire, the German Empire, and the Austrian Empire. More properly, these states might better have been called the realms of the Romanovs, Osmanlis, Hohenzollerns, and Habsburgs, respectively, for these empires actually were dynastic states built for the most part between the fifteenth and eighteenth centuries by the efforts of diverse groups of political entrepreneurs operating under the banner of a dynasty that in turn was sanctioned by the prevailing ethical institutions, political and religious, but most commonly Latin and Orthodox Christianity or Islam.

Although, at least for their era, these groups of political entrepreneurs were far from being homogeneous, they did represent a narrow (by modern standards) spectrum of interests, which permitted them to find a common vehicle within the umbrella of the dynasty that employed them and gave them leave to pursue their own private agendas. In time, out of their activities a certain cultural political order evolved. For central and eastern Europe this order became, albeit through many vicissitudes, the realms of the Habsburgs, Hohenzollerns, Romanovs, and so on. Descendants of these entrepreneurial elements, of course, became both the chief beneficiaries of and the articulate political element within those states that grew out of the activities of their forebears. But nevertheless in time, with the exception of the sickly Ottoman Empire, these dynastic states came to be parliamentary ones as well. Furthermore, the dynamics emanating from the diversity within, when combined with the stability derived from the stately order that embraced it, produced a vibrant civilization that not only spread its benefits within the boundaries of the respective states but transformed these limits to embrace Europe (and indeed, much of the world) as well.

Because this study will deal with Austria-Hungary and will focus on the era of Emperor Franz Joseph, it is concerned with defining and examining evolving Austrian political-culture perceptions during the reign of the last Habsburg patriarch. Regarding old Austria, there is little argument that the Dual Monarchy did become fertile ground for cultural achievement. Austria produced creative talent of the highest quality, talent such as that of Hayden, Mozart, and Brahms, Grillparzer, Hofmannsthal, and Schnitzler—talent that has left behind a heritage that very much enriches our world today. In addition, the realm of the Habsburgs established the circumstances that permitted a good many of her citizens to enjoy a high degree of material prosperity. One only has to recall, for example, the level of material well-being associated with the Austrian *Grunderzeit*.[22]

It is true, however, that Austria, like most states that evolved in the past, was constructed without reference to the nations that lived within them. Therefore in Austria, as in other states out of the past, an articulate minority of only limited diversity constructed a state over the heads, so to speak, of a large and diverse majority. That majority constituted a potentially centrifugal force with regard to the centripetal ones bringing about the state and holding it together. But it required the random unleashing of unprecedented forces in the course of the nineteenth century to activate the potential of these centrifugal forces. And thereby the story of political culture in central and eastern Europe in the course of the nineteenth century is that of the pull between centripetal and centrifugal forces, as the state tried to hold itself together while the nation was bent on dismantling the state. In time it was the centrifugal forces that prevailed.

Human beings, it seems, are assigned by destiny the Sisyphean task of re-learning the lessons of history. And perhaps too they must relearn that not all the diversity that dwells within a given order represents civilization. Central and eastern Europe had to endure revolution, war, and Holocaust following the great collapse that overtook the region during the years 1917 and 1918. Germany and Austria were seized by the Nazis, Russia by the Bolsheviks. Following the Second World War, the collapse of the German Third Reich led to the creation of the oppressive Soviet empire. But, more recently, the Soviet empire imploded, bringing about the collapse of the stately order that was founded out of the bloodletting that took place in the region between 1914 and 1945. But diversity let loose has not brought much joy. One result, for example, was those horrendous events sweeping through Bosnia.

This study attempts to make a contribution toward the understanding of events such as those coursing through what had been Yugoslavia by examining the issue of state against nation as these elements were synthesized and crystallized in the Austrian-Hungarian state chiefly during the years 1867–1918 and, thereby, give insights into the role played by political culture in the construction of states generally. That old Austria is an apt vehicle for the study of south-central Europe, including that part of the *Lebensraum* once occupied by Yugoslavia, is because the progress of the Habsburg realm was central to bringing into the region that order and those ideas that eventually were to fuse with more locally inspired perspectives to bring about what is often called the greater Serbian idea. The greater Serbian idea, in turn, has had an influence in the shaping of Europe during the twentieth century that is far greater than and grotesquely out of proportion to Serbia as a political power per se—not only because of the power of the Greater Serbia idea, but also because of how this perspective interacted with the foibles of the European great powers. In the final analysis it was these, rather than Belgrade, that permitted the Serbian perspective to become a catalyst in their ruin.

Notes

1. The spirit of this point of view is captured in Edward Crankshaw, *Vienna: The Image of a Culture in Decline* (New York: Macmillan, 1938).

2. See, for example, Otto Weininger, *Geschlecht und Charakter: Eine prinzipielle Untersuchung* (Vienna: Wilhelm Braumüller, 1908). This work, perhaps viewed today as "infamous" rather than "famous," demonstrated heavy doses of Jewish self-hate. See also Karl Kraus, celebrated feuilletonist and editor of the renowned *Die Fackel,* whose star, because it has come to be evident that he both demonstrated dislike of women and evinced Jewish self-hatred, also has fallen within contemporary academia. See, for example, Karl Kraus, *Literatur und Lüge* (Munich: Kösel Verlag, 1974).

3. The heir to the throne, Archduke Franz Ferdinand, seems to have been thinking, if only out of desperation, of establishing some sort of military dictatorship so as to override what he saw as Magyar intransigence. A post–World War II assessment of the archduke is found in Friedrich Wiessensteiner, *Franz Ferdinand: Der Verheinderte Herrscher. Zum 70. Jahrestag von Sarajevo.* (Vienna: Österreichischer Bundesverlag, 1983).

4. Hitler's views of his Vienna days is best viewed (in English) through his *Mein Kampf* (New York: Reynal and Hitchcock, 1941).

5. See Adam Wandruszka, "Die Habsburgermonarchie von der Grunderzeit bis zum Ersten Weltkreig," in Schloss Grafenegg, *Das Zeitalter Kaiser Franz Josephs: Teil 2, Glanz und Elend, 1880–1916* (Beiträge). (Vienna: NÖ Landesregierung, 1987), pp. 4–19.

6. A useful if general summary of this period is found in Edward Crankshaw, *The Fall of the House of Habsburg* (New York: Viking Press, 1965), especially pp. 78–99.

7. This Austrian view of these circumstances is best followed in Heinrich von Srbik, ed., *Quellen zur deutschen Politik Österreichs, 1859–1866,* 5 volumes (Osnabrück: Biblio Verlag, 1967).

8. Terminology was seemingly as convoluted as the organization of the dual state. *Austria* after 1867 refers to the crown lands, that is, the hereditary lands belonging to the House of Austria and ruled through the *Reichsrath* from Vienna. Less often these Austrian territories are referred to as Cisleitha (or Cisleithia); that is, the lands west of the River Leitha, which traditionally divides Austria from Hungary. Hungary (or the lands of the Crown of St. Stephen) is east of the River Leitha (Transleitha or Transleithia) and, from 1867, was ruled from Budapest. When in Vienna, Franz Joseph was emperor *(Kaiser)* and when in Budapest king *(König)*. Hence, joint institutions were known as *K.u.K. (Kaiserlich und Königlich)*, whereas Austrian institutions were known as *imperial-royal (Kaiserlich-Königlich)* and Hungarian institutions were *royal (Königlich)*. The whole, besides Austria-Hungary, often was referred to as the Dual Monarchy or the Habsburg Realm or even the Danubian state or Danubia.

9. These nations, which in time came to be called subject nations, were Croat, Czech, Italian, Polish, Rumanian, Ruthene, Serb, Slovak, and Slovene. The two ruling nations, of course, were the German and Magyar (Hungarian). The considerable number of Jews in the population are not included in this litany because they alone were not considered among the rooted nations; that is, they possessed no territory of their own in the sense of ethnic possession going back to time immemorial. For a summary of the evolution of Austria's Jewish communities, see William O. McCagg, *A History of the Habsburg Jews, 1670–1918* (Bloomington: Indiana University Press, 1989). For a view of the blind eye, see Joseph M. Baernreither, *Fragments of a Political Diary,* ed. Joseph Redlich (London: Macmillan, 1930).

10. The standard and still most useful discussion of the nationality question is found in Robert A. Kann, *The Multinational Empire,* 2 volumes (New York: Columbia University Press, 1950). See also Arthur J. May, *The Habsburg Monarchy, 1867–1914* (Cambridge: Harvard University Press, 1960).

11. The power game is best described in A.J.P. Taylor, *The Struggle for Mastery in Europe, 1818–1914* (Oxford: Clarendon Press, 1957).

12. For a short, cohesive summary of this dimension of foreign affairs, see Alan Sked, *The Decline and Fall of the Habsburg Empire, 1815–1918* (London: Longmans, 1989). A longer, scholarly analysis of the foreign policy of Austria-Hungary is found in F.R. Bridge, *The Habsburg Monarchy Among the Great Powers, 1815–1918* (Oxford: Berg, 1990).

13. A good discussion, albeit a highly opinionated one, of the changing nuances of the Serb (south Slav) question is found in Baernreither, *Fragments of a Political Diary.*

14. See the summary by Alois Mosser, "Die Wirtschaft im Habsburgerreich," in *Das Zeitalter Kaiser Franz Josephs,* p. 64. An excellent and very accessible summary of Austria's economic progress during this period is found in David E. Good, *The Economic Rise of the Habsburg Empire, 1750–1914* (Berkeley: University of California Press, 1984).

15. Ibid., pp. 65–66. On Austria's agrarian economy during the period of the Dual Monarchy, see Ernst Bruckmüller, "Die Entwicklung der Landwirtschaft Zwischen etwa 1880 und 1906," in *Die Zeitalter Kaiser Franz Josephs,* pp. 51–60.

16. Mosser, "Die Wirtschaft im Habsburgerreich," p. 63. See also John Komlos, ed., *Economic Developments in the Habsburg Monarchy in the Nineteenth Century* (Boulder, CO: East European Monographs, 1983).

17. See May, *The Habsburg Monarchy,* p. 336 and passim.

18. Ibid., pp. 401–402.

19. A standard discussion of the Austro-Czech question is seen in S. H. Thompson, *Czechoslovakia in European History* (Princeton: Princeton University Press, 1943). Also useful is Elizabeth Wiskermann, *Czechs and Germans* (New York: Oxford University Press, 1938).

20. Faced with overwhelming defeat externally and the onset of unruly disintegration internally, Emperor Karl I (successor to Franz Joseph and the last Habsburg monarch of Austria-Hungary) stepped aside on October 16, 1918. And while this move fell short of abdication, Karl, by his action, permitted Austria-Hungary's component parts to develop in their separate ways, and south-central Europe's successor states commenced what was to be their turbulent existence on the ruins of the Dual Monarchy. Hence October 16, 1918, can be viewed as the effective date marking the end of the realm of the Habsburgs.

21. See Douglas Botting, *From the Ruins of the Reich: Germany 1945–1949* (New York: New American Library, 1986), especially pp. 149–192.

22. The period of *Grunderzeit* is usually taken to be the years 1867 to 1873; that is, from the start of the *Ausgleich* to when Vienna's stock market collapsed in fiscal panic in May of 1873.

✧ 2 ✧
Nation and State in Danubia: Centrifugal and Centripetal Forces in Austria-Hungary, 1867–1914

Despite many illuminating volumes published on the subject, it remains unclear why the sanctity of the nation-state was the major ideological tenet to arise out of the political culture of nineteenth-century Europe. What is clear, however, is that this ideology possessed vast ramifications for the future of the continent. Much that came out of nationalism has proven not beneficial, and certainly not constructive. The strident ideology, because it serves as a convenient warrant for savage behavior, has been responsible for much human suffering. It has been rightly stigmatized for its role in justifying the violent wars and political terror that overtook Europe beginning in 1914. Certainly the visible wreckage in 1918 and 1945 of what had once held so much promise leaves us not a little perplexed and calls urgently for an understanding as to why such a calamity befell Europe.

We need to know about nationalism and the calamities it produced for the added reason that we find ourselves facing new conflicts arising out of it. Moreover, we have few ideas as to how to resolve these conflicts. To understand our condition is the first step toward resolution, and the first step toward understanding is to know from where national conflict arose. It is only natural to bring the past to bear in considering our present and thereby our future.[1]

One road from our present puzzle concerning the why of nationalism leads back over the past to the imperial city on the Danube—to Vienna. In the center of the venerable Danubian metropolis is a vast, rambling complex known as the Vienna Hofburg. Part of this labyrinth of brick and stone, constructed in various architectural styles, now serves as the official residence of the president of the Austrian republic. Other parts are used for governmental offices. Still other areas are given over to apartments for state retirees. Also, the state library, housing the scholarly accumulation of civilization, is found within its walls. But if space has been given over to the esoteric, the mundane has not been overlooked, for within other parts of the castle weary guides herd uncomprehending tourists through once rich apartments. Space that in the past was used for decorous state ceremonial has been set aside for conventions, and members of various professional and club groups rationalize the expense of a trip to Vienna by exchanging notes and pleasantries with their colleagues in the former *Rittersaal*.[2] A discussion of the history of old Austria might center on the former ruling dynasty that once occupied these spaces making up the Hofburg. Indeed, the House of Habsburg's pretensions harkened back to the seedbed of Western civilization, and icons of these are still visible in the building, albeit muted by the ravages of time. For example, the most recent wing of the Hofburg, its finishing touches put on just as the storm of the great war broke over Europe, was erected as part of a planned background to a grand imperial square that would give visibility to Austria's past glory and link it with the dynasty's hopes of future promise for its supranational Austrian realm—a promise that was to be heralded by an imperial paladin from a vast balcony situated so as to hold sway over the entire Burgplatz.[3] What actually came to pass was that the great square came to be filled with a fascist mob, Austrians all, paying homage to one of Vienna's adored own, Adolf Hitler. What is today visible to the knowing eye in that pile of old bricks and mortar lying in the center of Vienna—and this despite the egalitarian uses to which currently the old palace is put—are the empty echoes of an unredeemable imperial past and the horrors of the old capital's more recent Nazi past.

Perhaps no city is more symbolic of the disintegrated past European order than the former imperial capital on the Danube. For centuries Vienna had dominion over the lands of south-central Europe. Peoples from many nations had been drawn together within her walls, and over the years they wove a rich, diverse, and dynamic culture. This development was linked to the fact that after 1438, with one exception, the imperial crown of the German people belonged to the Habsburgs. As "holy Roman emperors," the Habsburgs elevated Vienna, in turn, to the status of *civile imperium*. However it was only after the seventeenth-century Austrian general Prince Eugene of Savoy pushed the Ottoman Turks out of the Danubian basin that the squares and streets clustered around the great, Gothic Stephensdom donned that baroque cloak that still gives the old city center a magical glow. The Hofburg, now bereft of the Habsburgs, may, in the minds of some observers, brood in the heart of Vienna. But, especially in the shadows of sunset, it still can conjure associations with the variegated old Austria of Maria Theresa, and of Hayden, Mozart, Beethoven, and so many others, the whole suddenly capable of transformation into enchantment under the captivating strains of Lanner and the Strausses.

From the settlement at the foot of the Kahlenberg, the Latinized Austrian culture, always in a German idiom, was extended south to the Save and east to Bakovina, beyond the Carpathians. Austrian influence leaped northward even into the heartland of Teutonic Germany, where it held sway until forcibly uprooted by the Prussians during the second of the three wars of German consolidation in 1866.[4] Even then, while Austria's political power had to beat a retreat, her cultural influence held fast. At the opening of the twentieth century one could still observe that Munich was far more Austrian than Prussian; that is, the city on the Isar was Catholic and south German, like the capital on the Danube. Indeed, that observation remains true today, for culture clings fast even where politics gives way. The difference between Vienna and Berlin is due to more than the traumatic division of Germany during the nineteenth century. Vienna will always remain linked with the spirit of Prague and Budapest. Vienna is tied to the Danube, which threads its way through the cultural variety of south-central Europe. Berlin is circumscribed by the Spree, which never leaves Brandenburg. Berlin is Prussian; Vienna, Catholic and cosmopolitan.[5] Hence

> There is only one imperial city.
> There is only one Vienna.
> There is only one nest of robbers.
> And that is called Berlin.[6]

The relationship between the existence of any given state and the cultural origins of the people residing within its borders is at best haphazard. And in any case, these relationships are not founded on some natural and immutable law. Austria-Hungary, for example, was the result of political fortune that embraced certain myths surrounding the Roman and Carolingian empires and the rise of Europe's Latin Christian commonwealth. It was these myths, growing out of the passing of time, which propelled an obscure but aggressive feudal family to found itself as a dynasty. As a dynasty, the House of Habsburg was the focal point of the territorial ambitions of other warrior families. Out of the interaction between these families rose a system of order embracing a territory occupied by a diversity of ethnic populations. This realm came to be called, after the establishment of the *Ausgleich* with the Magyars in 1867, Austria-Hungary.[7]

In its broad outlines, if not in its details, the origins of Austria-Hungary are no different than those of any other European state. In western Europe, however, the wide range of forces that eventually imposed a high degree of cultural uniformity on the peoples residing there had long been at work before these were discernible in central and eastern Europe.[8] Hence, the states in western Europe, including the German *Reich,* emerged in the modern era of industry and capital as nation-states because the overwhelming majority of their peoples were considered as possessing a common culture and ethnic heritage. The case was very different for the three empires or realms embracing south-central and eastern Europe: Austria-Hungary, the Ottoman Empire, and the Russian Empire. These states emerged in modern times as multinational states and, furthermore, ones in which subject nations were governed according to the interests of the ruling nation.[9]

By the middle of the nineteenth century, however, national consciousness loomed large in all of Europe, but perhaps most destructively in south-central Europe, where it became corrosive to the centripetal forces of state building. Indeed, while the Atlantic seaboard states were not immune to the centrifugal pull of rampaging nationalism, the very existence of the order and civilization of central and eastern Europe was called into question by it. After 1850, the three eastern states commenced to dissolve markedly under the pressures generated by the call—too often founded on dubious assumptions and hence doubtful perspective—demanding national renewal.[10]

Because the articulate classes in these states chose, not unnaturally, to fight back, the pressures and counterpressures yielded a deep (and eventually racially cast) antagonism that was the tinder ignited on June 28, 1914, when the Austrian heir to the throne was assassinated at Sarajevo. Nationalism, like the forbidden gold that Albrecht stole from the depths of the Rhine, turned out to be the curse that brought down Valhalla—that is, overturned the chief props of old Europe's order and engulfed her civilization in seemingly ceaseless conflagration, all beginning on a beautiful, sunny, otherwise innocuous June day.

There always exist vested interests, having deep economic and social roots, that wield enormous political power within the established and complex institutions in any given state order. These interests, of course, were structural in Austria-Hungary prior to the First World War and were mirrored in the Austrian tradition, a kind of patriotism given tangibility and continuity by the dynasty installed behind the baroque walls of the golden-hued Schönbrunn, the glitter and pomp that surrounded its court in the Hofburg, and, above all during the second half of the nineteenth century, by the romance and tragedy associated with the person of Austria's monarch, Franz Joseph I. In addition, the emperor was in possession of his army, which, supranational and imperial-minded to its core, was loyal to the black and gold banner of the Habsburgs. It was the nineteenth-century poet Franz Grillparzer who, while extolling Marshall Radetzky's victories in the Italian campaign of 1848, best described the link between army and state by reminding his readers that the emperor's soldiers reside in a "camp that is Austria."[11]

Much more gave substance to tradition than just the existing manifestations of Austria's past. There was, for example, the order issuing forth from the governments in state and provincial capitals. In 1907, Austrian administration was characterized by the future president of the second Austrian Republic, Karl Renner, as being more democratic than that of England and having more justice than that of France.[12] There was a network of transportation and communication that tied the lands of the realm together and advanced the benefits derived from the monarchy's near autarky in agriculture and industry. Her great cities, as diverse as Prague and Trieste, Vienna and Budapest, were centers not only of government and culture but also of industry and finance. All, however, were inextricably linked with the fortunes of one another, because the system out of which these urban centers developed was itself dependent on an ongoing social, political, and economic development comprehensible only within the Danubian realm of the Habsburgs.[13] The steel industry in Styria, for example, depended on coal mined in Bohemia. Exports manufactured at Prague's Skoda works were sent by rail to Trieste and thence, often in Austrian ships, to the markets of the world.[14]

Revenues drawn from commerce and industry produced great profits for a few and incomes for many, and so brought about a greatly enlarged Austrian middle class whose inclination toward self-indulgence was no different than that in any other state. Consequently, the Austrian bourgeoisie supported and increased the variety found in Austrian Danubia. Middle-class proclivities, for example, interjected energy in the artistic and literary endeavors of Franz Joseph's realm.[15] Fin de siècle Vienna, for all the official emphasis on the status quo, was alive with the new and innovative Weltanschauung pursued in her coffeehouses or in the studios of the Vienna Secession.[16] Straddling above, if somewhat aloof, stood a generally conservative aristocracy, which, although increasingly forced to share privilege with the haute bourgeoisie, still were considered representatives of old Austria and hence continued to exist as a feudal corporation enjoying the fruits of its privilege. In return, the aristocracy gave loyal, and oftentimes efficient, service to state and dynasty.[17] Below the middle classes, as in all of Europe, stood the usual large and insecure working classes, who, too often unseen by the great world, shared the meager fare spared to them by the beneficiaries of Austria's capitalistic development.[18]

Industrial development gave to national self-consciousness in south-central Europe a different connotation than was given to its counterpart in the more culturally assimilated areas of the West. Rather than the pride in state power that was so manifest north and west of the Danube, the chief vehicle carrying nationality within the ethnic riddle south and east of it was not technological development but culture. And as it became the measure of cultural self-consciousness, language came to be perceived as being endowed with all manner of cabalistic significance, became a tangible demonstration of ethnic uniqueness; even more, the superior strength of a given nation. In time, the lurking but inchoate centrifugal forces of nationalism drew both energy and focus from the mystique read into the meaning of language, and thereby cultural nationalism became a threat to Austria's political cohesion. Thereby too language came to be a standard-bearer for those who would destroy the very social progress and economic prosperity, drawn out of industrialization, that had generated national self-consciousness in the Dual Monarchy in the first instance.[19] Hence, in paradoxical fashion, nationalism, a product of the success of the state as a functional political entity, in Austria threatened to destroy that which had brought it about.

As industrialism took hold in old Austria, demographic shifts that resulted as peasants belonging to one language group sought work in industrial centers initially dominated by another language group brought about, as a certain but nevertheless unintended result, the intermingling of diverse national cultures. Hence, industry-driven emigration brought about national integration in these centers without at the same time bringing about a concomitant sense of cultural assimilation. Rather, a sense of cultural differentiation was sharpened among individuals within these groups. Hence, in the last analysis, emigration to the cities created (and, as it gathered momentum, exacerbated) social disharmony among the nations in the Dual Monarchy as a whole.[20] Czech peasants, for example, who emigrated from the countryside to centers such as Prague or Teplitz, came for the first time to perceive themselves as Czechs, because in Bohemia's cities they found it necessary to use the German tongue, which had long predominated in these places as the language of civic discourse, but they saw it as the most humiliating of yokes.[21] The industrialization of Bohemia, to remain with this example, rendered the region's harmonious administration increasingly more difficult. Indeed, it can be said of Austria-Hungary in general that wherever government successfully promoted a broad spectrum of social and economic advances in the name of progress, the very success of these endeavors tended to undermine the cohesion necessary to ensure the future security and well-being of the state. Modernism, in the form of social pressures generated out of industrialism and capital, thereby undermined the Dual Monarchy. But without embracing modernism, Austria-Hungary could not be expected to survive as a great power, if indeed she might survive at all. Certainly, nothing underscored more in Vienna the price to be paid if a state failed to modernize in order to live than the example of the growing debility of Austria's neighbor and once deadly enemy to the south: the Ottoman Empire.

It cannot be estimated with any precision the degree to which questions surrounding cultural nationalism constituted an immediate threat to the existence of the Dual Monarchy. Certainly, much that was written and spoken on this issue came from the elements within the waxing middle classes that apparently were materially prospering the most. Further, many of the more lugubrious pronouncements were mere rhetoric for political consumption in an era of spreading democracy and popular government. And much that has been written on the subject since the collapse in 1918 can often be seen as little more than justification after the fact.[22] Nationality strife, to be sure, was given vivid public demonstration; for example, more than one raucous riot paralyzed Austria's universities, and much unruly conflict took place in the otherwise sober rooms of state and provincial legislatures.[23] These antics shocked pre–World War I Europe, where the general perception was of an immutable order of things. To many foreign observers, and not a few from inside the monarchy, the rampant disorder seemed to presage the immediate breakup of the ancient realm. The view is quite different, however, from the perspective of post–World War II Europe. The trauma of a second world war followed by a cold war has made it less difficult today to understand that the discontent neither disrupted the day-to-day functioning of the state nor necessarily spelled its doom. We know only too well that life goes on even in the most difficult of circumstances. Perhaps it was Robert Musil who best summarized the contradictions within Austria's nationality question when he wrote: "In this country one acted—sometimes indeed to the extreme limits of passion and its consequences—differently from the way one thought or one thought differently from the way one acted."[24] Indeed, it was the apparent paradox between the reality of government, on one hand, and what passed in the streets, on the other, that led the writer Hermann Bahr to observe that although the city's inhabitants "aspired . . . all they really wanted was to live."[25] It was not national strife but more than four years of world war and revolution that brought down the Dual Monarchy. But, as historical hindsight verifies, much else came down with it. In point of fact, Austria-Hungary was merely one victim of the destructive forces created within the subterranean catacombs of industrial life and given force through the unleashing of the First World War.

All facets of the question concerning old Austria's durability in the face of the centrifugal forces of nationalism lead back to that of vested interests and the tenacity of those interests in the face of their opposition. Certainly, despite its complaints, the middle class as a whole was cognizant of its stake in the existing order. Perhaps it was for this reason that national rhetoric came not from bankers or industrialists. Rather, nationalism was articulated by those within the bourgeoisie having a political-philosophical bent, so as to elicit a passionate response among the restless and rootless always present in industrial, urban civilizations. By the same token, little of this nationalist rhetoric led to widespread political activism. If the strength of the centrifugal forces inspired by nationalism is to be measured against those working for the Dual Monarchy's preservation, then determination should rest on the fact that, prior to 1918, very little action was taken from within the Austrian population to bring down the state. Rather, most overt political action aimed at restructuring Austria-Hungary so as to ensure the preservation of the state. When viewed from within the context of the possibilities of the European state structure prior to World War I, the Dual Monarchy appeared sufficiently substantial and rational so that most would opt for its continued existence. Following the First World War, a Swedish diplomat observed to his Czech counterpart, who had been known for his constant carping against old Austria, "I do not understand the basis of your complaint for in [old] Austria you enjoyed security from your enemies and you had tranquility and well-being."[26] It is true that the dichotomy between the rising standard of living coming out of the status quo and the strident, threatening demands of the exponents of cultural nationalism did cast a discouraging pall over much of the positive activity going on within the monarchy. That Austria had her enemies, unreconcilable even in the face of progress and long before the First World War, is rendered patently obvious by the British journalist Henry Wickham Steed, who, in his introduction to Thomas G. Masaryk's *The Making of a State,* wrote: "Written by Masaryk as an authoritative record of the efforts by which the freedom of Czechoslovakia has been won . . . it is a discerning historical interpretation . . . of the process of Czechoslovak redemption from Habsburg servitude. . . . To Masaryk and the Czechs the name 'Austria' meant every device that could kill the soul of a people, corrupt it with a modicum of national well being . . . deprive it of freedom of conscience."[27] Indeed, the continued undercurrent of nationality strife was responsible for much of the pessimism expressed regarding Austria's future. But hope for the future also was implied at the same time by those selfsame sources who saw, once nationality reform had been brought about, a glorious forecast for all of Danubia's peoples living within the embrace of the monarchy. Still, the negative forebodings were many, and no less a personage than the Emperor Franz Joseph was subject to them. Yet the brilliant architecture of Adolf Loos and Otto Wagner, concomitant with the gifted, if more unsettling, paintings of the Vienna Secessionists, such as Gustav Klimt, Oskar Kokoschka, and Egon Schiele, stood as signs of Austria's dynamic inner creative forces. This era of rich and substantial creativity stood in marked contrast to the gloomy portents of decay, death, and collapse that have been used, for example, to explain the all too numerous suicides of Vienna's gifted men and women.[28] Again, it was Robert Musil who perhaps has best described the tenuous nature of the old Austria's substance:

> The Emperor and King ... was a legendary old gentleman. ... One knows exactly what he did, prevented, or left undone; but then ... younger people who were familiar with the current state of the arts and sciences were sometimes overtaken by doubt whether he existed at all. The number of portraits one saw of him were almost as great as the number of inhabitants of his realms; on his birthday there was much eating and drinking as on that of the Savior, on the mountains the bonfires blazed, the voices of millions of people were heard vowing that they loved him like a father. ... But this popularity and publicity was so over-convincing that it might have easily been the case that this believing in his existence was rather like still seeing certain stars although they ceased to exist thousands of years ago.[29]

During the first decade of the twentieth century, the working classes became a formidable factor in the political life of Austria-Hungary. In 1907, a democratic election-reform law had been set in motion in the Cisleithan half (crown lands) of the Monarchy; one was on the horizon for Hungary as well. The Austrian reform transformed the lower house of parliament in Vienna (the Reichsrath), which legislated for all the crown lands governed from the Austrian capital, into an egalitarian body resting on universal manhood suffrage according to the principle of one man, one vote. This restructured lower house (the Abgeordnetenhaus) came to be dominated by political parties representing the less affluent strata of society. Indeed, no political party benefited more or, for that matter, was more instrumental in launching demands for this reform than the Marxist-oriented German Austrian Social Democratic Workers' Party (Deutschösterreichischen Sozial Demokratisch Arbeiterpartei).[30] It was the Vienna-based leadership of the socialists who first issued the demand for general and equal elections and, having organized impressive public demonstrations in support of this call, was in great part responsible in convincing the government of the efficacy of this reform[31]—although it must be admitted that, faced with obstruction in the parliament, the actual decision was made by Emperor Franz Joseph in hopes of gathering the support of the masses for the state (because of the fact that so much of the bourgeois political leadership was permeated by nationalism).[32] In any event, the Social Democrats won the largest bloc of seats in the first parliament that met on the basis of the new elections law. Out of more than four and a half million votes cast in May of 1907, Austrian socialist candidates received slightly over a million votes and 87 seats in the 516-member lower house. Out of the total socialist vote, more than half a million went to German Austrian candidates, followed by the Czech socialists, with about two-thirds as many votes. Also receiving a small fraction of the seats given over to the socialists were Social Democratic candidates representing the Polish, Ruthene, Italian, and Slovene nations. In order to leverage their influence within Parliament as well as to give tangible demonstration of socialist international solidarity, even within the multinational Habsburg realm, the socialist deputies organized themselves into the Union of Social Democratic Deputies (Verband der Sozialdemokraten Abgeordneten). This union operated under the leadership of a steering committee of twelve members carefully selected so as to reflect the number and strength of the socialist deputies of each nation having seats in the parliament. In actuality, however, the steering committee was dominated by members of the Vienna-based German Austrian leadership, not only because German Austrians possessed the largest bloc of seats allotted to the Austrian socialists as a whole, but also because of the experience and sophistication of the German Austrians and especially of their widely respected leader, Dr. Viktor Adler.[33]

Second place went to the paternalistic and Catholic-oriented Christian Socialist Party, which not only had a large following among the less affluent elements of the middle classes, but possessed a degree of tacit support from within influential segments of officialdom, including that of the heir to the throne, Archduke Franz Ferdinand. It needs no saying that because of their Marxist orientation (which was reflected in much of its sanguine rhetoric), the Social Democrats neither enjoyed nor sought such support. But for their part, the Christian Socialists followed the lead of the popular and politically astute mayor of Vienna, Dr. Karl Luegar. "Schön Karl" perhaps was most responsible for the party's garnering slightly over half a million votes and sixty-eight seats in the new parliament. Following Luegar's Christian Socialists was the Catholic Clerical Party, especially popular among Austria's peasants, with a return of somewhat less than half a million votes.[34] The popular coloration of the new parliament was further underscored by its having slightly over three hundred deputies who never before had sat in the lower house. Further, the overwhelming majority of these new members had gained their seats at the expense of the older middle-class parties, especially those that were liberal and representative of the haute bourgeoisie. The new deputies, however, were not politically homogeneous and, beyond the Christian and Marxist socialists among them, represented splinter nationalist and labor groups as well as diverse agrarian and clerical interests having adherents scattered throughout the crown lands.[35]

Although it is slightly problematic to speak of the diverse attitudes represented within a political party while at the same time dealing with it as a whole, nevertheless it can be said that because the German Austrian Social Democrats did not advocate the breakup of the state, Austrian Marxism represented elements seeking to uphold, albeit by sometimes drastic restructuring and reform, the fundamental outlines of Austria-Hungary. But, by the same token, the party always sought—at least if its rhetoric is to be taken seriously—to organize the working classes against capital along Marxist principles. Hence, the party was generally identified by the majority as belonging to the revolutionary left and therefore being beyond the pale politically. It was unfortunate, as far as the party's influence on the possibilities of reconciliation among Austria's nations was concerned, that observers did not focus more on the Social Democrats' evolutionary, in contrast to revolutionary, tactic. Too little attention was given to statements like those of Viktor Adler, implying revolution, to be sure, but not now, only later. The party's founder and chief spokesman argued for patience, for example, when he told his following:

> We are ready to greet our soldiers and say to them: "Yes brothers, today you still must sacrifice your health, [and] your life for the policies of the great and powerful. [But] the time will come when you will no longer have to sacrifice for conceited honor [and] for false prestige . . . for policy. The time will come when we will stand together in sacrifice only for the honor of peoples; for one's true honor, for one's future, and for one's development."[36]

The Christian Socialists, not least because of their support of both the dynasty and the idea of Catholic Austria, of throne and altar, was not usually regarded as revolutionary, although it was both genuinely anticapital, German nationalist, and, at the same time, anti-Semitic as well. In fact, however, its anticapitalism, less dogmatic than that of its Marxist rivals, did not especially summon angst among the politically articulate, because its socialist tenets were couched in terms of a vague antimodernism rather than calling for struggle in terms of class consciousness. But its antimodernism also especially was reflected in its German nationalism and its sharp political (as against racist) anti-Semitism; for this reason, perhaps observers ought to have known that Christian Socialism possessed the potential for political revolution in a fascist sense. But, of course, given the time and place, this potential passed unrecognized not only by the party's leaders and following but by the bulk of Austrian officialdom as well. By the same token, its often racist German nationalist bent rendered Luegar's party the worst possible political vehicle with which to bring about reconciliation among Austria's nations.

The orderly evolution of Austrian political culture was hamstrung by the fact that the two popular political parties that emerged out of the 1907 elections reform were ill suited to resolving nationality conflict: one, because of its doctrinaire Marxism, which axiomatically rendered the Social Democrats political pariahs; the other, the Christian Socialists, because its superficial orthodoxy was in fact founded on a kind of hard-nosed bigotry that rendered it both hostile and unfit when it came to the necessary business of national reconciliation and harmonization. Yet the reform produced no other popular parties on the scale of Christian and Marxist socialism but rather only various idiosyncratic splinter or nationalist groups and declining former mainstream parties that had flourished during the days when the parliament represented privilege rather than egalitarian, participatory democracy. Franz Joseph therefore did not obtain what he most desired from the election reform: a demonstration of popular support for the state from the enfranchised masses, who presumably benefited from its organization and order. Neither did the new parliament bring an end to the habit of various elements of its dissatisfied membership of indulging in parliamentary obstruction, thereby making orderly legislative progress according to the precepts of liberal democracy impossible. There being no other obvious way out of rampant obstructionism in the parliament, the emperor too often was forced to rule by those powers permitted him by the emergency provisions written into Austria's constitution (Article 14) in the event of political breakdown. Hence, Austrians witnessed the irony of having their emperor in fact more authoritarian in democratic times than he had ever actually been in the period of neo-absolutism (1848–1860). But of course everyone recognized that this state of affairs could not go on forever if the state was to survive politically, although certainly on many other planes—economic, cultural, and social—it was flourishing as the twentieth century took hold.

There seemed, however, to be a sort of tacit agreement that the current modus operandi be allowed to continue during the remainder of the old emperor's lifetime. Many felt that it would be time enough to settle the business of structural reform at the moment of Franz Joseph's passing. But he lived more than the usual span of years, and hence the political atmosphere was saturated by a kind of poisonous miasma emanating from the general tenuousness of things political during the last decades of the emperor's life. Gloomy forebodings of doom too often seeped into the political arena from the sidelines, with the result that the healthy glow of prosperity and progress was heavily tinted with the hues of despondency and anxiety. As a result, too many Austrians came to live in the present while averting their attention from the future. But, as historians know, the present is in fact the future.

It should be underscored that Austro-Marxism went out of its way not to make use of the uneasiness among the nations to promote discontent toward the state. Rather, the party's leadership, for the most part ensconced in Vienna, did its very best to promote policies that might ameliorate such strife. In addition, it performed a great service to the downtrodden among the proletariat by working to improve their health and education. As a result, even if it did not have their confidence on the political plane, many among Austria's articulate did see in the Social Democrats a positive force for the Dual Monarchy on the plane of general human welfare. Otherwise, nothing can explain the upper social classes' respect for and the lower classes' veneration of Dr. Viktor Adler.

For its part, the Christian Socialists, beyond preaching a vague Christian-Catholic universalism, and despite some concrete material benefits brought by it to the inhabitants of Vienna, added very little substance to real political stability for the peoples of Austria-Hungary as a whole. Before the First World War, the party presented almost nothing to the body of ideas as to how the Dual Monarchy might be profitably restructured. Moreover, after the death of its charismatic leader, Dr. Karl Luegar, in 1910, the party suffered from a dearth of dynamic leadership. But this is not to say that Christian Socialism in its rarefied, ideal form (as against it as a political party) was never a salient political-cultural prop in support of the multinational Danubian realm. A few Christian Socialists did endeavor to pursue a social policy inspired by Thomistic theory, and a number of its adherents could be found among the more articulate members of Austria's intelligentsia. And there is no doubt that this was at least part of the reason why the very devout heir apparent, Archduke Franz Ferdinand, often was found to be in the Christian Socialist camp. The fact remains, however, that this level of political pursuit was not shared by the party's rank and file. And it is not without a certain irony, therefore, that Catholic social theorists finally did succeed in bringing many Christian Socialists to that ground of political-culture federalism long occupied by its secular Marxist rivals, though only under the press of the Dual Monarchy's last hour.[37] Of course, the last hour was too late for saving the monarchy, but at least the two parties did find some common ground, if only for a short time, and were able to give to the first Austrian Republic a somewhat more auspicious start (if ultimately a false one) than that enjoyed at the same time by the German Weimar Republic to the north.[38]

In its predominately popular, lower form, Christian Socialism stands condemned in history for its crude pro-Habsburg, pan-German outlook, heavily laced with political anti-Semitism. Because dislike of Austrian Jewry was linked in large measure to antimodernism—that is, to popular hostility toward capital and large industry, which was naturally vented toward large banks and manufacturing concerns apparently under Jewish control—Christian Socialism's anticapitalist tendencies took on a German folkish coloration when articulated by its less enlightened mass following. In addition, Austro-Marxism was liable to be tarred by the same brush used by Christian Socialist leaders to attack capital and industry; because many of these Marxists were known to be Jews, if not by faith, then by background.[39] Nevertheless, these macabre, politically self-destructive proclivities evident within the lower strata of Christian Socialist activists held only limited sway in pre–World War I Austria-Hungary for two reasons: Its leaders kept close rein over its potentially unruly following, and racism in any form simply was not acceptable to Emperor Franz Joseph. And while these deleterious traits perhaps were gaining a certain acceptability among elements within its younger generation, what was not acceptable to Franz Joseph was (officially at least) not acceptable at his court. By the same token, recognition at court was certainly the chief accolade desired by the upwardly mobile among the population in the period of Austria's *Grunderzeit*. Hence, the influence of the emperor was considerable in holding back these pernicious developments. In addition, traditional institutions, which were represented in the person of the emperor, also managed to hold anti-Semitism and unbridled pan-Germanism in check, that is to say, confining it to the streets even if these same proclivities did endure in the substrata of the party's political life. But so long as Austria's imperial institutions endured, the chance that an Adolf Hitler would preside from some governmental chancellery was highly unlikely. This circumstance was especially so because in the last analysis Christian Socialist thinkers such as Karl von Vogelsang and party activists such as Karl Luegar and Ignaz Seipel were black and gold to the core.[40]

Cultural divisions that by the turn of the century had become tangible in the form of self-conceived political groups threatening Austria's stability were found most often in Bohemia and Moravia. Reconciliation within these provinces between German Bohemians and Czech Bohemians thereby became increasingly unlikely as nationalist-driven groupings—represented by the likes of the Party of Young Czechs, Czech National Socialists, and especially those noisy pan-German Bohemians who in 1904 organized themselves as the German Worker's Party (Deutsche Arbeiterpartei)—took positions that could only intensify the swirl of centrifugal forces surrounding the so-called Bohemian question. These strident cliques, however, must be understood as an only-to-be-expected end result of the long-simmering struggle between Germans and Czechs in Bohemia and Moravia for cultural domination of the provinces. In hindsight, it is difficult to see how a modus vivendi between the two nations could have been arrived at in an era of intense nationalism-driven struggle for control of the cultural turf in the two unfortunate provinces. But in any event the dispute was only escalated when the strident call of *"Los vom Rom!"* (away from Rome") from the German Worker's Party, led by the obstinate Bohemian aristocrat Georg von Schönerer with the help of his even less savory lieutenant Karl Hermann Wolf, urged German Bohemians to tear away from the Habsburg realm, taking all of Bohemia and Moravia with them, and join with their fellow nationals in the German *Reich*.[41]

The apparent initial strength of the party of Schönerer and Wolf had two sources: the reality, after 1871, of the united German Second Reich under Berlin's Hohenzollerns, and the flood of Czech-speaking Bohemian peasants into what had been the German-dominated industrial centers in Bohemia and (to a lesser extent) in Moravia. Czech Bohemians often displaced German-speaking blue-collar workers because, accustomed to a lower living standard, these peasant emigrants would work at lower wages, thereby maximizing the profits of their (most often) German Bohemian employers. In any event, the rank and file of German Bohemians were brought to the jolting realization that despite the veneer of centuries of Teutonic culture in Bohemia, German Bohemians in fact were a minority living in an alien land.[42]

Not only did internal Czech emigration generate cultural self-consciousness among German Bohemians, but the Czech threat to hitherto perceived German cultural hegemony was underscored by the outbreak of language conflict in the lands of the Crown of Saint Wenceslas. Up until the last quarter of the nineteenth century the language of civilization in the provinces generally had been thought to be German, not only the German Bohemians but Bohemians of other nations as well took on the language as their first tongue. The newly arrived Czech Bohemians from the rural regions of the two disputed provinces, however, spoke not German but their own Slavic tongue. Finally, and especially galling to the traditionally culturally dominant German population, members of the rising Czech intelligentsia, who in fact had often grown up using German as their first language, now insisted that the language of civilization in Bohemia and Moravia be Czech.[43] As the language dispute intensified, it was handed over to the imperial government to settle. But despite its attempts (perhaps in hindsight too tenuous but sincere enough for all that) to settle the issue in a manner acceptable to both sides, the emotionalism that was bound to travel hand in hand with cultural questions of this magnitude sabotaged Vienna's efforts. The consequence of this failure has rested heavily upon both the German and Czech nations throughout the course of the twentieth century.[44]

The polarization between German and Czech in Bohemia and Moravia overflowed into the remainder of German Austria and into the activities of other groups of pan-Germans. In addition, their activities in upper and lower Austria and in Carinthia fused together so as to reinforce those of Georg von Schönerer. The loose agenda uniting these groups of German nationalists was to detach all of the German-speaking lands under the scepter of the Habsburgs so that these same lands, but including also all of both Bohemia and Moravia, might be joined with the German *Reich* to form a single, united greater Germany.

These irredentist efforts, often embellished by the term *Anschluss* (connecting up) and pursued within an anti-Catholic *"Los vom Rom!"* idiom, proved to be loud and extremist, but the cry never took extensive root within the German-speaking population as a whole. Nevertheless, the rhetoric surrounding the *"Los vom Rom!"* idea was unsettling to the status quo and moreover (and again in hindsight) established an unfortunate precedent, one that eventually disturbed the post–World War I equilibrium in central Europe. But even before the great war, the work of these raucous pan-Germans resulted in the formation of the Union of German Nationalists (Verband der Deutschnationalen) and imbued it with the lugubrious Christian Socialist spirit of anti-Semitism cum antimodernism.

A union of German Nationalists suffused with Schönerer's angst should not be confused with another, more moderate group of German Austrians, the German People's Party (Deutsche Volkspartei). While somewhat sympathetic to a

German nationalist program, the German People's Party had its origins previous to the launching of dualism in 1867 and expressed in a German genre the support of these Germans for a rebirth of Josephistic centralism. But this sort of Austrian centralism, especially after the collapse of Austrian hegemony in Germany with her defeat at Königgrätz in 1866 and the establishment of the dualistic state structure of 1867, harkened back to the reign of Maria Theresa and was ill suited to the diffuse sentiments of *la patrie* that grew out of the French Revolution—ill suited because, patently, such a perspective could not be applied to an ethnically diverse Danubia, even in an era of popular nationalist politics, within a framework of bourgeois industrial capitalism.[45]

It is true, however, that during the middle third of the nineteenth century, a majority of German Austrians (drawn from the bourgeoisie or the German-identified aristocracy) desired a centralized state organized generally along the lines of the first French constitution or the 1814 French charter. In addition, many among the bourgeoisie, and more than a few aristocrats, wanted a secular state as well—that is, a monarchical state, but not one founded on the altar. Unfortunately for such aspirations, the German nation possessed insufficient weight, especially so because of the declining German Austrian population in relation to the growing non-German population, to enforce ideas of a Josephistic centralized state over the unwilling non-Germans. Most non-Germans opposed Austrian centralism not because they wished to leave the state but because they saw in such an organization no room for their own cultural development; in other words, non-Germans, and especially the politically articulate among them, wanted Austria's cultural diversity recognized within the realm's fundamental political structure.

The one major exception to these non-Germans were the Magyars, or at least elements among the Magyar gentry, who would have, if left to their own devices, opted for something other than mere equality within the common state. Indeed, as time passed, these Magyar elements not only grew in numbers but became both unyielding and obstreperous as well. The German Austrians, as a result, simply were unable to override Magyar demands not only for equality with them but also for superiority over all remaining Austrian nations. What was worse, as chance would have it, the dynasty was forced to deal with the hardheaded Magyars in the face of its defeat by Prussian arms in the Seven Weeks' War of 1866. The end result, as is well known, was the so-called *Ausgleich* (compromise) of 1867, whereby the dynasty divided cultural hegemony and civil governance of the state between the Germans in the west (Transleitha) and the Magyars in the east (Cisleitha), to the civil exclusion of the nine remaining nations residing in the state. While the Magyars were never really satisfied with the arrangement, the *Ausgleich* did minimally meet their demands. But it did so at the cost of stirring up resentment within the excluded nations, which, of course, only increased nationalism's centrifugal pull. And while it was true that the question was one of culture rather than civil rights, it can be argued that at bottom inferior cultural status did in fact work to create inferior civil status. That is, the issues surrounding the *Ausgleich* may have explicitly involved questions relating to the structure of the state, but implicitly, because the compromise in fact placed cultural limitations on nine of Austria's eleven nations, it became a de facto question of civil rights. To maintain otherwise, as many within the ruling circles did, was only begging the question. In any event, the *Ausgleich* put an end for all time to the dream of a Josephistic, centralized German state ruled from Vienna and embracing all the nations living within Danubia. In addition, because it was itself a kind of restatement of Josephistic principles, but in a German-Magyar dualistic sense and written up as a basic law, the *Ausgleich* shattered forever the dream of Austria's liberals of refiguring the monarchy as a single state along the lines of Enlightenment principles. From the moment of the concluding of the *Ausgleich,* political liberalism could no longer be part and parcel of the Dual Monarchy's political mainstream. At the same time, no other solution emerged that might pacify the nine subject nations while at the same time satisfying the expectations of the ruling German and Magyar nations. Hence the centrifugal pull of nationalism waxed, and by 1900 Austria-Hungary was forced to deal with the other great powers on the diplomatic field while hobbled by nationality strife from within. Although ranked among the great powers, Austria-Hungary in actuality was something less than a great power. It was the specter of this humiliation, when viewed within the broad framework of diplomatic relations among the European great powers as a whole, that played a great part in Vienna's role in bringing on the First World War.[46]

The collapse of a German-oriented centralism, however, did not push the bulk of German Austrian liberals into deserting the dynasty. Many instead turned to search for other means that would satisfy the desire for political wholeness while at the same time accommodating the monarchy's ethnic diversity. Such solutions usually called for substituting for the *Ausgleich* some sort of federative structure that would provide both political autonomy and cultural equality for all of Austria's nations. But because the German Austrian ruling classes tenaciously clung to the *Ausgleich,* these attempts produced sharp clashes, especially with the Magyar leadership. Nevertheless, these disputes were both ongoing and undecided at the outbreak of the First World War.[47] Schönerers and Wolfs represented only a minority of German Austrians, and few German citizens of the Austrian state saw their salvation in the breakup of the Dual Monarchy and a constitutional link with the great German *Reich* to the north. Most German Austrians were proud of their Austro-German cultural heritage, and this heritage also signified for them loyalty to the House of Habsburg. In this sense, Austria (in a German idiom) came first for German Austrians. Being German came second. It was only for those few pan-Germans blinded by Teutonic fervor (and their Magyar counterparts) that the Danubian realm could offer no home and hence no future.[48] Moreover, the attitudes of the German Austrian majority were essentially no different after the collapse of the Dual Monarchy and the overturning of its dynasty.[49]

The picture is less clear regarding both the Magyars and Austria's other remaining non-German nations. For example, because Schönerer's German Bohemian Deutsche Arbeiterpartei urged that German employers should hire only workers of German stock and because the bulk of employers in Bohemia and Moravia identified with German culture, the German Worker's Party may have sparked a kind of Hegelian antithesis in the formation of the counterposed Czech National Socialist Party. But it is also clear that this Czech party also grew out of the earlier, somewhat more moderate Young Czech movement (a Czech equivalent to the German People's Party), operating concurrently throughout the crown lands. Like their counterparts in the German People's Party, the Young Czechs might have been content with a degree of cultural autonomy, but only if they could have been fully satisfied that their cultural development as Czechs could be wholly obtained within the framework of a Habsburg Danubia. By the same token, if the Czech National Socialists seemingly were more unyielding than their Young Czech forebears, so too, did the Young Czechs seem to have been more unyielding than *their* political forebears, the so-called old Czech movement. In summary, as Czech national self-consciousness evolved after 1850, each successive generation of non-German Bohemian movements proved more unyielding on the Bohemian question than its ideological predecessors. This evolution brings up the question of whether Czech National Socialism represented an evolution on its own account and hence was something more than merely a Czech reaction to the likes of Schönerer's party. (This same question can be turned around and put to the origins of the German Worker's Party.) However, there can be no doubt that ultimately the Czech National Socialists, the party that originally had the allegiance of Thomas G. Masaryk and Eduard Beneš, among others, proved to be the carrier of an anti-German independence movement.[50] Further, the Czech National Socialists were in constant, unruly dispute with Schönerer's adherents. The interaction of the two parties therefore was typical of the political fallout from the Dual Monarchy's centrifugal forces. The "socialism of the stupid fellow," as some called the platform of these two parties, combined elements of cultural nationalism with certain paternalistic tenets not unlike the social programs associated with Austro-Marxism.[51] As such, unlike the Social Democrats, both German and Czech national socialism can be viewed as harbingers of a darker future that was soon to overtake central Europe. At the turn of the century, however, that future still lay hidden, for in 1907, when the elections reform went into effect, Schönerer's group was able to claim only three seats and the Czech National Socialists nine, and this within a broadly democratic process that elected 516 deputies. Hence, contemporaries might be excused if, in 1907, they viewed the Vienna parliament as not the end of but a new beginning for the ancient realm of the Habsburgs.[52]

The bulk of the Austrian people stood between the Social Democrats and the Christian Socialists, on the one hand, and the various pan-nationalist parties, on the other. Some were affiliated with the shifting programs of the twenty-five remaining political groups operating within the crown lands; many, however, linked themselves with no political movement and were content to contemplate nationality not just within Habsburg political culture, but on the assumption that the monarchy would continue to exist. To be sure, as the twentieth century wore on, the probability that the state would be restructured had increased for two main reasons. First was a desire to find a federative pattern that would satisfy Austria's ethnic mix, if not conform to its geographic distribution, which was not static but always in flux because of demographic changes as well as ones related to the development of Austria's economic infrastructure.[53] In addition, many realized that it was necessary to face down Magyar opposition to any change in the basic order as defined in the 1867 *Ausgleich,* while at the same time, many on both sides of the Leitha agreed that to stubbornly stay with the terms of the 1867 compromise was inimical to all concerned.[54]

The posture of the government in Budapest, dominated by the Magyar gentry, was especially damaging to Croats and other south Slavs, who, fated to live in the Hungarian half of the Dual Monarchy, had become hostile to the entire constitutional framework because of Budapest's insistence on a policy of forced Magyarization for those non-Magyars historically residing within the lands of the Crown of St. Stephen. Indeed, the infamous Agram treason trial of 1909 caused the deepest discouragement among otherwise Habsburg-loyal south Slavs because the outcome underscored the apparent unwillingness of the tired old emperor to make use of the dynasty's authority to defend Hungary's subject peoples from the obtuse cultural programs imposed on them by the hardheaded and inflexible Magyar minority, who were unfortunately in control of the kingdom's constitutional processes.[55] On the other hand, the heir to the throne, impatiently surveying the rule of the Hofburg from his heights at the Belvedere, was known to be a bitter opponent of the stubborn Magyar oligarchy and determined to deal with them so as to favor the cultural aspirations of the Croats and Slovenes.[56]

To be sure, no one knew with absolute certainty what program the Magyarphobic Franz Ferdinand would pursue. But from what he and members of his entourage had said, there were indications that the heir to the throne would work for a strong centralized state that would, at the same time, permit cultural development of all of Austria's peoples—a kind of shared nationalist dictatorship. Moreover, his reform would embrace not only the crown lands but the lands of the Crown of St. Stephen as well. And while it remains moot as to how such an oxymoronic arrangement might have been introduced, its existence as an abstract idea demonstrates that there existed, even up until 1914, hope among many that Austria might live. Even if the eighty-three-year-old Emperor Franz Joseph was unlikely to initiate a restructuring of his realm, waiting in the wings was the moody, irascible, but capable Archduke Franz Ferdinand. In addition, the archduke already possessed a shadow government made up of skilled and knowledgeable men anxious and ready to renew the monarchy.[57] Hence it was not all gloom in the Transleithan lands of the Crown of St. Stephen. The constellation of time and man implied that while the hour was late, time had not run out for Hungary's south Slavs to find redress within a Habsburg-led Danubian realm.

There were external factors working for the preservation of the Dual Monarchy as well. For example, Austrians had long come to fear Russian imperialism, which was especially unpalatable because of its associations with the dark, byzantine forces surrounding the proverbial despotism of its czars. But Austrians also had come to fear the domination that might be expected from the drive of the new German *Reich*'s economic imperialism.[58] Hence there still was much life in the traditional perspective that Austria was a necessary counterweight in Europe to the German and Russian empires. At the same time, Habsburg Austria was thought to be the best possibility for ensuring the free development of the peoples residing in Danubia without at the same time sacrificing what they might achieve and possess collectively. The sad events that brought about the great war in August of 1914 and the military alignments surrounding them too often have obscured these fundamental verities, though events since 1918 have upheld their importance. Freedom was not found in the alternatives to the Dual Monarchy that emerged between the end of the First World War and the collapse of the Soviet empire seventy-seven years later. And although today these circumstances may finally come about, events in the former Yugoslavia and in the Caucasus are not reassuring. And certainly what may be today's sunrise neither blots out nor justifies the terror and the bloodshed that coursed through south-central Europe after the Peace of Versailles.

Despite the undoubted centrifugal pull, a number of fundamental factors motivated the accommodation, and even resolution, of the monarchy's difficult nationality questions within the outlines of the existing state. There was, for one, the fact of a certain inertia borne on tradition that, with no clear-cut alternative, seemed preferable to a step in the dark. There was also the undeniable economic benefits that much of the population enjoyed as a result of the existing political synthesis and that promised to continue. And last, there was the brutal logic (and logistics) associated with the current European great-power political system; that is, international diplomacy perhaps required Austria's preservation and renewal. Austria was squeezed between two powerful empires, both rendered relentlessly expansive by the uncontrolled internal dynamic of modern power, and there were few who did not believe in Frantisek Palacky's words to the effect that if Austria did not exist, she would have to be invented.[59] Given the growing confidence in the permanency of the European state system, it was with some justification, therefore, that the majority of Franz Joseph's subjects looked to their futures within the Habsburg realm. Indeed, these masses were like all majorities everywhere. That is, they were without the financial and psychic means to play a great role on the political stage. On the other hand, in Austria they remained reasonably loyal to the rule of their emperor and king. This is not to say that they did not look to the future with a certain degree of anxiety. But they also were not without that fundamental, not always unfounded, optimism that is the possession of the misused citizenry of all times and in all places.[60]

Hence, if political angst was threatening not only the outer corpus of the Dual Monarchy but its very soul, there also was still in place the core of continuity that resided at the center of the dynasty, for the kaiser still sat at his desk struggling to put right what had fallen out of sorts. There still remained the hope that the chief of the Habsburg dynasty—whichever Habsburg might be carrying the dynasty's heavy burden at any given moment—could exert the necessary authority that would act as a centripetal counterweight to those things that seemed to be pulling the state apart. The hope was that the dynasty might infuse into the machinery of state the strength to overcome those obstacles thrown up against it by the enemies of Austria.

Notes

1. The tenor and the processes (but not the origins of the underlying assumptions) by which human emotions were manipulated toward accepting nationalist ends are clear enough. Take, for example, a pamphlet put forth by the irredentist National Rumanian League in 1892. This small booklet, *Die Rumanien Frage,* whips up a sense of chauvinist passion by convincing the reader that Rumanians in Hungarian Transylvania have been intolerably victimized by the Magyars and that, given the latter's total rejection of reasonable Rumanian demands for national-cultural recognition, no option remains but the de facto secession of Transylvania from the Hungarian state.

The first step in this argument is to identify Rumanians as opposed to Magyars (for both were constitutionally considered Hungarians) through a construction of the self (Rumanian) as opposed to the other (Magyar). So, for example, in appealing to the editor of London's *Athenaeum* to promote the English edition of *Die Rumanien Frage,* the discussion suggests, taking great pains to appear straightforwardly rational, that the Rumanians are a distinct and oppressed group of Hungarians deserving of outside support from civilized peoples for "what may we not hope from your philantropical [sic] sentiments when you learn that not individuals, but a whole race are groaning under the yoke of the oppressor, and that millions of men, women and children are looking with anxious eyes to Europe to put an end to the odious sufferings to which they are subjected." (See letter by the secretary of the Antwerp [Belgium] section of the National Rumanian League to the editor of the *Athenaeum,* dated February 1893 and enclosed with the English edition of *Die Rumanien Frage,* on file in the Institute for Social History, Amsterdam, The Netherlands.)

This first step, addressed in this example to a Britisher residing in an imperial capital that had subjected nearly a quarter of the earth's land surface to Britannia, thereby distinguishes self and other, oppressed Rumanians against oppressor Magyars. The discussion then turns to stereotyping the other by rhetorically asking "how it can be imagined that the [Magyar dominated] government [is] completely ignorant of [Rumanian] wants and aspirations [and] can feel for them [not] the slightest compassion in their distress." The Magyars collectively thereby are made not only obdurate, but unfeeling and insensitive as well. The victims, that is, the Rumanians, are then cloaked in mainstream west European historicism, for they are portrayed as "people of Roman Dacia who, at the present time, after 17 centuries of suffering, still speak a Roman language derived from the Latin rustic tongue." In other words the Rumanians are not only oppressed by a non-Western nation, culturally speaking, but they themselves are really culturally western

Europeans, victims longing for liberation from the hands of heathens. Using a generic plot from well-known fairy tales that, for example, were part and parcel of the childhood of politically articulate English people, the appeal goes on to argue that "the Magyars . . . treat Rumanians in the same way a stepmother who loves her own offspring gives to her other children a piece of bread and her contempt, [and] so the Magyar government not only protects its own people and advances them as a people seeing in us but the intolerable obstacle in its path, and never ceases to treat us as traitors." Beyond pitching its tale of woe to a wider audience, this fairy tale motif sets the stage for the final escalation, the demonization of the oppressor. This begins with a listing of the civil sins committed against the Rumanians by the Magyar government: rigged elections, forced Magyarization through public instruction, fanaticism of the Magyar press, and so on. Then this litany jumps into a macabre finale by accusing the Hungarian state of orchestrating "barbarous acts against the Rumanians by . . . gendarmes" and including "rape, torture and massacres." The English reader, whose correct emotional buttons have all been pushed while he is comfortably taking tea (imported from another one of Britain's foreign holdings), is brought to perceive the Magyars, collectively and hence individually, as demons.

Taken all together, the document that purportedly seeks cultural recognition for Rumanian Transylvanians within the existing Hungarian state nevertheless ends up on a note that strongly implies that such a goal in reality is too limited given the magnitude of actual Magyar transgressions. Indeed, added to the explosive mixture of sins and demands are the words of the Rumanian nationalist Terenzio Maniani that "lapse of time never changes violence into rights!" The appeal then adds Maniani's comment on the circumstances under which Transylvania was joined to the Crown of St. Stephen: "The annexation of [the province] to Hungary [was] against the will of the majority of inhabitants of Transylvania." This ignores, however, the fact that the entire process was carried out within the framework of the medieval era and hardly can be comprehended (as implied) in terms of the dynamics of modern, democratic government. One can conclude thereby that the goal of the Rumanian National League was not limited reform, but rather an irredentist agenda of bringing about the breakup of the Hungarian state for the profit of the kingdom of Rumania. This is not to whitewash Hungarian conduct toward their subject nations, but only to point up the political problem for existing state communities created by nationalism and irredenta when these goals were openly pursued and packaged in such fashion that, while claiming to seek a compromise resolution, in fact uses rhetoric clearly intended to short-circuit compromise. Moreover, in all probability the words were designed also to elicit a harsh Magyar reaction, further justifying the need to disassemble the current Hungarian state. See Anonymous, *The Rumanian Question in Transylvania and in Hungary: Reply of the Rumanian Students of Transylvania and Hungary* (Vienna, Budapest, Graz, Cluj, Antwerp: Jos. Theunis, 1892). This was printed in five languages: Russian, French, English, Italian, and German.

2. On the evolution of the Hofburg through time, see Moriz Dreger, *Baugeschichte der K.u.K. Hofburg in Wien* (Vienna: Anton Scholl, 1914).

3. See Elizabeth Springer, *Geschichte und Kulturleben der Wiener Ringstrasse* (Wiesbaden: Franz Steiner, 1980), pp. 596–598. This monograph, after its publication, came to constitute volume II of *Die Wiener Ringstrasse: Bild einer Epoche,* ed. Renate Wagner-Rieger, 10 volumes (Wiesbaden: Franz Steiner, 1980).

4. For an overview of the Habsburg state in this context of nationality, see Friedrich Heer, *Die Kampf um die österreichischen Identität* (Vienna: Hermann Böhlaus, 1981). On the evolution of Vienna, see Hilde Spiel, *Wien: Spektrum einer Stadt* (Munich: Biederstein, 1971) and Ilsa Barea, *Vienna* (New York: Alfred E. Knopf, 1966). Also of interest in terms of nostalgia is Edgard Haider, *Verloren Wien: Adelspläste Vergangener Toge* (Vienna: Hermann Böhlaus, 1984).

5. This difference has long been observed by others. See, for example, Alfred H. Fried, *Wien-Berlin: Ein Vergleich* (Vienna: Josef Lenobel, 1908). Toward the turn of the century the ethnic makeup of the Dual Monarchy was as follows: Germans:10,170,00; Magyars: 6,542,000; Rumanians: 2,623,000; Italians: 755,000; Slovenes: 1,280,000; Ceho[Czech]-Slovaks, 7,140,000; Poles: 3,255,000; Croatian-Serbs: 2,918,00; Russians [Ruthenes]: 3,158,000. Jews were counted within that national group within whose territory they resided or to which they belonged by attribution. Note too that Czechs and Slovaks often were grouped together at that time, belying the consciousness for separation that arose in 1990. See H.F. Brachelle, *Statistische Skizze der österreich-ungarischen Monarchie,* 12th ed. (Leipzig: Heinrich, 1889), p. 2.

6.

Es Gibt nur eine Kaiserstadt

Es Gibt nur ein Wien,

Es Gibt nur ein Rauberstadt,

Und das heisst Berlin

Cited in Arthur J. May, *The Habsburg Monarchy, 1867–1914* (Cambridge: Harvard University Press, 1960), p. 309.

7. See Friedrich Heer, "Österreich nicht Ostmark" in his *Der Kampf um die Österreichischen Identität*, pp. 23–39.

8. On the early Middle Ages, see Karl Lechner, *Die Babenburger: Markgrafen und Herzoge von Österreichs* (Vienna: Böhlau, 1976) and Alphons Lhotsky, *Europaisches Mittelalter: Das Land Österreich* (Munich: R. Oldenbourg, 1970); also Heinrich Fichenau, *Von der Mark zum Herzogtum: Grundlagen und Sinn des* privilegium minus *für Österreich* (Munich: R. Oldenbourg, 1970). For the early modern period see R.J.W. Evans, *The Making of the Habsburg Monarchy, 1526–1815: An Interpretation* (Oxford: Oxford University Press, 1979). A less sympathetic view is presented by Victor S. Mamatey, *The Rise of the Habsburg Empire: 1526–1918* (New York: American Heritage Press, 1971). For the evolution of the consciousness of the non-German Austrian nations, see Robert A. Kann and Zdenck V. David, *The Peoples of the Eastern Habsburg Lands: 1526–1918* (Seattle: University of Washington Press, 1984).

9. Perhaps the best example of this perspective is a multivolume work carried out under the guidance of Crown Prince Rudolf, titled *Die österreich-ungarische Monarchie in Wort und Bild,* 11 volumes (Vienna: Druck und Verlag der K.K. Hof-und Staats Druckeri, 1887). A thorough study of the Austrian nations for the years 1848–1918 is Adam Wandruszka and Peter Urbanitsch, eds., *Die Habsburgermonarchie 1848–1918,* volume III, *Die Völker des Reiches* (Vienna: Der österreichischen Akademie der Wissenschaften, 1980).

10. In 1910, Franz Joseph was said to have told Theodore Roosevelt, "The reason for my office is to protect my peoples from their politicians." Quoted in Georg Markus, ed., *Der Kaiser: Franz Joseph I in Bild und Dokumentes* (Vienna: Amalthea Verlag, 1985), p. 174.

11. See Ilse Barea, *Vienna,* especially pp. 114ff. On the general topic concerning the creation of a modern army for Austria-Hungary, see Scott W. Lackey, *The Rebirth of the Habsburg Army: Friedrich Beck and the Rise of the General Staff* (Westport, CT: Greenwood Press, 1995).

12. Karl Renner, "Sympathien und Antipathien," *Der Kampf* VIII (1908–1909), p. 164.

13. See, for example, Otto Bauer, "Die Bedingungen der Nationalen Assimilation," *Der Kampf* V (1912). See also more recent summaries: Alois Mosser, "Die Wirtschaft im Habsburgerreich," pp. 60–72, and Gerhard Maresch, "Industrie und Technik," pp. 73–82, in Schloss Grafenegg, *Das Zeitalter Kaiser Franz Josephs, Glanz und Elend: 1880–1916,* vol. I (Beiträge) (Vienna: Nieder österreichische Landesausstellung, 1987).

14. See Lawrence Sondhaus, *The Naval Policy of Austria-Hungary, 1867–1918: Navalism, Industrial Development and the Politics of Dualism* (West Lafayette, IN: Purdue University Press, 1993), especially pp. 142–153.

15. See James Shedel, *Art and Society: The New Art Movement in Vienna* (Palo Alto: Society for the Promotion of Science and Scholarship, 1981); a somewhat different summary is in Carl Schorske, *Fin-de-Siècle Vienna: Politics and Culture* (New York: Knopf, 1980). Also of interest in this regard is Lillian Langseth-Christensen, *A Design for Living* (New York: Viking, 1987) and Schloss Grafenegg, *Das Zeitalter Franz Joseph*, vols. I (Beiträge) and II (Katalog). See also Robert Waissenberger, ed., *Wien 1870–1930: Traum und Wirklichkeit* (Vienna: Residenz Verlag, 1984), especially Eduard F. Sekler, "Josef Hoffmann," pp. 131–136, and Elizabeth Schmuttermeier, "Die Wiener Werkstätte," pp. 145–150. See also the very lively account of the many dimensions of bourgeois life presented in Erich Alban Berg, *Als der Adler noch zwei Köpfe hatte: Ein Florilegium, 1858–1918* (Vienna: Verlag Styria, 1980); see especially "Wiens Burgertum—Eine Kleine Auswahl von Grossen Originalen," pp. 48–64. Also of interest is Hermann Swistun and Heinrich Baltazzi-Scharschmid, *Die Familien Baltazzi-Vetsera im kaiserlichen Wien* (Vienna: Hermann Böhlaus, 1980). The Baltazzis and Vetseras were on close terms with aristocrats (one of the Vetseras being the infamous Marie of Maylering), but in fact did not belong to that first society; rather, they orbited out of the upper crest of the second.

16. See, in addition to that cited above, Gerbert Frodl, "Die Maleri: Künstlerhaus—Secession—Hagenbund" in Schloss Grafenegg, *Das Zeitalter Franz Josephs*, Beiträge, pp. 231ff.

17. Two autobiographies that sustain this truism are Nora Fürstin Fugger, *Im Glanz der Kaiserzeit* (Vienna: Amalthea Verlag, 1980) and Erwein Lobkowicz, *Erinnerungen an die Monarchie* (Vienna: Amalthea Verlag, 1989). See also Gunther Martin, ed., *Als Victorianer in Wien: Erinnerungen des britischen Diplomaten Sir Horace Rumbold* (Vienna: Österreichischer Bundesverlag, 1984).

18. See Roman Sandgruber, "All Tag des Fin-de-Siècle—Wiener Glanz und Elend," *Die Zeitalter Franz Josephs*, Beiträge, pp. 138–151. See also, Robert Waissenberger, "Eine Metropole der Jahrhundertwende," *Wien, 1870–1930*, pp. 7–20, and Berg, *Als der Adler noch zwei Köpfe hatte*, pp. 171–180.

19. See Otto Bauer, "Das Bedingung der Nationalen Assimilation," *Der Kampf* V (1912), pp. 246–263.

20. Ibid. See also Erno Deak and Richard Gisser, "Bevölkerungsentwicklung in der Monarchie nach 1880," *Das Zeitalter Franz Josephs*, vol. II, pp. 19–24. Perhaps the most useful, and in some ways definitive, analysis of this phenomena remains Otto Bauer, *Die Nationalitätenfrage und Sozialismus* (Vienna: Volksbuchhandlung, 1907).

21. Bauer, "Die Bedingung der National Assimilation," *Der Kampf*, V (1912). Bauer emphasizes here that it usually was the second generation of emigres that felt this humiliation, as the first was more concerned with material matters like employment. Moreover, Bauer notes that members of the third generation, especially if they had orbited upward into the bourgeoisie, loudly proclaimed the necessity that the cultural nation of their grandparents, as defined by language, receive civil recognition. That is, the first generation emigrated and the second assimilated, while the third dissimilated.

22. See, for example, Thomas Garrigue Masaryk, *The Making of a State: Memoirs and Observations, 1914–1918* (London: Frederick A. Stokes, 1928).

23. Insights into this well-documented difficulty are offered by the emphasis on tactics from the perspective within the political parties in Lothar Höbelt,"Parliamentary Politics in a Multinational Setting: Late Imperial Austria," Working Paper in Austrian Studies (Minneapolis: Center for Austrian Studies, University of Minnesota, 1993).

24. Robert Musil, *The Man Without Qualities* (New York: Capricorn, 1965), pp. 33–34.

25. Quoted in Hilde Spiel, ed., *Wien: Spektrum einer Stadt* (Munich: Biederstein, 1971), p. 41.

26. Alfons Clary-Aldringen, *Geschichten eines Alten Österreichers: Mit einem Vorwart Golo Mann* (Frankfurt am Main: Ullstein, 1977), p. 158. The Czech diplomat to whom these words were addressed answered back, "Yes, but the caged lion has tranquility enough to eat and it is secure from its enemies. But the Bohemian lion loves freedom even more." Feelingly, the Hungarian ambassador (who was also present) interjected, "But what if the Hunter comes?" Clary-Aldringen then commented, "And since then, the hunter has come twice!"

27. Quoted in Masaryk, *The Making of a State*, pp. v–xiv.

28. See Fritz Judtmann, *Mayerling Ohne Mythos: Ein Tatsachenbericht* (Vienna: Kremayr and Scheriau, 1968). The author, Arthur Schnitzler, a medical doctor and psychiatrist by training, wrote much fiction dealing with suicide as well as sketching an accurate perspective of life in Vienna. For the author's early life and an outline of his writings, see Arthur Schnitzler, *My Youth in Vienna* (New York: Holt, Rinehart and Winston, 1970). An antidote to the canon of pessimism is observed in James Shedel, "Variatione zum Thema Ornament. Kunst und das Problem des Wendels in Österreich der Jahrhundertwende," in Alfred Pfabigan, ed., *Ornament und Askese im Zeitgeist des Wien Jahrhundertwende* (Vienna: Brandstätter, 1985). See, in addition, James Shedel, "Emperor, Church and People: Religion and Dynastic Loyalty During the Golden Jubilee of Franz Joseph," *Catholic Historical Review* 76 (1990).

29. Musil, *The Man Without Qualities*, p. 93.

30. See William Alexander Jenks, *The Austrian Elections Reform of 1907* (New York: Columbia University Press, 1950).

31. See Peter Schöffer, *Der Wahlrechtskampf der Österreichischen Sozialdemokratie: 1888/89–1897* (Wiesbaden: Franz Steiner Verlag, 1986). See also Hans Mommesen, *Die Sozialdemokratie und die Nationalitätenfrage in Habsburger Vielvolkerstaat* (Vienna: Europa Verlag, 1963).

32. This well-known fact is verified in still another way from a record of a conversation that took place between Prince Karl von Schwarzenberg and Kaiser Franz Joseph in which Schwarzenberg stated that when he spoke to Franz Joseph "about not permitting the 1907 elections law because it would destroy the aristocratic large land owners *[Grossgrundbesitz]*, a power that supports Austria. The kaiser answered, 'Believe me, the only means by which the east can be saved lies in the introduction of the general elections law *[allgemein Wahlrecht]*.'. . . These words, spoken in the year 1907, cut me to the quick since I recognized from them how great the concern *[Sorgevolle]* with which Kaiser Franz Joseph viewed the future." See memo (incomplete) of Prince Karl von Schwarzenberg in Austrian States Archive, N.P.A. (o1/41a), Karton 448, ff. 1–125.

33. Ludwig Brügel, *Geschichte der österreichischen Sozialdemokratie*, vol. v (Vienna: Wiener Volksbuchhandlungen, 1925), pp. V, 33–53.

34. Ibid., pp. 40–41. See also Jenks, *The Austrian Elections Reform of 1907*.

35. See Peter Urbanitsch, "Politisierung der Massen," *Das Zeitalter Kaiser Franz Josephs, Beiträge*, pp. 106–125, especially pp. 122–124.

36. *Arbeiter Zeitung*, July 29, 1914. See also Brügel, *Geschichte Österreichischen Sozialdemokratie*, V, 171–173.

37. See Friedrich Funder, *Von Gestern in Heute: Aus dem Kaiserreich zu die Republik* (Vienna: Verlag Herold, 1963), especially pp. 85–130. Also, Klemens von Klemperer, *Ignaz Seipel: Christian Statesman in a Time of Crisis* (Princeton: Princeton University Press, 1972, pp. 3–73. For a glance at the national perspective of the future clerical

fascists, see Ignaz Seipel, *Staat und Nation* (Vienna: Braümuller, 1916). Old Austria's last hours from the view of its last minister-president are described in Heinrich Lammasch, *Europas Elfte Stunde* (Munich: Verlag für Kulturpolitik, 1919). See also Paul Molisch, *Geschichte der deutschnationalen Bewegung in Österreich von ihren Anfang bis zum Zerfall der Monarchie* (Jena: Gustav Fischer, 1926).

38. David Strong, *Austria: October 1918–March 1919* (New York: Columbia University Press, 1939) and (for Germany) Richard M. Watt, *The Kings Depart, The Tragedy of Germany: Versailles and the German Revolution* (New York: Simon and Schuster, 1969).

39. See Andrew Gladding Whiteside, *Austrian National Socialism Before 1918* (The Hague: Nijhof, 1962). See also Bruce F. Pauley, *From Prejudice to Persecution: A History of Austrian Anti-Semitism* (Chapel Hill: University of North Carolina Press, 1992).

40. See Kurt Schuschnigg, *The Brutal Takeover: The Austrian Ex-Chancellor's Account of the Anschluss by Hitler* (New York: Atheneum, 1971). See also E.H.P. Cordfunke, *Zita: Keizerin van Oostenrijk koningin van Hongarije* (Amsterdam: De Bataafsche Leeuw, 1986), pp. 171–182.

41. See Andrew Gladding Whiteside, *The Socialism of Fools: Georg von Schönerer and Austrian Pan-Germanism* (Berkeley: University of California Press, 1975), and his *Austrian National Socialism Before 1918*. An interesting point of view on these issues is seen in Wenzel Jaksch, *Europas Weg nach Potsdam* (Stuttgart: Deutscher Verlag, 1959). See also Clifton Earl Edmondson, *The Heimwehr and Austrian Politics, 1918–1936* (Athens: University of Georgia Press, 1978). See also Gary Cohen, *The Politics of Ethnic Survival: Germans in Prague, 1861–1914* (Princeton: Princeton University Press, 1981).

42. For example, on November 21, 1902, Count Franz Thun remarked to Freiherr Aloys Lexa von Aehrenthal that "The political situation is without consolation. . . . [Koeber's] speech was a masterpiece and it made a great impression at the moment it was given. But it didn't make things any better, because men do not wish it to be better, they all live only to be dissatisfied politically and to hate on the basis of nationality. The radical elements on both sides are so strong that rational *[ruhigen]* persons have no room in which to maneuver." See Ernst Rutkowski, *Briefe und Dokumente zur Geschichte der österreichisch-ungarischen Monarchie unter Besonderer Berucksichtigung des bömisch-mährischen Raumes,* "Der Vafassungstreue Grossgrundbesitz, 1880–1899" (Vienna: R. Oldenbourg, 1983), II, p. 639. Of course, this ethnic chemistry was not limited to Czech German lands but was widespread. For example, by 1880, when Vienna had become a metropolitan city, one out of every three Viennese was Czech; that is, a Czech-speaking Austrian citizen. But by 1950, there were only 3,950 Czech Viennese. Changing political culture had its reflection in changing demography. See Spiel, *Wien: Spektrum einer Stadt,* pp. 34–37. The bourgeois perception of the relationship between national culture and the political state was one where every national culture, as measured by the language in use, required its own state. In other words, language in use implied not only culture but race as well. Further, this perception thereby implicitly called for the breakup of multinational political entities like Austria-Hungary into its national-territorial components. This sort of deconstruction, of course, was far easier to achieve as an abstraction than it was in political reality. See, for example, Johann Christoph Allmayer-Beck, *Ministerpräsident Baron Beck: Ein Staatsmann des alten Österreich* (Vienna: R. Oldenbourg, 1956), especially pp. 9–17. In fact, as with Baron Beck, many old Austrians were descended from more than one of Austrian's nationalities, this descent was, so to speak, a genetic reflection of old Austria. This fact, although a historical truth ignored by nationalist ideology, caused considerable confusion. See, for example, the very interesting article by Gerald Stourzh, "Ethnic Attribution in Late Imperial Austria: Good Intentions, Evil Consequences," in Ritchie Robertson and Edward Timms, eds., *The Habsburg Legacy* (Edinburgh: University of Edinburgh Press, 1994), pp. 67–83. This tendency is illustrated in

the post–World War I era by the following examples: the president of the Austrian (First) Republic, Dr. Michael Hainisch, was asked by the Czech Academy, in 1925, to contribute to a *Festschrift* to be presented to the president of the Czech Republic, Dr. Thomas G. Masaryk. Hainisch was assured the work would be printed only in German, because he had been in the same class as Masaryk in the Academic Gymnasium in Vienna. In other words, because both once had been Austrians and friends. (See Austrian State Archive, PA-I, Karton 208, Liasse Österreich 1/1, 1920–1930, f. 42). In 1934, a furor broke out between Prague and Vienna because the Czech newspapers maintained that the Austrian chancellor, Wilhelm Miklas, really was Czech. An embarrassed and angered Miklas was forced to defend himself in the Austrian newspapers, writing that although his mother was German, his grandfather had been born in "Cernetic by the mill" (Mühle/Miklas), but he had come to Vienna as a very young man, where "generally he only spoke German" (ibid., ff. 435–450).

43. Ernst Rutkowski, *Briefe und Dokumente zur Geschichte der österreichisch-ungarischen Monarchie,* II, pp. 664–670, in which appears the minutes of a conference of "reconciliation" wherein representatives of German and Czech political fractions laid out their grievances. The Czech delegate, Dr. Pacak, strenuously demanded recognition of Czech speech at every level of activity where historically German speech had been the common usage. See also Hugo Hantsch, *Die Nationalitäten frage um alten Österreich: Das Problem der konstruktiven Reichsgestatung* (Vienna: Herold Verlag, 1953). See also Whiteside, *National Socialism in Austria.*

44. The sad end result is summarized in Douglas Botting, *From the Ruins of the Reich: Germany 1945–1949* (New York: Meridian, 1986), especially pp. 149–192. And indeed, Czech perceptions of mistreatment did not always withstand scrutiny. For example, German politicians in the disputed lands complained that the Taaffe government in Vienna (1879–1893) made excessive concessions to the Czechs in matters of education. And these complaints were on the mark, for even by the early and mid-1880s statistics suggest that the Czechs had already made great gains relative to the Germans in education; that is, under German liberal control before the Taaffe era and before Czech politicians were actively pressing Vienna for concessions favoring Czech nationals. See Gary B. Cohen, "Education and Czech Social Structure in the Late Nineteenth Century," in Hans Lemberg et al., *Bildungsgeschichte, Bevolkerungsgeschichte, Gesellschaftsgeschichte in Den Böhmischen Ländern und in Europa: Festschift für Jan Havranek zum 60. Geburtstag* (Vienna: Verlag für Geschichte und Politik Wien, 1988), pp. 35–36. General support for this view is presented in the same volume in Robert Luft, "Politische Professoren in Böhmen 1861–1914," pp. 16ff.

45. See Paul P. Bernard, *The Limits of the Enlightenment: Joseph II and the Law* (Urbana: University of Illinois Press, 1979). See also Derek Beales, *Joseph II: Under the Shadow of Maria Theresa,* and Christopher Duffey, *The Army of Maria Theresa: The Armed Forces of Imperial Austria, 1740–1780* (New York: Hippocrene Books, 1977) .

46. See F.R. Bridge, *The Habsburg Monarchy Among the Great Powers, 1815–1918* (Oxford: Berg, 1990), especially pp. 345–371. See also Fritz Fellner, "Der Zerfall der Donaumonarchie in weltgeschichtlicher Perspektive," in Richard Georg Plaschka and Karlheinz Mack, eds., *Die Auflösung des Habsburgerreichs: Zusammenbuch und Neu-orientaerung im Donaurum* (Vienna: R. Oldenbourg, 1970), pp. 32–41.

47. See L. Katus, "Über die Wirtschaftlichen und Gesellschaftlichen Grundlagen der Nationalitätenfrage in Ungarn vor dem Ersten Weltkreig," in Akadémiai Kiadó, *Die Nationale Frage in der österreich-ungarischen Monarchie* (Budapest: Verlag der Un-garischen Akademie der Wissenschaften, 1966), pp. 149–216.

48. See Whiteside, *The Socialism of Fools.*

49. In the fall of 1918, the choices then confronting Austria-Hungary were laid down

in stark relief by the Social Democratic writer Karl Mann. In sum, Mann stated simply that if Germany won the world war, Austria would live; if not, Austria would die. See Karl Mann, "Die Selbstbestimmungsrecht der österreichischen nationen," *Der Kampf* XI (1918).

50. The first and second presidents, respectively, of the first Czechoslovakian Republic.

51. See Whiteside, *The Socialism of Fools*.

52. See Franz Ludwig Carsten, *Faschismius in Österreich: von Schönerer zu Hitler* (Munich: Wilhelm Fink, 1977), especially pp. 25–29. See also Richard S. Gehr, *Karl Luegar: Mayor of Fin-de-Siècle Vienna* (Detroit: Wayne State University Press, 1990), especially pp. 143–169; Bruce F. Pauley, *Hitler and the Forgotten Nazis: A History of Austrian National Socialism* (Chapel Hill: University of North Carolina Press, 1981); Whiteside, *The Socialism of Fools*.

53. One example of the confusion between abstract claims for national territory and the demographic realities will suffice to illustrate the point. Prior to 1918, Slovakia belonged to the Hungarian state, a constituent part of the lands of the Crown of St. Stephen. But the Slovakian people were primarily a peasant people residing in the rural areas, while German and Magyar minorities gathered to form a majority in Slovakia's market towns and administrative centers such as Bratislava (Pressburg). But by 1900, under the press of industrialization, many of the Slovaks left the countryside to find jobs in cities, but not in the largest Slovak one (again Bratislava), which retained its German majority (52.5 percent) or in the second largest, Kosice, which retained its Hungarian majority (66.3 percent). Rather, the largest concentration of Slovaks in any one city, some 50,000, was to be found in the Hungarian capital, Budapest. See Owen V. Johnson, "Newspapers and Nation Building: The Slovak Press in Pre-1918 Slovakia," in Lemberg et al., *Bildungsgeschichte, Bevölkerungsgeschichte, Gesellschaftsgeschichte in Den Böhmischen Ländern und in Europa*, especially pp. 160–178.

54. This point brings us back to the discussion of the Rumanian question in note 1 for this chapter and to the question of what was the seed of modern nationality discord. What was the origin of the politics of victimization, which made use of nationalist sentiment? The answer to these questions has to be in the social dynamics of modernism, in the social manifestation of capital and industry. This manifestation is seen in the rise of a literate bourgeoisie whose livelihood was founded on industry and commerce. Being literate, this bourgeoisie was both armed by and reachable through the written word, presented by the popular press. But the popular press wasn't free; it belonged to various agenda-driven communities, with the result that this press attempted to manipulate as often as it attempted to inform. Thereby arose not merely the issue of cultural nationalism but its use in conducting the politics of victimization, of the emergence of self-perceived groups of victims that, when put together, gave popular political leaders those majorities need to maintain and increase their position as brokers of political power.

55. For example, spokesmen of Hungary's minorities pointed out that Article 44 in Hungary's 1886 Nationality Act started from the fiction that the peoples occupying the lands of the Crown of St. Stephen constituted an integral Hungarian political nation. The act then went on to permit the use of different languages represented within those same peoples, but with a caveat, for it allowed the free development of the nationalities only as collective entities and then only on the cultural level and only to a limited extent. Further, because the act stressed the indivisibility of the Hungarian political nation, it implicitly rejected the national individuality of the Slovaks, Rumanians, Serbs, Germans, and Ruthenes living within the Hungarian state. See Laszlo Szarka, "The Dimensions of Small Nation Identity: Slovakia as a Nationality Region of Pre-1918 Hungary," in Lemberg et al., *Bildungsgeschichte, Bevölkerungsgeschichte, Gesellschaftsgeschichte in Den Böhmischen Ländern und in Europa*, p. 185. On the trial, see Joseph M.

Baernreither, *Fragments of a Political Diary,* ed. Joseph Redlich (London: Macmillan, 1930).

56. See Robert A. Kann, "Franz Ferdinand der Ungarnfeind?" in his *Erzherzog Franz Ferdinand Studien* (Vienna: R. Oldenbourg, 1976), pp. 100–126.

57. See especially Allmayer-Beck, *Ministerpräsident Baron Beck,* pp. 90–121.

58. See Ottokar Czernin und zu Chudenitz, *Im Weltkreig* (Berlin: Ullstein; 1919), especially pp. 21–26. See also Gary W. Shanafelt, *The Secret Enemy: Austria-Hungary and the German Alliance, 1914–1918* (Boulder, CO: East European Monographs, 1985).

59. This old *Staats idee,* naturally associated with the *Legitimisten* after World War I, remained whole within certain quarters long after the monarchy's disappearance. For example, following the assassination of Engelbert Dollfuss, the *Österreicher,* a journal belonging to the monarchists, reminded any who would read it that "only the monarch alone can put an end to the horror and guarantee peace and order. 'Give the people a kaiser.' These words are on the lips of everyone! Give us a kaiser so that we can believe again in our fatherland. Our independence can only be complete under the Habsburg monarchy. We should not fear the threats of our neighbors. It is a matter for us alone to decide how to build our house and what to put under its roof. Let's let the kaiser come to his realm and the Stephensdom will be filled with the prayers of the people giving thanks to God for allowing his return. . . . The destiny of Austria is inextricably linked with the Habsburgs!"

60. For a review of the Habsburg contribution, see Bruce F. Pauley, *The Habsburg Legacy, 1867–1939* (New York: Holt, Rinehart, and Winston, 1972).

✧ 3 ✧
Kaiser as Political Icon

onventional wisdom tends to heap the blame for the final collapse of Austria-Hungary on the last Habsburg patriarch, emperor, and king, Franz Joseph I. The policies of this unfortunate monarch, to continue with the usual cant, were the product of his imperious but mediocre mind; when combined with the old emperor's vaunted arrogance and cold-blooded selfishness, it goes far toward explaining the final disaster that overtook the Austrian state and the ancient House of Habsburg. It is said that further evidence of the extent of Franz Joseph's misanthropy is the fact that personal misfortune visited those whose lives in any way touched upon the emperor's.[1]

This hostile view of Franz Joseph was created, for the most part, since his death in 1916. The states that replaced the Dual Monarchy desired to defame the old as much as possible so as to justify the new state order associated with the settlement of the First World War. In fact, Franz Joseph, by the very fact that he stood at the helm of his dynasty, was Austria-Hungary's chief political icon; his towering visibility exerted immense centripetal political pull. His presence—indeed, the very thought that he existed—gave legitimacy to that political order often referred to in the vernacular as the Habsburg empire or the realm of the Habsburgs. The kaiser's role as chief prop in the ceremonial that gave life and color to Austrian political culture came about not because of any prescribed cult of personality, but because he personified those historical forces that had brought together and continued to sustain the Danubian realm. Moreover, the kaiser's persona carried the weight of that hoary political tradition, conjuring up in the minds of those who looked upon him as continuity between present and past as well as expectation of the future. This distinction between persona and office, one which combined in the emperor an unusual, not always easy mix of folksy informality and a near holy presence, is illustrated in a famous letter by Empress Maria Theresa to her son, Joseph, in which the mother, not the empress, wrote:

> You have enjoyed yourself putting the dagger into the heart, ironically and with reproaches too extreme for people for whom you yourself believe to be the best. . . . How I fear that you will never find friends who will be attached to Joseph. . . . For it is not the Emperor or co-regent from whom these biting, ironical mischievous shafts come, it is from the heart of Joseph, and this is what alarms me, and this is what will bring, ill fortune into your life, dragging the Monarchy and all of us with you.[2]

The august presence of Kaiser Franz Joseph as political icon similarly is leavened by his self-knowledge, manifested in his personal letters. Franz Joseph was acutely conscious of his image, and faced it with a wry, self-deprecating humor as when, for example, he spoke of being trapped within his nimbus[3] or when he signed his letters to his empress as "your little one."[4] It was Franz Joseph the man, not the emperor and king, who poured out his profound and private grief over the loss of his only son in a letter to Elizabeth: "Tomorrow is the painful day when our thoughts will unite us in prayer for our dear Rudolph. Seven years have passed, the pain has become milder, but the tragic memory and the view of the irretrievable future remains."[5]

Certainly, the old emperor's political career was far from being happy, and at the same time Franz Joseph's private life was marked by tragedy. Yet, whatever the true causes of his misfortunes, they were the unhappy result of neither cold-bloodedness nor arrogance; nor were his policies the product of a mediocre mind. Franz Joseph's misfortunes both have their source in and derive their magnitude from circumstances far greater than the sum of the men, individually and collectively, who dealt with them. Indeed, the difficulties besetting the Dual Monarchy during the era of Franz Joseph were far larger than all of Austrian society itself.

The historical image of Emperor Franz Joseph for the most part comes from contemporaries inherently opposed to those principles for which the monarch stood. Although these critics often were accomplished men of integrity and intellect, their perspective was forged from differing circumstances of experience and environment. Most often the emperor's contemporary critics belonged to a small circle of Viennese intelligentsia within the haute bourgeoisie; by nature this group was critical of most everything external to its world, to the point of alienation. And because their orbit was narrowly circumscribed by their esoteric proclivities, members of this intelligentsia tended to reinforce one another's distortions. The end result of their deliberations sometimes was profound; often, however, the ideas emanating out of this intelligentsia were convoluted and self-centered and led to conclusions devoid of objectivity. So, for example, it was the famed critic and writer of feuilletons Karl Kraus who once characterized Franz Joseph as "that great and evil demon, a nightmare whose pale presence oppresses the land and eternally grasps it by the throat so as to prevent its quiet sleep and peaceful development."[6] On the other end of the spectrum are panegyrics written either by men of the emperor's own caste, who were thereby constitutionally unable to set their observations within the broad framework necessary for understanding, or by flatterers. The real Franz Joseph, both the emperor and the man, lies somewhere in between, captive of his own inherited perspective. That captivity explains how men, even when possessed of sufficient ability, unfailing integrity, and the greatest goodwill, take actions shown in hindsight to have been unwise.

In the first place it must be recalled that Franz Joseph was not bourgeois. He was neither born nor raised in the middle class; neither did he travel socially within its circles. Not unnaturally, the emperor had little empathy with the bourgeois perspective, especially the materialist views of those involved in industry and capital. Neither could he share the often subjective outlook encased in their positivism, which often rested on the shifting sands of a value-free relativism.

Experience had been very different for Franz Joseph. Born in 1832 as an aristocrat, the first son of a Wittelsbach princess and a Habsburg archduke standing near the Austrian throne, Franz Joseph grew up in the afterglow of the victory of conservatism over Napoleon. Like most aristocrats of that era, he came to distrust anything that hinted at popular government. It was a young Franz Joseph who once wrote to his mother during the tumult of popular rebellion in 1848 of the necessity "that we put an end to those excesses that take place in our lands having constitutions. . . . We must govern energetically and those who disobey, be they prince or clergy, must relentlessly be pursued and punished."[7] These harsh words must be judged within a perspective that takes into consideration that it was not until midcentury that the Apollonian Napoleonic myth arose. Before then, Europeans, or at least the majority of those among the politically articulate, recalled mainly the misery and tyranny that resulted as war followed democracy and, in the company of his marshals, the French Caesar led a Gallic tide of revolution across the continent of Europe.

More than a few saw in the equilibrium established by the Congress of Vienna a liberation and a return to harmony under the benign aegis of a refurbished old order. The vast, undulating political forces that even then were being forged out of the Industrial Revolution were as yet undetected; hence the self-assurance of the Austrian court that it represented the best of all possible political worlds. The Catholic Church also had received new life out of the failure of the French Revolution to produce the Nineveh of the *philosophes*. Thereby too was strengthened a faith in a secular political hierarchy under monarchs who, in turn, had been anointed by the Christian God. The world of the young Franz Joseph, unlike the rising bourgeois world, was not relative; rather, it rested on the certainty of the absolute.

Chance had decreed that Franz Joseph be born a dynast and, moreover, inculcated with a perspective born of the certainty that one day he must shoulder the responsibility of championing God's order against those democrats who bided time in Europe's subterranean political cellars. Here is the central theme of Franz Joseph as emperor: Throughout his sixty-eight-year reign, one that extended from the rebellious days of December 1848 to the overwhelming catastrophe of modern war, the monarch never deviated from his rooted conviction that the well-being of his peoples rested on the welfare of his dynasty and, to the extent that God had placed its future in his hands, upon his judgment. Not only was the emperor's concept of his duty an awesome burden, it was challenged by nearly every aspect of the unfolding contemporary world. To the degree he understood these challenges, Franz Joseph was forced to twist and turn on their account; so it was that from time to time he gave concessions to the mounting pressures of democracy. To his mind, however, these concessions were secondary to his first priority: preserving the order of Habsburg *Hausmacht*.[8]

The emperor's hidebound Weltanschauung not withstanding, democracy had waged a successful offensive between 1860 and 1900 within the realm of the Habsburgs. And indeed, after 1907, the Cisleithan half of the Dual Monarchy was constitutionally as democratic as any state in Europe, while internal political pressures within Transleitha were rapidly pushing the Kingdom of Hungary along the same political path already taken by Austria. Hence, there is not a little irony in the fact that the stormy political stalemate emanating out of the nationality question within the democratic Austro-Hungarian political arena allowed the emperor to govern more absolutely in the democratic era than previously, when the state was grounded on the principles of monarchical absolutism. The paradox emanating out of parliamentary confusion only served to reinforce the emperor's conviction regarding the source of his authority. Indeed, the more deeply liberal democracy took root in Austria, the more its bourgeois parliamentary life appeared threatened by disruption; this underscored the primary role of the emperor in the constitutional processes of the state and only strengthened the faith of many of his subjects in the substance of the opening words of Franz Joseph Hayden's famous popular hymn: *"Gott erhalte unser Kaiser, Gott beschutze unser Land."*

Many other factors beyond structural ones within his makeup played a part in shaping Franz Joseph's perspective of his role; for example, the uncomfortable elegance of Schönbrunn or of the Hofburg; the tiresome Spanish court etiquette, which was designed to accentuate the dignity of the monarch but which harkened back to a more remote past; and lastly, the baroque genre of the Roman Catholicism to which it was tied. Perhaps central to the formation of the character of the young Franz Joseph, however, was the overweening role of his mother in framing her son's Weltanschauung. The Archduchess Sophie, a clever Wittelsbach princess, came to the Austrian court in 1828 as the wife of Emperor Franz's second son, the Archduke Franz Karl. What Sophie found in Vienna was a government and court in the hands of an elderly camarilla headed first by the aging Metternich and later, after Emperor Franz's death in 1835, presided over by the amiable but feebleminded Emperor Ferdinand I. Indeed, she discovered that even her own husband was himself rather feeble in mind and body; more frightening, there appeared no other leadership within the imperial family other than a few aged and sometimes rather dotty archdukes. It was these circumstances that drew Sophie into the vacuum at the center to become, as it was said, "the only man in the court."[9]

Although very clever and energetic, Sophie was typical of the aristocratic women of her time in that she was neither schooled in the art of politics nor otherwise in possession of the skills of governance. Still, many came to see her as the only instrument possessing the intellectual strength and determination that might ensure that her oldest son would someday succeed to the Habsburg inheritance. This perception of Sophie was reinforced by the fact that the reigning Ferdinand evidently would produce no heirs and that her husband, the emperor's brother and next in line to the throne, was only marginally better suited to exercise sovereignty. The weakness in the reigning line of the House of Habsburg brought inordinate focus not only on the archduchess herself but also on her oldest son, he who was to become Kaiser Franz Joseph I.

Archduchess Sophie took command of her son's upbringing and education, and the fact that she did so gave her enormous political leverage in the otherwise vacuous court. And so it was that she could wrap her son's perspective within that of her own. The boy's view of things was flawed by being locked within those factors that distorted the Weltanschauung of the mother, an energetic, clever, haughty aristocrat, but nonetheless a somewhat frightened woman still recoiling from the social upheavals during her youth. Not unnaturally, therefore, Sophie was blind to the real character of those socioeconomic forces then coursing through the realm of the Habsburgs and transforming south-central Europe into a modern industrial society dominated not by an aristocracy of antediluvian outlook, but by an aggressive, innovative, and upwardly mobile bourgeoisie. Too often, rather than viewing constitutional questions within the framework of the rational needs of the then emerging organic nation-state, such questions were viewed by Archduchess Sophie, and by court aristocrats of her ilk, merely as matters concerning an artificial dynastic state, matters overly focused on issues of etiquette, precedence, and dynastic prerogatives. Neither were the dimensions of external political questions sufficiently appreciated by the archduchess. More destructive to the harmonious evolution of the state was that all too often, socioeconomic pressures closing in on the court were seen only as questions relating to the troublesome parvenu. Indeed, his mother's views survived to set the course the son would take even after Sophie's death. Shortly before the event, Sophie had written Franz Joseph a "farewell" letter in which she admonished him: "My valued Franzi, since you are charged with a heavy responsibility for your Catholic empire, which you must *most of all* keep Catholic, though at the same time you will bestow paternal care on several millions of different faiths. . . . Only weakness . . . on the part of the well intentioned . . . encourages the pioneers of the revolution."[10]

The atmosphere pervading the Austrian court did not prevent the young Franz Joseph from exposure to a most rigorous intellectual training, and Sophie did see to it that her son was instructed closely in languages and political science. But Franz Joseph received this instruction framed in timeworn, outmoded social prejudice, with none of the latitudinarianism that marked, for example, the court of Maria Theresa or the upbringing of Joseph II and his brother, Emperor Leopold II. But if it was framed in outmoded values, Franz Joseph's education nevertheless was intensive. For example, at the age of six the little archduke was compelled to speak only French every second day. Very soon after, while the

English language was passed over because it was not the language of any of his subjects, he was made to take up Magyar, followed by Polish, Czech, and Italian. At seven years, the boy began a regimen first laid down by Joseph II, which called for formal instruction first eighteen and then thirty-two hours a week; at twelve years, the hours spent on instruction were increased to fifty a week, including three set aside for the study of music. The future emperor at fifteen years of age began his study of law and political science, but in such fashion that less emphasis was placed on the ideas associated with the humanities, because these were considered dangerous to understanding, while more was placed on the technical aspects *(Realien)* of statecraft thought necessary for a chief administrator. Although his mother's hand shielded Franz Joseph from an even more strenuous program urged on him by Emperor Franz, there can be no doubt that parent and guardians had assiduously prepared the boy Franz Joseph for those responsibilities that he looked to assume as a man. Indeed, toward the end of his formal instruction, perhaps in an effort to leaven formal learning with experience, the young prince was made to spend Sundays on the *Rennweg* with old Prince Metternich. There the grave former chancellor treated his young listener to discourses on both the art of government and the depravity of human nature. No doubt too, the old man castigated new trends emanating out of the spreading bourgeois world. One cannot know whether the boy took all of Metternich's words in with fascination during those long Sunday afternoons or whether his mind wandered to things at the same time more compelling and prosaic. Nevertheless, the elderly oracle could have done little other than to have convinced the young archduke of the need to view the future uneasily through the prism of the past.[11]

No archduke's upbringing was thought complete without a thorough exposure to the military arts, and to these Franz Joseph took especially well. Indeed, his favorite role—and he did come to understand role playing as a necessary part of his metier—was that of supreme warlord. So it was that the monarch appeared always most at ease among the manly comradeship of the bivouac. By the same token, Franz Joseph was no militarist, no bombastic or strutting martinet; rather, he shared in the romantic chivalric traditions of his caste, which, moreover, was required of him by the general population that had been imbued with the martial spirit of the Napoleonic era. At the same time, the emperor carried out his duties as chief military showman with a seriousness tempered by quiet dignity that won him general respect along with the deepest loyalty from the army's rank and file. Indeed, by the time of the old emperor's death in November of 1916, it was these qualities, and especially his devotion to the concept of duty, which he always carried out with unfailing courtesy, that had won over his subjects to him even when they did not share his known political views.[12]

On the public side of Franz Joseph's personality, all too often his self-conscious role playing imbued his presence with a certain artificiality and remoteness, the result of his seeming compulsion to dwell upon Olympian heights constructed by himself, aloof from ordinary mortals. But, beyond the nature of his upbringing, a good deal of Franz Joseph's apparent aloofness had to do with his innate character and was not the solely the outcome of either design or the self-consciousness that was part of the proud Habsburg tradition. By nature, Franz Joseph was both introverted and introspective. In addition, his tastes were Spartan; he eschewed banquets and balls, bouts of heavy drinking as well as haute cuisine. Neither did the emperor possess empathy for the ornate, baroque backdrop provided by his inheritance. And while he understood the political utility of this high-flown staging, he never was easy in these surroundings. Indeed, shyness and a disinclination to be demonstrative underscored his seeming discomfort before the public. So it was that the emperor's public appearances took on a quality of polite stiffness, which, while impressive as a clear demonstration of the emperor's goodwill, gave him the posture of a mannequin contrived to fit a role, and it was this quality in him that stood as a bar against the revelation of the inner man.

In contrast to his practiced role playing, the quality of the emperor's statecraft is open to question. However, whatever its lacks, there is little room for claiming that its failures were the product of insufficient education or of inattention to his lessons. As in so many human endeavors, more is involved in statecraft than the depth or breadth of learning, for the potential statesman's experience and perspective, along with intelligence and character, combine with education to produce the total man. Unlike the subjects selected for study, however, the fundamentals of perspective are formed within an environment over which the individual, particularly as a child, has little control. Further, like character, perspective resists yielding to knowledge. Formal knowledge may endow an individual with technical competence but has less influence on the circumstances within which this competence is put to use. This limitation is imposed upon all humankind. It is perhaps the tragic stuff from which history flows.[13]

However, it is also apparent that the old Franz Joseph had been leavened, so to speak, by life's experience. By contrast, that youth who at eighteen became kaiser on December 2, 1848, appears to have been unpleasantly lordly and imperious for an otherwise somewhat unprepossessing stripling. The roots of this unpleasantness were in that hidebound outlook brought about by his having been driven by his education too far into his imperial nimbus. The result was that Austria possessed a sovereign fatally unsuited to the tasks that lay before him; he was fundamentally unable to operate constructively within the developing milieu in which his tasks would have to be carried out. Yet at the same time Franz Joseph was in no way inherently disagreeable or contumelious. Nor was his attitude linked with a contempt for knowing. On the contrary, Franz Joseph appears to have been personally amiable and reasonably curious. In addition, he was loyal, dutiful, hardworking, incorruptible, and conscientious to a fault. And, while Franz Joseph always remained to some extent that product which had emerged out of Austria's *biedermeier Hofstaat,* nevertheless by his late seventies Franz Joseph had come to be perceived as something other than priggish. He had become the beloved old emperor. And by his late eighties he had been transformed into Austria's last patriarch, remote and still isolated within his imperial nimbus but at the same time at least sometimes able to reach outward and even downward. He revealed himself to be a not insensitive human being who, in point of fact, was not so inherently different from many among his subjects. Further, he even appears by then to have embraced an outlook that was, at least in many of its dimensions, haut bourgeois rather than aristocratic.[14]

It might be argued that some of the popularity surrounding the old kaiser, but noticeably absent from the young Franz Joseph, might be simply because, by the turn of the century, his image evoked continuity for many Austrians, tying their present with their past. In other words, the emperor had endured, his life spanned the decades, and so the state's chief liturgical prop also became its chief artifact; simply because of that, Franz Joseph both generated sentiment and drew sympathy toward his being. But the world of the late nineteenth century had come to be far different from that of midcentury, and the cultural ambiance that provides the prism through which existence is perceived had changed as well from what was in place when the young Franz Joseph assumed the throne. By 1900, Austria-Hungary was becoming a part of the world of industry and capital, and the power unleashed by these forces was uprooting the traditional ways of the Slavic and German peoples alike, transforming their landscape from the bucolic ones painted by artists such as Peter Fendi and Jakob Alt to one of proletarian grime. To the extent that the dynasty was perceived as rooted in the past, hewn out of the now decaying pillars of throne and altar that nevertheless had assumed the status of a romantic chimera in the face of the industrial present, old Austria had come to symbolize in the popular mind all those vague but comforting things that had been said to have been lost to the rampaging forces of modernity. And so the arrogant young kaiser was transformed into the kindly father of his peoples; he alone, both in his persona as kaiser and in the imperial court as an institution, symbolized the rights of the traditional communities as they stood confronted by the incomprehensible but powerful and impersonal forces seeking their destruction.

Certainly, as is so often the case with individuals who have transcended their eras, the difference between the young and old Franz Joseph also may be related to that process of mellowing, which undoubtedly comes as a consequence of surviving and surmounting both private and public tragedy. But perhaps in Franz Joseph's case his evolution toward a more humane form was spurred by the death in 1872 of she who had been both his savior and burden: his mother, Archduchess Sophie.

As emperor, and hence head of the House of Habsburg as well as monarch, Franz Joseph orbited within three concentric and concurrent spheres of activity, all of which related to the imperial house, the court, and the state (known respectively as the *Hausstaat, Hofstaat,* and *Staat*). In pursuing his daily routine within these three spheres of activity, the emperor considered himself bound by his understanding of the duties and traditions associated with each of them. Hence to this extent Franz Joseph's personal perspective was a not inconsiderable factor in the day-to-day functioning of the state, under all the constitutional guises that Austria took on during his lifetime.[15] The truism has been stated often enough that the dynasty served as the most persuasive symbol and thereby the most tangible link holding together the ramshackle Austrian realm, because in it the nations perceived those historical forces that had brought them together in the state. Consequently, it fell to the emperor—to whomever wore the crown of the Habsburgs—to transform himself symbolically from mere mortal into the personification of the historic centripetal force pulling together the otherwise divergent realm.

Franz Joseph carried out his task well, and his role playing as emperor and king recalls, perhaps even inspired, the words of Hugo von Hofmannsthal, who, in writing his *King Candaules,* noted that where all is moving, slipping, and sliding *(das Gleitende),* kingship provides focus and unity for otherwise disparate elements by serving as that vehicle through which all can take part in the ceremony of the whole. In this way, separate, seemingly divergent elements, such as those in nationality-troubled Austria, are given visible demonstration that in fact all are part of the same whole, that each is destiny to the others. Kingship, Hofmannsthal maintained, provides tangibility to what otherwise is elusive in the heterogeneity of modern society; that is, all individuals are members of the same political community symbolized by the institution of the monarchy. Great rulership depends on continued recognition of the aesthetic component of the form, with the king "the high-priestly, no-longer-human essence, the son of gods." Kingship, as viewed by many Austrians and reflected in the writings of Hofmannsthal, is an art whereby the monarch, serving as a liturgical instrument, extends himself into political society on the basis of the perceived traditions surrounding his dynasty, linking the elements of that society together by larding it with a sense of community. Hence, in the face of sociopolitical diversity, kingship gives a "ritual form of politics from which none feel excluded and thereby the inchoate energies of [conflict] . . . may be harmonized."[16] Franz Joseph, even in old age, played his assigned role well. And so to the public the old Franz Joseph invariably appeared the correctly remote last patriarch, who, if not in possession of charisma, at least possessed the confidence of Austrian citizens, who for the most part had come to view him as a dependable role model, a fit liturgical prop for the ceremonial of throne, altar, and state.

In addition to its emperor-king role player, the dynasty required a mechanism that would render it a force when extended into the life of the nations; that is, it required a ritualistic vehicle by which liturgy might infuse life into its symbols. The primary task of the court—indeed, the reason for its very existence—was to satisfy this need. Hence, at least by the twentieth century, the Austrian *Hofstaat* had come to be a sort of theater, providing a stage from which the dynasty might reach out to touch the emotions of the people. The court, therefore, is to be understood as generating those centripetal forces necessary to give life force to the state by staging solemn rites that would draw in individuals viewing them from afar by giving them a sense of vicarious participation in the state's history as well as in its present. This ceremony of the whole required in turn an apparatus in which the commonweal might perceive itself upheld, while at the same time politically sensitive special interests were favored. The dynasty served as the focal point of the state, while the court served as the prism through which the dynasty was to be observed. However, the dynasty also was to justify its continued existence within the state by demonstrating not only efficacy but efficiency as well, through a bureaucracy created by it for the administration of the state.

The *Hofstaat,* literally "court-state," must be properly understood if its internal function (in contrast to the external one of providing the ceremony of the whole) is to be appreciated. Each archducal house possessed its own court, involving great numbers of people, buildings, and acreage. The status of these archducal courts was determined by the rank of the archduke in question within the hierarchy of archdukes. The first *Hofstaat* of the realm was that belonging to the emperor and king of Austria-Hungary. Generally speaking, the second court of the realm, if only because of the political clout lodged within it, was that of the heir to the throne, Archduke Franz Ferdinand, and the third belonged to Archduke Friedrich of Habsburg-Teschen. Purists, however, might rank Friedrich's court before that of Franz Ferdinand's because of the fact that the heir to the throne's wife, the Duchess of Hohenburg, ranked below the Habsburg archduchesses. The court provided the immediate entourage for its chief liturgical prop, as well as separate ones for his spouse and children. Members of this entourage (*Hofdamen, Palästdamen, Adjutanten,* and the like) were ranked against one another in the strictest order. In addition, these individuals were often the constant companions of the member of the imperial family to which they were assigned, and hence shared the life of their master or mistress at a intimate level. It went without saying, therefore, that members of this entourage were drawn from only the high aristocracy because of the loyalty implicit in this caste's link to the crown. This relationship provided employment (if not always exciting employment) to many members of the aristocracy who otherwise might be forced to live in straitened circumstances. More important, however, this relationship renewed generation by generation the necessary bonds between dynasty and aristocracy so as to tie together the aristocratic net that had originally formed the state.

The *Hofstaat,* of course, involved more than personal entourages. Menial functions were performed not by members of these entourages but by an administrative apparatus—menservants, chambermaids, and the like—drawn from the lower levels of society but nevertheless carefully selected, trusted, and valued because of the necessary familiarity that they must have with their employer. For example, the emperor's court (that is, the one operating out of the Vienna Hofburg, in contrast to his court housed in Prague or the one housed in Budapest) included cooks, gardeners, masons, lawyers, accountants, bankers, general administrators, security guards, imperial and royal bodyguards, opera singers, actors and actresses, concertmasters, art historians, curators, restorers, and all the other personnel necessary to care for or conduct the court opera, court theater, various picture galleries (the Kunsthistorische Museum, for example), and the maintenance of various palaces and castles or the administrations of various estates *(Güter)* scattered throughout the realm, as well as to manage the income derived from the latter.

This vast and diverse apparatus had to be both structured and organized and then administrated in turn by the likes of the *Obersthofmeister* (chief court chamberlain), *Obersthofmarschall, Oberstallmeister,* and so on. These administrative positions always went to members of the high aristocracy, again providing responsible and lucrative employment to those who might naturally be expected to be chief supporters of the dynasty and renewing the bonds of that social net, made up of the high aristocracy and dynasty, that had been cast over the realm centuries before to form the state. In addition, two purely state (as against court) functions fell within the imperial and royal Hofstaat: the military chancellery, through which the emperor acted as supreme warlord, and that, which provided Franz Joseph with the personnel, the *Hofbeamten,* for civil administration.[17]

Franz Joseph, like all members born into the dynasty (with the exception of its female members once they had married out of the sovereign house), was at least nominally governed through a unique code known as the house law *(Hausrecht).* The house law, in turn, had been codified under the office of the Obersthofmeister, in February of 1839, into a kind of standing order called the family statute *(Familienstatut).* Unlike the *Hausrecht,* which had evolved out of the kaiser's authority over the dynasty *(Hausgewalt)* as well as the state *(Staatsgewalt),* the family statute was secret. The *Hausrecht* in reality was nothing more than an inchoate collection of precedents and traditions rendered coherent through the family statute. In any event, house law had nominal primacy for those under it in the case of contradiction between it and the general constitutional law prevailing within the Dual Monarchy. This primacy, however, probably was not constitutionally legal in the strictest sense after 1867. Nevertheless, because the emperor had possession of the family's purse, adherence to the house law was required if the family member concerned was to expect sustenance from the family funds.[18] Further, the application of *Hausrecht* to new circumstances—and there were many as democratic and industrial society increasingly overwhelmed the mores of the old order—ultimately was determined by the chief of the House of Habsburg, that member of the family who ruled from Vienna and Budapest as *Kaiser und König.*[19] In the last analysis, therefore, the dynasty was a dictatorship of the most authoritarian sort, and the emperor was its generalissimo. Members of the dynasty therefore can be thought of as having had to exist within the proverbial gilded cage.[20]

Habsburg *Hausrecht* was enforced by the emperor, but he especially relied on the advice of the archdukes, usually members of an even older generation, who surrounded him. To this extent, the older archdukes might be considered as the chief magistrates of their house. The doyen of the House of Habsburg, until his death in 1896, was the Archduke Albrecht, the crusty and hard-nosed victor of the Battle of Custozza. By dint of this victory over the Italians in 1867 and of being the son of Archduke Karl, the supposed victor over Napoleon in 1809, Albrecht had great influence over Franz Joseph. There was nothing that Albrecht's Habsburg cousins feared more than a confrontation with the stiff-necked archduke, given the blows that could be expected through the emperor should the former's august wrath not be assuaged. So, for example, the young Archduke Johann Salvador found himself stripped of all rank and privilege when, after years of fruitless feuding between the young, somewhat liberal-minded archduke and the more hidebound members of his family, the young archduke renounced his position and entered into the shipping business by acquiring a sailing vessel in London. Whatever the merits of the young man's conduct, Albrecht would not countenance a member of the dynasty forgoing the preordained circumstances of his birth by joining the haute bourgeoisie and indulging in unholy commerce. Not only did Johann Salvador find himself drummed out of his house (and then took the name of Johann Orth), but in contradistinction to the constitutional rights guaranteed Austria's ordinary subjects, he lost his citizenship as well. Even fate appeared to side with the House of Habsburg, for in 1901 the unfortunate Johann Orth lost his life when his ship, the *Saint Margaret,* sank at sea during a violent storm off the Cape of Good Hope. So was the ultimate price paid for the attempt to adulterate the ancient mystique surrounding Austria's imperial dynasty.[21]

Unlike in the eighteenth century, when a lack of male Habsburgs was at least a partial cause of two of Austria's major wars, there was a plethora of archdukes by the opening of the twentieth century. Forbidden by house law to follow the usual professions open to the sons of the haute bourgeoisie, and even denied the latitude given to sons of ordinary aristocrats, these archdukes had too little to occupy them and far too often ended up leading indolent lives, too often within the capital's sensuous hothouses alongside Vienna's demimonde. Yet, in truth, there was little else these superfluous ones could do. Untrained in the arts and sciences as well as unaccustomed to the ways of the unfolding twentieth-century professional world, it was difficult for the young Habsburgs to find a meaningful way in which to serve the state in the bourgeois era. Indeed, these imperial and royal scions were reduced to being nothing more than a decorative backdrop for court ceremonial. Little wonder that not a few of these privileged Habsburgs fell prey to an enervating and self-destructive ennui. Little wonder too that the easygoing, bittersweet Viennese, despite some quite vocal criticism concerning archducal deportment, were more often than not sympathetic to the position in which collateral members of the ruling house found themselves.

The maintenance of the dynasty required both large expenditure and considerable man-hours. The very size of the house demanded numerous residences, summer as well as winter ones, along with chamberlains, hunt masters, equerries, and the like, so that each family satellite might have its small court reflecting the archaic grandeur of the chief one ensconced in the imperial Hofburg. Without doubt these lesser courts provided employment for a variety of impecunious and not always able ladies and gentlemen collected about them. But their financing could constitute a sharp drain on the imperial Austrian purse. In an effort to free himself, his immediate family and the state from having to sustain the lifestyle expected of his nephews and cousins, Emperor Franz I had established a separate fund, that came to be called the *kaiserlich und königlich Familien Fond*, for their support. A part of a larger reorganization of imperial finances following the Napoleonic Wars, the imperial and royal family fund was capitalized through resources that had been gathered by Europe's oldest reigning dynasty throughout the centuries.[22] Once established as an endowment for the support of the house, the fund was put on a businesslike basis under the auspices of financial experts in Europe's most prominent and successful banking houses. The result was the continual increase in the wealth of the house as a whole. In this way the welfare of all members of the imperial house was secured without straining what had come to be understood as the public (state) purse. The emperor also possessed a private purse, but not until 1879, on the death of the Emperor Ferdinand I, did Franz Joseph have possession of real personal wealth. Indeed, up until that time the finances of his immediate family were always somewhat strained, especially as it was not too clear that Ferdinand, living in Prague's Belvedere, would will the personal fortune surrounding his throne to he who had been forced upon him as his political heir in December of 1848. But once this wealth was inherited by Franz Joseph, this too was turned over to professional bankers, with the same good results enjoyed by the family funds.

While Austria's ruling house benefited from the fiscal arrangements for its wealth, cooperation with the dynasty in these matters had great advantages for the banking houses themselves. For one thing, the reigning house was, if only indirectly, the source of useful and privileged information, and for another, what was good for the client obviously was good for the counsel.[23] Indeed, like all sovereigns of his era, Franz Joseph was less conscious of what today passes, at least officially, for conflict of interest. But offsetting this was not only the fact that Franz Joseph was not versed in business matters but also his social disdain for the world of commerce. Indeed, although quite conscious of its beneficial necessity, Franz Joseph personally was interested neither in money nor in how it was obtained. By the same token, it passed unquestioned, even by a man intrinsically as full of an old-world sense of honor as the emperor, that his house should benefit from any fiscal opportunity that might fall before it.

Because it related to his control over his house, Franz Joseph closely followed expenditures made from the family fund, even if he was rarely party to investment decisions for it. Members of his extended family therefore were uncomfortably aware that their own fiscal security rested upon the emperor's active

goodwill. For his part, because he was acutely conscious of his sovereign obligations toward his house (and never did Franz Joseph use or consider the family
funds his in a personal sense), the emperor well understood that his fiscal power
over the family purse constituted leverage over the conduct of members of the
dynasty. Further, this leverage played a fundamental role in ensuring the functioning of the *Hausrecht* and the preservation, at least from the emperor's point
of view, of the external order and sanctity of Austria's ruling house. All parties
involved were only too aware of that same link between the emperor's financial
power over them and what was expected of them insofar as their conduct in
public was concerned; the power of money over men worked well to ensure an
orderly house, especially if the men involved were somewhat enervated by the
inherent restrictions on their lives.

Affairs related to the state were pursued within the framework of civil and
military cabinets. Each, in turn, was divided into an Austrian and a Hungarian
section. Potentially at least, cabinet directors possessed great influence in political decision-making processes, because all written reports from the lower eche-
lons of the bureaucracy had to pass through the hands of the appropriate cabinet
chiefs if these were to find their way to the emperor and king. However, Franz
Joseph understood the nature and tactics of bureaucratic infighting, where the
power to censor is the power to mold, and he successfully outflanked his cabinet
chiefs through the informal practice of permitting heads of government departments to orally report directly to him. The emperor imposed one inflexible
proviso on this procedure, however: Each minister was admonished to report
solely on his own responsibilities and to strictly abstain from all comments on
those of another. Not only were the cabinet chiefs held in check, but because
only he could put together the pieces of the puzzle gleaned from various oral and
written reports, Franz Joseph gained paramount influence as the sole orchestrator
of the state's bureaucratic apparatus. In this manner, Franz Joseph alone came to
be seen as standing above politics (if, however, not always as an impartial
observer) in favor of the welfare of Austria-Hungary.[24]

The price, in both personal as well as public terms, for functioning as Austria-
Hungary's chief arbitrator was a heavy one, for the task required that the emperor share his Olympian sphere with no one, whether from the public or private
sectors or from his immediate family and personal acquaintances. Further, when
he did descend into ordinary, day-to-day activities, for example, holding audi-
ences or opening exhibitions, Franz Joseph had to do so using the greatest of
tact, least he appear to favor one man over another. The end result was that too
often the emperor appeared infused with imperial arrogance and ingratitude;
however, there was no other way, for the Emperor Franz Joseph could have no
confidants, no intermediaries, and certainly no political friends. He could possess
only servants. Indeed, the sheer weight of the documents that passed over his
desk and the volume of the words that reached his ears each day reached tidal
proportions, to a point far beyond what a human mind, even if it had God

standing behind it, could assimilate. Hence, the ultimate cost of the emperor's holding the balance of the decision-making power in his hands was a dangerous oversimplification of complex matters. Yet Franz Joseph, imbued with the perspective and practices of an earlier era, could find no better procedure; so it was that the emperor worked in isolation, carrying a burden that, despite its weight, he failed to recognize as being too great for a single individual.

The merits emanating out of Franz Joseph's administrative procedure should not be overlooked. The sovereign did manage to free himself to a large degree from the usual machinations that habitually surround imperial chiefs as the ambitious vie with one another for a share in the imperial nimbus. In turn, in his isolation Franz Joseph also obtained some peace of mind. Beyond time spent alone—not too onerous for a shy man given to introspection—there was consolation for loneliness in his perception that he was fulfilling his duty to his subjects and to his God. Too, Franz Joseph's entourage consisted not of courtiers but of officials who, as good Viennese subjects, came to appreciate their emperor as they comprehended the nature of his exertions for them. So, for example, on a beautiful spring day,

> around 2:30, I went with four horses *à la daumont* to open the exhibition in the Prater. The entire way over the Ringstrasse to the Prater was decorated with flags and garlands of leaves *[Laubgewinden]*, all the houses displayed banners and tapestries [and] members of the Veterans Union stood all along the way and also there were firefighters from all of the provinces of the crown lands in the thousands; there really was an unbelievable number of loudly cheering people and proper saluting men in the windows. I had not expected it, but rather the opposite in this time of wailing, vexation and trouble! The archdukes, diplomats, and high officials as well as countless of the elegant public awaited me at the rotunda. It was very well and successfully arranged.[25]

Beyond administrative procedure, cabinets, and departments, there existed in Austria-Hungary constitutional elements of government. These elements, which of course came into being only erratically between 1848 and 1907, and even then begrudgingly as far as court and emperor were concerned, nevertheless were not ineffective in rooting the traditions surrounding the throne in popular government. Indeed, once those elements had come into being, Franz Joseph, as was consistent with his sense of the honorable, strove to live up to his constitutional obligations, and so the Dual Monarchy's two parliaments, one sitting in Vienna, the other in Budapest, also came to be an invariable factor in the daily routine of the emperor. Each parliament had the divisions usual for European states in that era: an upper, privileged house and a lower one, the latter with unclear powers of legislative initiative and dependence on varying degrees of popular suffrage. The terms of the *Ausgleich* called for a cabinet more directly dependent on the outcome of elections for parliament in Hungary (albeit if on a narrow franchise), and hence the emperor was forced to confront that body more often, and this within the context of the convolutions typical of Magyar politics, than its Austrian counterpart. And while on the surface the complexity of Franz Joseph's task in Hungary ought to have been offset by the fact that the assembly in Budapest rested on the narrowest of franchises, despite its institution of ministerial responsibility, politics in the lands of the Crown of St. Stephen tended to focus on the turbulent and unruly Magyar gentry, and so Franz Joseph's task there was often most difficult. But the one obligation, also in connection with the 1867 *Ausgleich,* that Franz Joseph found most onerous was that he should spend half of every year in his royal seat in Ofen (today's Buda), which was high above the Danube and in the midst of his Hungarian subjects. It did no good that the Magyars rewarded his promises with a goodly refurbishing of Maria Theresa's old palace, facing out toward Pest; the monarch never was easy with his difficult, darkly tempestuous subjects. Whenever he could, Franz Joseph found urgent business requiring him to hurry back to Vienna, and he once told Elizabeth that he was always unstrung when in Hungary: "I don't find many joys here. If it goes smoothly and peacefully with parliament, the communist and socialist peasant movements in a few districts are very shrill, and in one troops had to be used. As with everything in this land, all is extreme. Generally there is an atmosphere of overbearing dread."[26]

After 1907, at least, it was different with the parliament for the hereditary crown lands, sitting in Theophil Hansen's great classical building on Vienna's Ringstrasse. In the first instance, the lower house, the Abgeordnetenhaus, while elected on the basis of universal manhood suffrage, did not possess ministerial responsibility. The emperor therefore could name his own ministers, and he often did, without direct reference to the party politics surrounding the Vienna parliament. Secondly, he normally met with its leadership only a few times a year— predictably when the parliament was invited to the great *Rittersaal* in the imperial Hofburg to hear the annual speech from the throne, and at various other times when an effort was made to demonstrate solidarity between the crown and the parliament by the emperor's presenting a fête for the latter's more visible leadership through formal dinners or by having them included in the guest list for the annual court ball. Token demonstrations, to be sure, but perhaps better than none, and in any event time-consuming ones for Emperor Franz Joseph. Indeed, it was not through any design of the crown that the Vienna parliament ultimately exerted less influence than it might have over Austria's political life, and certainly its failure to have a positive and enlightening effect on Austrian affairs was both a great worry and disappointment to the emperor. However, the Abgeordnetenhaus, convulsed by nationalist-inspired obstruction, found it impossible to work in an orderly and constructive fashion. Parliament would not govern. And in its absence, the emergency provisions provided by Article 14 of Austria's constitution demanded that the emperor govern in its place; so he did, and, moreover, with more influence than in the days when Habsburg monarchs had no parliaments with which to contend. But the situation hardly was a cause for joy; for example, the emperor lamented, in connection with the storms that focused around the question of the "Badeni language law," whereby the prime minister had attempted to give the Czech language equal legal status with the German language in Bohemia, that

> [the] minister . . . sees me daily, he has brought no unity to the parties in the House of Delegates since the German Progressive Party will have none of it as usual and so nothing is resolved and here we govern for a time without parliament according to decree. Now in Hungary the extreme left [takes the opportunity to make] great difficulties. . . . I hope that the other parties will stand up to them. There is much worry and the only consolation is in the splendid deportment of the troops through all this business when they are called to intervene.[27]

Perhaps the single most popular forum (if a limited one) provided by Austria-Hungary's *Ausgleich* where Franz Joseph might have been forced squarely to confront all of his peoples as a whole was the House of Delegates. This device—not a legislative body; its eighty members elected only indirectly through a popular vote, with forty members elected by the lower house in the parliament of each half of the Dual Monarchy—was the body in which joint issues such as intrastate fiscal relations, foreign affairs, and military policy were reconciled. But in practice these sorts of issues rarely were fully aired, as the House of Delegates too often was ensnared in that nationality obstruction that reflected the order of the day in the Vienna parliament (and to a lesser extent the Budapest parliament). So this third body proved no bar, the constitutional era notwithstanding, to the monarch's authority. Indeed, the very diversity of the Dual Monarchy seemed heightened in the twentieth century by its parliamentary bodies, inasmuch as these became mirrors reflecting the animosity felt by the Austro-Hungarian nationalities, or at least by their spokesmen, for one another. Government therefore remained in the hands of those who could successfully manipulate the bureaucracies of the two states. Because the strings leading from such manipulation eventually wound up in the hands of the emperor and king, Franz Joseph I, it was in fact the emperor himself who decided what was best for the rambunctious peoples living within his heritage.

The reality of the emperor's authority leads to one further observation: Unlike Austria's politicians, who might come in and out of office and thereby get out from under the weight of political decision making, Franz Joseph never was free of this weight. He was born, so to speak, on the throne. He could never avoid its responsibility except through death. Day and night from the time he was nineteen to his death in his eighty-sixth year, Franz Joseph had to be responsible, a lightning rod, for all the political heat generated by the changes emanating from the Industrial Revolution. If from time to time he took an easier path for himself or if he made an unwise decision, these factors have to be balanced with an understanding of the constant and continuous burdens of a monarch who had sole ultimate authority but nonetheless lived within the complexities of an industrial, capitalistic, and democratic era. Of all the individuals living within his land, therefore, Franz Joseph was the most unfree of all. And so it was too that, in an era when Austria-Hungary seemed threatened with perpetual tumult, to many it was the imperial house and its chief that appeared to be the only political institution standing for stability and continuity. Paradoxically, because the sanctity of private property appeared to rest on this stability and continuity, the House of Habsburg came to stand for Austria-Hungary's bourgeois order. In the center of the ruling house stood that living symbol, he who at the same time was both chief executive and chief liturgical prop for Austria's dynastic idea: Franz Joseph. Indeed, in the eyes of many of his subjects, "the Austrian emperor . . . was the constitution. He signified protection and well-being. The citizen had the feeling when he sat himself down at the breakfast table and took pleasure in the burning dialogue that had occurred in the debate at parliament . . . given in his newspaper, that Franz Joseph, who already had been busy at work . . . had taken precautions to protect law and order."[28]

Notes

1. The emperor's brother was executed in Mexico in 1867 by order of General Benito Juarez, the rebel leader whose nationalist-inspired forces seized the Mexican government, permitting him to proclaim himself president of the republic, and who, in turn, declared the deposed emperor of Mexico a traitor because of Archduke Ferdinand Maximilian's attempt to establish a Mexican empire under an imperial scepter of his own through the aegis of the French emperor, Napoleon III. Franz Joseph's son died of self-inflicted gunshot wounds to the head in somewhat mysterious, if sordid, circumstances in 1889, when Crown Prince Rudolf's body was found alongside the naked one of his poisoned lover, seventeen-year-old Marie Vetsara, in his hunting lodge at Mayerling bei Wien. Empress Elizabeth died at the hands of an assassin, the Italian anarchist Lucheni, in 1898 in Geneva as she was boarding a lake steamer.

2. Quoted in Derek Beales, *Joseph II,* volume 1, *In the Shadow of Maria Theresa, 1741–1780* (Cambridge: Cambridge University Press, 1987), p. 147.

3. See Jean de Bourgoing, Evabeth Miller Kienst, and Robert Rie, trans., *The Incredible Friendship: The Letters of Emperor Franz Joseph to Frau Katharina Schratt* (Albany: State University of New York Press, 1966). See especially p. 53, where the emperor apologizes to his very close friend for not daring to step out and speak with her during an imperial appearance. A more recent, fuller discussion of these letters, along with the letters themselves, is Brigitte Hamann, *Meine liebe, gute Freundin!: Die Briefe Kaiser Franz Josephs an Katharina Schratt aus dem Besitz der österreichischen Nationalbibliotek* (Vienna: Ueberreuter, 1992).

4. This usually was signified by the words *"Dein Kl[eine]."*

5. Georg Nostitz-Rieneck, ed., *Franz Josephs Briefe an Kaiserin Elizabeth,* 2 volumes (Vienna: Herold, 1960), II, p. 130.

6. Quoted in Hilde Spiel, "Der Liebe gute alte Herr," *Wien: Spektrum einer Stadt* (Munich: Biederstein Verlag, 1971), pp. 81–82. For more aphorisms by Karl Kraus, see Harry Zohn, ed. and trans., *Karl Kraus: Half Truths and One-and-a-Half Truths* (Montreal: Engendra Press, 1976), and Harry Zohn, ed., *In These Great Times: A Karl Kraus Reader* (Montreal: Engendra Press, 1976).

By the same token, it was that very same Karl Kraus who won loud acclaim from his friends by reducing "creative energy" to being "nothing more than [to] show that there is a distinction between an urn and a chamber pot and that [those who fail to make this distinction] are divided into those who use an urn as a chamber pot and those who use the chamber pot as an urn." Quoted in Allan Janik and Stephen Toulmin, *Wittgenstein's Vienna* (New York: Simon and Schuster, 1973), p. 89. See also Karl Kraus, *Werke*, ed. Heinrich Fischer, 14 volumes (Munich: Köesel, 1952–1966), III, p. 341. Karl Kraus was hailed by many contemporaries despite the contradictory views he aired from one writing to another and despite his misogyny and his Jewish self-hate cloaked in anti-Semitic rhetoric. Indeed, many of his contemporaries closely identified Kraus with Austria's "intelligentsia." The writer achieved his notoriety because of his sharp-witted opinions and incisive, pungent writing style. For example, Kraus wrote the above words on chamber pots and urns while defending the architect Adolf Loos from the latter's many detractors.

7. Otto Ernst, *Franz Joseph as Revealed by His Letters* (London: Methuen, 1927), pp. 45–58.

8. There are many works dealing with Emperor Franz Joseph. But many of these contain inaccuracies or points of view no longer completely tenable in view of the unfolding understanding in more recent studies of the history of Austria-Hungary. Still one of the more solid overviews of the emperor is found in Egon César Conte Corti and Hans Sokol, *Kaiser Franz Joseph* (Vienna: Styria, 1965). More recent is Jean-Paul Bled, *François-Joseph* (Paris: Fayard, 1987); an English translation is available (Jean-Paul Bled, *Franz Joseph*, trans. Teresa Bridgeman [Oxford: Blackwell, 1992]). Insights into the life and times of Franz Joseph is also found in a more recent work: Ernst Trost et al., *Franz Joseph I von Gottes Gnaden Kaiser von Österreich apostolischer König von Ungarn* (Vienna: Fritz Molden, 1980). Also useful are the reminiscences written just after the First World War: Josef Schneider, *Kaiser Franz Joseph und sein Hof* (Vienna: Leonhardt, 1919), and, if used with care, Albert Alexander Vinzenz, Freiherr von Margutti, *Vom alten Kaiser: persönliche Erinnerungen an Franz Joseph I, Kaiser von Österreich und apostolischen König von Ungarn* (Leipzig: Leonhardt, 1921). A standard, if somewhat dated study, of the emperor is Josef Redlich, *Kaiser Franz Joseph of Austria* (Berlin: Ullstein, 1929). Recent studies are Steven Beller, *Franz Joseph* (London: Longmans, 1996), and Alan Palmer, *Twilight of the Habsburgs: The Life and Times of Emperor Francis Joseph* (New York: Grove Press, 1995). For short but very useful overviews, see Adam Wandruszka, "Kaiser Franz Joseph als Herrscher und Mensch," in Schloss Grafenegg, *Das Zeitalter Kaiser Franz Josephs: Von der Revolution zur Grunderzeit*, 2 volumes (Vienna: NÖ Landesmuseums, 1984), I *(Beiträge)*, pp. 17–23, and Brigitte Hamann, *The Reluctant Empress*, trans. Ruth Hein (New York: Alfred A. Knopf, 1986, pp. 23–42. For a discussion of the circumstances surrounding his son's suicide, see Fritz Judtmann, *Mayerling Ohne Mythos* (Vienna: Kremayer and Scheriaw, 1968). Works dealing with the emperor on a more intimate level are Friedrich Saathen, ed., *Anna Nahowski und Kaiser Franz Joseph: Aufzeichnungen* (Vienna: Böhlaus, 1986), and Brigitte Hamann, ed., *Meine liebe, gute Freundin!: Die Briefe Kaiser Franz Josephs an Katharina Schratt*. See also Erich Alban Berg, *Als der Adler noch Zwei Köpfe hatte* (Vienna: Styria, 1980). Two works that shed light on the mundanities of the emperor's everyday life are Eugene Ketterl, *The Emperor Franz Joseph I: An Intimate Study by His Valet du Chambre* (London: Skeffington, no date), and Josef Cachee, *Die Hofküche des Kaisers: Die K.u.K. Hofküche, die Hofzuckerbäckeri und der Hofkeller in der Wiener Hofburg* (Vienna: Amalthea, 1985).

9. On Sophie see Corte and Sokol, *Kaiser Franz Joseph*, pp. 1–31.

10. Quoted in Brigitte Hamann, *The Reluctant Empress* (New York: Knopf, 1986), p. 199.

11. Heinrich Benedikt, *Die Monarchie des Hauses Österreich: Ein historisches Essay*

(Munich: R. Oldenbourg, 1968), pp. 123–124. See also Franz Schnürer, *Briefe Kaiser Franz Josephs an sein Mutter: 1838–1872* (Munich: R. Oldenbourg, 1930). The historian Jean-Paul Bled maintained that "Franz Joseph would always keep in mind Metternich's assertion that a Constitution founded on the principle of representation would be incompatible with the pluralist nature of the Austrian Monarchy." See Bled, *Franz Joseph*, p. 7.

12. Perhaps nowhere are these attributes of Franz Joseph better spelled out than in the novel by Joseph Roth, *Radetzky March* (Berlin: Gustav Kiepenheuer Verlag, 1932). See also Hamann, *The Reluctant Empress*, especially pp. 207ff.

13. For an excellent discussion on the psychological circumstances shaping conscious choices, set in Vienna and in the time frame of the rule of Franz Joseph, see William J. McGrath, *Freud's Discovery of Psychoanalysis: The Politics of Hysteria* (Ithaca: Cornell University Press, 1986), especially the discussion on pp. 59–151. See also P.S.F. Falkenberg, "Arthur Schnitzler's Literary Diagnosis of the Viennese Mind," in Mark E. Francis, ed., *The Viennese Enlightenment* (New York: St. Martin's Press, 1985), pp. 130–142. Not to be overlooked in regard to this topic is Carl E. Schorske, *Fin-de-Siècle Vienna: Politics and Culture* (New York: Knopf, 1981), especially "Politics and the Psyche: Schnitzler and Hofmannsthal," pp. 3–23.

14. A display of the aristocratic perspective toward the imperial house and, in particular, Emperor Franz Joseph is seen in Ernst Rutkowski, ed., *Briefe und Dokumente zur Geschichte der österreichischen-ungarischen Monarchie unter besonderer Berücksichtigung des bömisch-mährischen Raumes,* Teil I: "Der Verfassungstreue Grossgrundbesitz, 1880–1899" (Munich: R. Oldenbourg, 1983). See, for example, p. 543, when, in writing to Prince Max Egon zu Fürstenburg, Count Oswald Thun cites, with obvious affection, Franz Joseph's "great spirit and courageous heart." See also Ernst Bruckmüller, "Zur Sozialstrukur der Habsburgermonarchie," in Schloss Grafenegg, *Das Zeitalter Kaiser Franz Josephs,* I, pp. 99–112; Friedrich Edelmayer, "Das Bildungsbergertum," in ibid., pp. 197–201; Waltrude Heindl, "Die höhere Bürokratie in Österreich: Entwicklungs Linien seit 1848," in ibid., pp. 207–211; Moritz Csaky, "Adel in Österreich," in ibid., pp. 212–219.

15. A precise legal relationship between the House of Austria and the constitutional processes of the state never was clearly stated. Rather, this relationship rested on evolution and precedent. The Austrian constitutional processes were grounded on the October 1860 and February 1861 imperial patents, which were handed down from the throne to establish the terms for a constitutional monarchy. And while these processes were amended from time to time, most recently in 1907 regarding elections reform, the grounding set forth by the two imperial patents remained the basis on which the constitutional process was viewed up until the end of the Dual Monarchy in 1918. That the constitution provided for the direct rule of the kaiser in times of continued parliamentary breakdown (Article 14), indicated that the kaiser intended to reserve for himself, if only in extreme circumstances, ultimate plenipotentiary authority. The constitutional relationship, on the other hand, between the king and Hungary (lands of the Crown of St. Stephen) was rather precisely defined in the 1867 *Ausgleich* and is rather more explicit on the prerogatives belonging to the Hungarian crown. Clearly here the crown was ultimately subordinate to the political process of a parliament elected on a narrow franchise.

16. Quoted in Carl E. Schorske, *Fin-de-siècle Vienna: Politics and Culture,* pp. 18–22. See also Franz Dirnberger, "Das Wiener Hofzeremoniel bis in die Zeit Franz Josephs: Überlegungen über Probleme, Entstehung und Bedeutung," in Schloss Grafenegg, *Das Zeitalter Franz Josephs,* I, pp. 42–50. See also Ketterl, *The Emperor Franz Joseph: An Intimate Study,* especially pp. 262–333, and Elizabeth Grossegger, *Der Kaiser Hüldigungs Festzug* (Vienna: Österreichischen Akademie der Wissenschaften, 1982).

17. See Vilmos Heiszler, Margit Szakács, and Károly Vörös, *Ein Photoalbum aus*

dem Hause Habsburg: Friedrich von Habsburg und seine Familie (Vienna: Böhlau Verlag, 1989), especially pp. 30–41.

18. See Friedrich Tezner, Die Wandlungen der österreichischen-ungarischen Reichsidee (Vienna: Manz, 1905), pp. 59ff. Tezner's account does not consider the Familienstatut, as it was still secret. For a good, and more recent, discussion of the intricacies of Austro-Hungarian state and dynastic law, see Johann Christoph Allmayer-Beck, Ministerpräsident Baron Beck: Ein Staatsmann der Alten Österreich (Munich: R. Oldenbourg, 1956), especially pp. 32–57.

19. Too often various members of the court, through intrigue, got involved in the process. See Allmayer-Beck, Ministerpräsident Baron Beck, pp. 32ff.

20. See Janik and Toulmin, Wittgenstein's Vienna.

21. Lavender Cassels, Clash of Generations: A Habsburg Family Drama in the Nineteenth Century (London: John Murry, 1973).

22. A summary, dated December 20, 1918, of the properties belonging to the House of Habsburg-Lorraine and the organization of the same for administrative purposes is found in the Austrian State Archives, NPA 208/Liassen Österreich 1/2–1/5, ff. 553–556. See also H.L. Mikoletzky, Kaiser Franz I. Stephen und der Ursprung des Habsburgisch-lothringischen Familienenvermögens (Vienna: Österreich-Archiv, 1961). See also Schloss Luberegg, Kaiser Franz und seine Zeit: Von der Franz. Revolution bis zum Wiener Kongress (Marbach/Donau: J. and H. Sandler, 1991).

23. Margutti, Vom Alten Kaiser, pp. 238–239.

24. See Erich Graf Kielmansegg, Kaiserhaus, Staatsmänner, und Politiker (Vienna: Verlag für Geschichte und Politik, 1966), especially pp. 174ff. See also Max Herzog, ed., Viribus Unitis: Das Buch vom Kaiser (Vienna: Herzig, 1898).

25. Georg Nositz-Reineck, Franz Josephs Briefe an Kaiserin Elizabeth, II (Vienna: Herold, 1960), 403.

26. Ibid., p. 362.

27. Ibid., p. 325.

28. Heinrich Benedikt, Die Monarchie des Hauses Österreich, p. 124.

✧ 4 ✧
The Austrian Idea

While much has been said about the centrifugal nationality forces under-mining the cohesion of the Dual Monarchy, it also must be remembered that there existed concurrent, opposing centripetal cultural forces. These forces were to be found in that psychic grip fashioned by and out of history: a teleologi-cal political perspective, which might have held together the Austrian synthesis (and hence those discordant parts always inherent in any synthesis) if it had been able to inspire the fervor of a single, emotive issue, like nationalism did. But the Austrian idea had its source in a number of wellsprings located throughout Austria's cultural past, and so, its centripetal pull came not from a single idea, party, or agenda. Because Austrians were represented by a number of different, even antagonistic, cultural icons emanating out of a variety of past experience, they possessed a variety of perspectives as to who they were and a variety of game plans for winning state recognition of their self-perceived status. Where there was agreement among these groups and agendas, it was in the desire to keep Austria-Hungary whole. This goal of maintaining social assembly (or, more to the point, not promoting social disassembly) required a certain degree of tolerance by each group for the others, not least a refusal to stereotype and demonize others. That this assembly failed to take place is history; today the Austrian idea is long dead. Nevertheless, the Austrian idea merits examination if for no other reason than to comprehend the dimensions of the civilization lost when old Austria went to the ground in 1918.[1]

Before 1918, one was Austrian by virtue of possessing citizenship in any of the lands ruled under the scepter of the Habsburg emperor ensconced in the imperial Hofburg in Vienna.[2] Similarly, one was Hungarian if one possessed citizenship in any of the lands of that same Habsburg sovereign reigning as king from the royal castle in Budapest.[3] Moreover, both Austrian and Hungarian together were Austrian-Hungarian, because they shared the same sovereign, he who was emperor when in Vienna and king when in Budapest. Hence both shared in the common traditions of their common historical experience as mani-fested in the dynasty; and because they stood together under the umbrella of state created by the House of Habsburg, Austrian-Hungarians shared the Austrian idea. Robert Musil perhaps best described the actual muddle involved in being Austrian-Hungarian in a nationalistic era when he wrote:

[The] sense of Austro-Hungarian nationhood was an entity so strangely formed that it seems almost futile to try to explain it to anyone who has not experienced it himself. It did not consist of an Austrian and a Hungarian part that, as one might imagine, combined to form a unity, but of a whole and a part, namely of a Hungarian and an Austro-Hungarian sense of nationhood; and the latter was at home in Austria, whereby the Austrian sense of nationhood actually became homeless. The Austrian himself was only to be found in Hungary, and there as an object of dislike; at home he called himself a citizen of the kingdoms and realms of the Austro-Hungarian Monarchy as represented in the Imperial Council, which means the same as an Austrian plus a Hungarian minus this Hungarian, and he did this not, as one might imagine, with enthusiasm, but for the sake of an idea that he detested, for he could not endure the Hungarians any more than they could endure him, which made the whole connection more involved than ever. As a result, many people simply called themselves Czechs, Poles, Slovenes or Germans.[4]

Perhaps confusing its genesis with his realm's maturity, Emperor Franz Joseph held that the Austrian idea as symbolized and served by his dynasty continued to be the best possible means by which the disparate national components might be bound together. In his view, Austria-Hungary was both a viable state and a necessary one. Franz Joseph maintained that the dynastic principle depended not upon national ties but upon loyalty forged between it and its subjects, which would transcend the barriers of cultural-national community threatening to divide the realm. According to the emperor, one could possess patriotic sentiments toward the dynasty, and hence be a good Austrian, while at the same time having love for one's homeland in the sense of cultural identification within the territory belonging to one's national community.[5]

In any event, political identification in old Austria, by definition, referred not to one's ethno-cultural background but to one's membership in a political organism, a supranational state. The Austrian idea had evolved into a self-conscious attempt to transcend the narrow ethno-cultural limits of modern national identity in Europe by focusing around the historically sanctified institutions attached to the Catholic Habsburg dynasty and thereby also to the Roman Catholic church; that is, around throne and altar. The Austrian idea, although in the main assuming a perspective shared especially among Austria's privileged aristocracy and by the intellectual heirs of Josephism, was more than merely a political emotion belonging to that elite; further, this perspective, as is always the case in the fabrication of cultural icons, was felt to be a social reality despite the fact that historically the Austrian idea had its origin in the concrete self-interests of this same elite. And indeed, by the turn of the century, the Austrian idea had gained a mass following, gaining widespread support especially among German-speaking Austrians belonging to elements of the peasantry and the petite bourgeoisie. Unfortunately, during the last decades of the Dual Monarchy, these lower-middle classes tended to follow the political leadership found in parties such as the Christian Socialist party, whose ideology, especially when in the hands of the likes of Karl Luegar, embraced elements of religious fanaticism and anti-Semitic bigotry that rendered their support of the dynasty a mixed blessing at best because it threatened to drive away support of Austria's non-Germans, especially the Protestants as well as many of the secularists among them.[6]

As is well known, the *K.u.K.* army joined with the aristocracy and the Roman Catholic Church to complete the social triad of traditional support for the dynasty and hence, for the Austrian idea. The Church, by definition, was multinational and, at its governing level, aristocratic. Indeed, in some ways the Church can be viewed as having been at the high point of her existence a kind of superstate that served Europe's social as well as spiritual needs. What she lacked, however, was the sword, and therefore ultimately her primary influence gave way to that on which she depended for her protection as an institution, the rising secular state. Thereby, while theoretically inferior to the church state, the secular state, because it possessed the army, emerged in practice superior to the church in modern times. The army was the true bridge in modern times between church and state in the context of Austrian civilization.

Like the church, the governing level of the army, that is, its officer corps, historically was aristocratic. But it was largely bourgeois by the twentieth century; nevertheless, these middle-class members of the officer corps still took, as in the chivalric past, a personal oath of loyalty to the monarch, not to the state or to its constitution.[7] This ancient framework for perceiving military loyalty continued to exist right down to the end of the Dual Monarchy; the theoretical bond that tied army officers to one another as well as to the state was their personal oath to obey the kaiser and king, to obey he who was their *Allerhöchstkriegsherr* (supreme warlord). Because of this, much of the command vehicle through which the imperial and royal government operated to maneuver the army was a part not, strictly speaking, of the state apparatus, but of the court *(Hofstaat)*. And hence, also right down to the end, matters of command and promotion never were easily in the grasp of that civilian jurisdiction normally associated with the constitutional apparatus of modern European states. So the potential existed, had all other factors been equal and the supreme warlord been willing, for Austria-Hungary to have turned into a kind of military dictatorship grounded on her dominant nations. But, of course, precedent had run in the other direction in Austria during the nineteenth century, and precedent is a very strong building block in the fabrication of political culture. Nevertheless, given this militarist backdrop, the rise of fascist dictatorships in central Europe in the wake of the collapse of almost everything of the political order following the First World War perhaps was not surprising.

The army's effective functioning had been a result of the common experiences and perceptions of its leaders. As long as the army was a relatively small, mercenary force, funded by the imperial treasury, its leaders could be certain of the soldiers' motivation and esprit de corps. In modern times, however, not only did the function of the army become more complex and diverse, requiring the division of its officer corps by specialization, but it increasingly depended for its rank and file on a general conscription of young males in the population. In time, therefore, the army's officer corps came to be filled with men drawn not only from the upper strata of the bourgeoisie but also increasingly from its lower strata, while the rank and file consisted largely of young men who did not necessarily want to be there but who were, in contemporary parlance, doing their time.[8] As in the sphere of politics, the popularization of the army by necessity brought about a transformation of its inner spirit. The old outward forms remained, but these were increasingly hollow, as the substance of its esprit de corps was drawn from broad and diverse sources, producing an aggregate of different experiences and hence a potpourri of contradictory perceptions and expectations. In addition, funding for the army became a matter for the parliament, and hence part of the proverbial political football after 1859, and especially after the initiation in the Austrian crown lands of the equal and general elections reform in 1907. Henceforth, while narrow matters of command might still be pursued by the *Allerhöchstkriegsherr* through his *Hofstaat,* that all-important bottom line slipped out of his hands and fell into the hurly-burly of Austria's tumultuous political currents.[9]

Archduke Franz Ferdinand clearly expressed these concerns (along with others that unsettle the contemporary reader) when he wrote to the emperor, in 1908, that

> it is a sorry thing that everyone works against the army. The present government with [Max Vladimir von] Beck at its head is known to be hostile to the military [and] the Hungarian government does everything that it can to bring the army to ruin. The goal, which everyone works for in common with all their might, is to rob it of its esprit de corps and render the officers incapable . . . of giving the monarch help if he now or in the future requires the army to [help him] in maintaining his throne. It absolutely no longer can be allowed that [the army] be used as the poor football for those destructive elements that would destroy it. Hungarians, Freemasons, and socialists are at work to undermine the support of the throne and that is the reason why all turn toward destroying the army.[10]

It was not only the cohesiveness of the army that was undermined by the advent of modernism. The rank and file of the Catholic Church was broadened to the extent that on the local level, it largely ceased to be aristocratic. Much of the local clergy, for example, fell into various democratic nationalist currents, so as an institution, the Church was no longer homogeneous in her political perspective. Hence neither was it possible for the church leadership to support the throne, as in past centuries, by fabricating a uniform but broad-based political program that would generate support for the dynasty among the population at large through the help of the lower clergy. As the nineteenth century passed over into the twentieth, not only had the old symbiotic relationship between church and army been broken, but the triad of church-army-aristocracy that supported the dynasty, and hence held up the traditional Austrian idea, was weakened at its base.[11]

Almost from the beginning, therefore, the Austrian idea experienced a certain tension with the growing realities of mass political culture evolving out of the industrial capitalist era. The Austrian perspective—at least at the level of its most socially privileged articulation—required a tolerant, even liberal, view of cultural diversity, that is, a vision unencumbered by narrow-minded bigotry or mindless chauvinism. This supranational state, as against the multicultural state, required the fusion of all its parts into a whole under the umbrella of a great idea that transcended narrow self-identification, be it ethnic or otherwise; the resultant whole had to be, not an amalgam of still-identifiable parts, but a seamless fusion, founded on a common idea of the state. But much of the popular following of the Austrian idea came from segments of society created out of the dynamics of industrial capitalism and having precisely that narrow self-identification. In addition, during the nineteenth century the Austrian idea became embroiled in a confrontation between feudal loyalty (a concept with its roots in the history of Danubia going back to the fifteenth century) and ethno-cultural identification. Trying to retailor the idea of Austria as a single entity to these two apparently incompatible constructs required the negotiation of hitherto unfamiliar political-ideological patterns arising out of the century of industry and capital.[12]

The historical origins of feudal loyalty clearly grew out of the highly abstract idea of fealty, which was the rather soft adhesive of political society before the advent of the modern nation-state. Although its explanation customarily was cloaked in religious mysticism, fealty was in fact a product of practical utility. Society, while always fragile, was especially vulnerable during the period of the European Middle Ages because of its endemic political dislocation and its having been grounded in an era lacking viable means for quick and sure communication. In the absence of both such a means and a broad rationale for tying together society, there was still a felt need by rulers and ruled alike for order; the politically articulate fell into marrying general need with self-interest so as to produce government through subinfeudation. Because the political product inherently was unstable, subinfeudation was a poor expedient. But during the feudal era it was the best society could do. And so it was that the responsibility for territorial governance was divided among feudal lords according to a haphazard, always convoluted system of lord and overlord, tenuously linked by common self-interest and extending on up to an anointed monarch who sat at the apex of the feudal pile, with scant recourse available to those actually dwelling upon the land. This feudality at the same time was divorced from the tribal instincts of the people over which it purportedly governed, and many times even from knowledge of these people. Thereby two separate avenues to political consciousness were laid down: that belonging to a bellicose and aggressive feudality founded on personal loyalty generated out of self-interest and promoted by war as well as cemented by mutual authority over land, and that tribal instinct belonging to the tillers of the soil, who, lacking the means to make their voices either heard or politically relevant, kept their cultural-national identification to themselves and hence out of history. In time, this feudality evolved into a more high-flown aristocracy, and as it did so, it became the articulate sociopolitical outer layer that subsumed the politically voiceless peasant who worked beneath and remained unseen as far as the manifestations of high culture, political and otherwise, were concerned.[13]

The evolution of the feudal aristocracy into the Austrian higher nobility is exemplified by the Clary-Aldringen family. By the nineteenth century, the Clary-Aldringens were counted as aristocrats of noble lineage, and the family quite naturally fitted well within the context of the Austrian idea, viewing the Dual Monarchy as both fatherland and homeland *(Vaterland und Heimat)*.

Count Alfons Clary-Aldringen wrote with pride of his immediate forebears, who in turn were descended from politically entrepreneurial knights hailing from south Germany. It was his seventeenth-century ancestor, Count Hieronymus Clary who, through marriage and adventure, established the family on its great estates in Bohemia. The family also prudently associated itself with the fortunes of the House of Habsburg when the dynasty, during that same century, aggressively engaged its resources in the task of carving out a vast domain in south-central Europe, mostly at the expense of the Turks. The Clarys emerged into the eighteenth century thoroughly woven into the aristocratic net that at that time held together the results of the Habsburg state-building enterprise. Moreover, once in possession of what might be thought of as the dividends from its participation in the political adventures of Austria's Habsburgs, the Clarys succeeded in clinging to the bulk of its *Fideikomiss* (entailed property), centered at Teplitz, throughout the vicissitudes of the first half of the twentieth century, down until the fateful spring of 1945. Bohemia became the family's homeland because Schloss Teplitz was the Clarys' home, the place where their hearts were. The family "loved its Schloss, the landscape, the forest, the Erzgebirge, and even the air permeated with coal dust . . . for Teplitz had a special charm which was felt by . . . guests [from] near and far."[14] But of course Austria was always the Clarys' fatherland, for it was Austria, not Bohemia, that rendered the Clarys not only men of power, but "good and cheerful people" who, while pursuing the hunt, did not neglect art and music.[15] So it was that Friedrich Chopin and Franz Liszt played Schloss Teplitz's piano and the dyspeptic Beethoven often visited the estate's waters fruitlessly seeking a cure for his loss of hearing. So too did the incomparable Goethe find hospitality at the castle and took the deepest pleasure in its then still bucolic environs.[16]

During the nineteenth century, however, Austria emerged not only as a cohesive state but, by 1860, as a territorial-parliamentary one as well. Further, the diversity within the state, at least at certain social levels, blended together to create a dynamic and variegated culture that one might call Austrian. Because human beings are the carriers of culture, the manner in which diverse elements combined to create Austrian culture is best understood by exploring the comings and goings of her citizens as they wandered across Austria's territorial landscape over time.

Take, for example, the illustration supplied by the family history of one of Austria's future minister-presidents, Baron Max Vladimir von Beck. Born in 1854 in Wahrung bei Wien, Beck was given the name of Josef Marie Johann Wladimier by his parents, Dr. Anton and Hersilia (neé Hagenauer) Beck.

Anton came from southern Moravia, where the family had evolved out of German- and Czech-speaking peasant stock. Anton entered into the Habsburg state bureaucracy and rose to the rank of knight by the year 1877. It was his mother's family who came from Czech-speaking Moravia, and Anton, for reasons of his own, underplayed his paternal German-speaking heritage and came to consider himself a Czech, by which he meant that his fatherland was Austria but his people were Czech and his land was Moravia. It was for that reason that he included the Germanized name Waldimier (for Vladimir) among the names given his son, underscoring that his son was Austrian by state but German and especially Czech by nation. Indeed, young Beck's mother came from an old Salzburg patrician family. She, however, was born in Trieste and grew up in Austria's Italian-speaking territories; she spoke both French and Italian better than German. As young Beck would have it, then, his father might be understood culturally as possessing a German and Czech background whereas his mother might best be understood as being *südlandisch* (from the southern lands), but both Becks were Austrian.[17] Moreover, Anton Beck's career was pursued, and very successfully so, in Vienna, within the framework of German Austrian culture. In a word, young Max Vladimir Beck was an individual manifestation of the Austrian idea as it had evolved by the mid-nineteenth century; he himself took the view that he was Austrian, and he dedicated himself to the mission of creating a living space within which the small nations in south-central Europe, Slavic and non-Slavic alike, might develop their culture free of domination by *Deutschtum* from the northwest and by an aggressive Russo-Slavism from the east. In so viewing the Austrian mission in this fashion, it should be added, Beck shared with many Austrians of his generation a new perception of that mission that differed from an older, German centralist one, going back to the era of Josephism, whereby Austria was to carry European civilization in the German idiom down along the Danube to the shores of the Black Sea.[18]

Max Vladimir Beck, like his father before him, was both beneficiary and product of the Austrian state in that the Becks' rise out of their peasant background was through the avenue provided by the state bureaucracy. Able men with good minds, both pursued educational opportunity now open to them in an era of spreading liberal democracy, and both found careers as civil servants. Young Max, moreover, not only scaled the highest ranks of Austria's bureaucracy, but in the course of his work entered into the inner spheres of the dynasty itself and was ennobled in 1903. The ascent of the Becks underscores the role of the state as an avenue for social mobility and how this served as a cohesive element holding the state together. It is little wonder, then, that young Beck took a liberal view—that is, a centralist perspective—of the Austrian mission. But Beck's view was revisionist in that he sought not only to uphold the unified Austrian state but also to maintain it as a space in which all Austria's national cultures could exist. Nevertheless, because the driving forces of nationalism, concomitant with the spread of industrialism, were rapidly changing political expectations, Beck's perspective, to the minister-president's own surprise, was transformed into an ultraconservative one by the opening of the twentieth century. Perceiving himself as an Austrian and as the upholder of a unified Austrian state, Beck, although he began his career within the liberal vanguard of Austrian political ideology, found himself ending up "a reactionary."[19] But in any event, Beck's view did coincide broadly with Franz Joseph's stated perception of Austria-Hungary's raison d'être, for the emperor saw that

> more than historical events of the past have brought our peoples together. [They have been brought together] also by the absolute necessity of their present and future well being. The Monarchy therefore is not merely an artificial creation, it is an organic one, and as such even doubly necessary, for it is a refuge—an asylum for all the national splinter groups in central Europe, which, if they stood alone, must lead a doubtful and troubled existence, as they would become a football for their more powerful neighbors.[20]

For his part, looking back past the trauma of the events preceding and during the First World War, it is little wonder that Count Alfons Clary-Aldringen took a benevolent view of the way life had been at Teplitz and toward the Austrian idea of political statehood. Like others among the aristocracy, he had lost much with the collapse of the old society and the way of life associated with it. For beyond property, Clary had lost his Josephistic bearings and hence that stately identification that he associated with his Austrian fatherland—that deference that had accompanied his person, which to his mind's eye was part and parcel with the Austrian culture of baroque and rococo, extending out of the era of Maria Theresa. But by the same token, if the forces and events leading up to an unfolding in the course of the First World War were an accurate manifestation of the attitudes of others, Clary's Austria apparently had never been the Austria of her non-German masses. He came to realize, if only in hindsight, that beneath Prague's golden spires there lived not one people but three: German, Czech, and Jew. He had thought that the Bohemian capital was the home for all three nations, that they were all Prague's joint proprietors *(Miteigentümer),* but he belatedly came to realize that in fact Prague was only the place where their houses were located, not where their hearts were. It seemed that Prague belonged to only one of them and not to the other two.[21]

Clary's visit to Prague in 1918 was his first after many months at the battlefront during the First World War. Hence, perhaps he did not have a chance to notice the changes, observed by others, sweeping the Czech-speaking population under the press of hunger and when Austria labored under the specter of defeat. A fellow aristocrat, Count Erwein Lobkowicz, no less wedded to the Austrian idea and also loyal to the kaiser to the last, was more attuned to the shifting nuances in Bohemia, and so while for many, defeat meant an end to war and a return to the good old days, for Lobkowicz it meant a uncertain future. He was well aware, thanks to his close contacts with government officials in Prague, that the loyalty of many Bohemians to old Austria was increasingly doubtful. Hence, Lobkowicz, after hearing of the state affairs from the likes of the state chief of police in Prague, Count Reinhold Boos-Waldeck, "could focus on the future only with the greatest apprehension."[22]

In the view of a Clary or Lobkowicz, to be Austrian was to be loyal to the kaiser and therefore to possess feelings about the fatherland focused around a German dynasty. These feelings were at odds with the ethno-cultural nationalism of non-Germans. So, for example, Clary extolled the memory of an Austro-Polish friend, a professor at the University of Cracow, because he stood for "all that was beautiful and noble; a passionate Polish patriot and an imperial true Austrian."[23] As for himself, the count felt as much at ease in Italian Trieste, a part of what had been his broad fatherland, as he did in Polish-dominated Cracow, which also lay within the parameters of Franz Joseph's realm.[24] Clary suffered none of the contradictions felt by those standing on the nation-state principle, none of that pull between loyalty to one's state and loyalty to one's nation. By the same token, once the count became aware of the nationalist perspective, he had nothing to offer, no new idea, that might bridge the tension between nation and state. Rather, Clary's perspective only became increasingly outdated and irrelevant as the modern clashed with the old.

The deconstruction of those social-political perspectives that created a career like that of Max Vladimir Beck's or the lifestyle of the Clary-Aldringens and Lobkowiczs proved, after the collapse of the Dual Monarchy in November of 1918, painful for many Austrians. And this new reality was true not only for the privileged but for little people as well. Take, for example, the case of Herr Markus Laufer. In March of 1919, Laufer wrote to Friedrich Adler, then a socialist member of the National Assembly of the provisional Austrian republic, begging him for help in keeping both his job and national identity. It seems that Laufer was discharged in December of 1918, from his job as a *K.u.K.* postal clerk in Vienna and advised to return to either his native Poland or to Czechoslovakia. Thereby the unfortunate man lost his future along with his job and political identity, for he lost his pension right as well. Laufer appealed the decision to Chancellor Karl Renner through the offices of the barrister Dr. Egon Zweig. Renner rejected Laufer's appeal, telling him "that he could not be considered German Austrian because he had been born in Lemburg in the year 1910 (sic) where the first language was Polish. . . . A further [factor working against him] related to the fact that his people were Czech."[25] Poor Laufer went on to explain that he had spent his entire adult life in Vienna and that he himself had nothing in common with those Czechs "who seem to have just sprouted up." The clerk continued that his ancestors had been Germanized over two thousand years ago as a result of "Roman legions having destroyed the [ancient] Jewish realm. What," Laufer pleaded to Adler, "am I to do?" Adler, without evincing the slightest sympathy for the poor unfortunate, evidently thought nothing was to be done. He conveyed this opinion to Laufer while further pointing out that both the chancellor as well as a high official in the chancellery, the socialist Dr. Ellenbogen, were agreed that the former postal clerk was actually Polish.[26] In this case one can see how the nation-state principle overwhelmed an Austrian who, because he lived in the wrong time and place and now did not belong to any articulate group, had made an unfortunate mistake in taking the Habsburg state for granted.

The nation-state idea, while perhaps no less abstract than the feudal idea, may reflect, if factors of common culture such as language and religion are present and operate in synergistic fashion with the de facto possession of territory by a given ethnic group, what apparently is a more instinctual political identification.[27] Indeed, it is especially the sense of tribe that is the central substance of that ethno-cultural political perspective that in modern times has come to be the fundamental rationale underlying Europe's nation-state principle. In this principle's exaggerated form, blood too has been added to the ideological mix— nowhere more fatally articulated than by that Austrian who later became the Mephistophelean leader of the modern German nation. It was Adolf Hitler who hailed the nation-state idea as one wherein "the highest purpose of the . . . state is the care and preservation for those primal racial elements which, supplying culture create the beauty and dignity of a higher humanity. We . . . therefore only are able to imagine a state which safeguards . . . nationality."[28] That this perspective of the nation-state challenges in every respect the Austrian idea is self-evident. And although many nations succumbed to the yoke created out of Hitler's rhetoric, no nation among those formerly under the Habsburg scepter experienced that yoke more fatally than did old Austria's Jewish subjects. But long before the Holocaust cast its dark shadow over Danubia, some saw the dolorous possibilities as the Austrian idea commenced to give way to the nation-state principle. Robert Musil was surely prescient when he described Frau Klementine Fischer, a daughter of a high civil servant, as being ensnared in a fatal trap when

she had married Leo . . . first of all because the families of high civil servants sometimes have more children than means, but secondly, too, out of romanticism, because in contrast with the meticulously thrifty narrowness of her parental home banking appeared to her a latitudinarianism . . . and in the nineteenth century a cultivated person did not judge another person's values according to whether he was Jew or Catholic—indeed, as things were then she practically felt that there was something particularly cultivated in disregarding the crude anti-semitic prejudice of the common people. . . . Later the poor woman found a spirit of nationalism welling up all over Europe, and with it a surge of hostility to Jews, which transformed her husband, so to speak in her arms, from a respected liberalist into a member of a destructively analytical-minded alien race.[29]

The writer Hugo von Hofmannsthal, if less plaintive than Musil, also saw the deleterious ramifications of the spreading confrontation between the Austrian idea and the nation-state principle. Indeed, in 1913 Hofmannsthal saw that Austria stood on the brink of catastrophe. Writing to his friend, the poet Leopold von Andrian, he said, "We must understand that we have a home *[Heimat]*, but no fatherland *[Vaterland]*, as . . . [Austria] is only an apparition *[Gespenst]*. It is bitter to contemplate that at least one more time one must give over the blood of his children for this apparition."[30] Andrian was perhaps a bit too optimistic in responding to his friend, but in its own way, his too was a prophetic note. Andrian reminded Hofmannsthal that Austria signified an ideal that transcends the idea of the simple nation-state. It is, he went on to write, "the cooperation and partial blending of the genius of the people whose existence is possible only within a great realm *[Reich]*." Therefore, while Hofmannsthal thought he possessed no homeland, his friend at the same time saw Austria as his only possible homeland.[31]

As is seen from the above exchange, the Austrian idea generally was an elitist one that had but weak drawing power among most of the enfranchised masses, particularly among Austria's non-Germans. Indeed, the undermining of the Austrian idea and the concomitant development of the nation-state principle began when the self-conscious participation of the masses became necessary to the conduct of states and when the press of popular political culture broke through the elitist network that in the past had spoken for it, if not actually subsumed it. At this moment in time, the instant when the political-economic dynamics resulting from the Industrial Revolution pushed the masses into the decision-making processes of the state, the ethno-cultural perspective of community was thrust upon the political consciousness of that self-organized minority that so long had governed over it. Because of its paradoxical nature, the Industrial Revolution proved fatal to Austria. The position of the state in the European political world came to depend on this multifaceted technological and socioeconomic development, but the socioeconomic upheavals generated a mass political culture that was anathema to the existing elitist state's essence, its restrictive hierarchy.[32] Thus the assumptions shaping the perspective of Austrian identification were at the same time both destroyed and transformed by the advent of the new, industrial capitalism–driven popular political community. The members of such a community, by definition, are consumers, and so popular politics came to the fore in another way also as popular culture burst through the net of elitist culture.[33] Further, popular political culture proved to be grounded in ethnocentrism.

One observer stated that the collapse of old Austria was comparable to the falling of the theater "curtain without applause. . . . the monarchy evoked few tears for [Austria] as well as her emperor had lived beyond their era."[34]

Thomas Garrigue Masaryk, born within his Bohemian homeland as an Austrian, certainly did not begin his political career as a champion of the nation-state principle; it was only over time that he came to accept it as the rationale for state building. In 1915, Masaryk revealed the nature of that mundane political road he had been traveling when he observed:

> Till recently mankind was divided and organized into states and churches without regard to Nationality. The modern era is characterized by the development of various nationalities, as strong political and state-forming forces. In practice, language, as the medium of common cultural life and effort, is the best test of Nationality. Besides Nationality, in modern times, economic development, as well as provident care for the masses—not merely for aristocratic minorities—has become a great political and racial force. . . . The watchword "National-States" sums up the tendency of modern political development.[35]

Masaryk's statement certainly contrasts with that made by Prince Alain Rohan in 1897, that Austria required "unswerving *[unverrückbare]* loyalty to our dynasty, to our Austrian fatherland and to the German population in Bohemia."[36] Indeed, if one takes Rohan's perspective as a starting place and Masaryk's as an ending place, then the road between them, traversed by both the fading aristocracy and the up-and-coming bourgeoisie at overlapping moments in time, reveals the demise of the Austrian idea and its replacement by the nation-state principle.

The rise of the masses, however, was not initially perceived as an alarm signifying the immediate demise of the old elites and, hence, the old Austrian state. The elite continued their lives focused around Austrian land and capital; the masses gathered together, faceless, in her burgeoning cities. But central to the transition that would lead to the triumph of the nation-state principle was the emergence of the bourgeoisie, that class new in terms of both lifestyle but especially perspective, that unwittingly brokered the demise of the Austrian idea and thereby made way in Danubia for the nation-state principle. The bourgeoisie had emerged from the masses but at the same time wished its material success both acknowledged and accepted by the older elites. Thereby, this new class unwittingly constituted itself as a bridge or mediator between the masses, on the one hand, and the old elites and the Austrian state, on the other. Moreover, an especially crucial role in this transformation was played by a specific element within this new class, the industrial bourgeoisie, and more precisely the haute bourgeoisie among them. As this group won the economic means that propelled them both politically and socially upward, they came into close contact with the old elites. And as was only natural, this contact caused this bourgeoisie to want to emulate the lifestyle of their social betters. But as these newly emergent prosperous classes reached out toward the older elites, aristocrats such as the

Clary-Aldringens and Lobkowiczs or *Kunstadlen* (the highest rank of accomplished and recognized artists in the field of high culture), like the Hofmannsthals, they deserted the hearth of their peasant grandfathers. But their desertion was not their only effect on these peasant communities. Through the industrial bourgeoisie's control of industry and capital came the transformation of those same rooted communities they had left behind, for they used their economic leverage, again unwittingly, to make the agrarian proletariat of these communities the economically oppressed industrial proletariat of the cities. As capital and industry destroyed the paternalistic stability underlying the old social order, new social issues emerged, most obviously the spreading disaffection of the urban proletariat. Thus the popular politics of social reform was born. The new urban masses became adherents of the newly emergent popular political parties, parties such as the socialists, the German People's Party, and the Christian Socialists, which purported to be seeking help for the people's lot. Further, these political parties, be they Marxist, nationalist, or Christian, were all focused around socialism; with them came the advent of the dynamics that would destroy not only the old Austrian synthesis, but also the new, still evolving bourgeois order, even before the process of its creation had been completed.[37]

The family of Habsburg-Teschen demonstrates the anomalies that developed as the worlds of industry and capital converged on the traditional one belonging to the high aristocracy.[38] This branch of the dynasty, at the head of which was Archduke Friedrich, sometime inspector general of the *K.u.K.* army, possessed entailed estates that had originated as gifts by Maria Theresa to her daughter during the first half of the eighteenth century.[39] By 1900 these estates were the focus of extensive development in agricultural industry and mining, which rendered this branch of the family immensely wealthy in the sense of modern entrepreneurial capitalism. And although Archduke Friedrich employed a workforce of about eight hundred, many of whom were educated members of the bourgeoisie trained in engineering and in the ways of finance, Friedrich himself, also formally conversant with high finance and engineering, kept a very sharp eye on the ledger books as well as on possible avenues of further entrepreneurial activity. For example, Friedrich developed his dairy industry to the point that it had a near monopolistic hold over the profitable market of nearby Vienna.

At the same time that the family of Habsburg-Teschen was plunging into the fiscal ways of the industrial haute bourgeoisie, it also showed itself to be influenced by the contemporary currents of nationalism. Archduke Friedrich himself was proudly descended through his mother from the Hungarian branch of the dynasty, founded by the fifth son of Emperor Leopold II, Joseph, Palatine of Hungary. His wife, Isabella, Princess of Croy-Dülmen, claimed, in the idiom of chauvinism, descent from the ancient Hungarian Apárd. In addition, Isabella spent much of her considerable energy in developing local Hungarian handicrafts and marketing them throughout Europe. Her children, six of whom survived into adulthood, were schooled in Magyar and steeped in Hungarian history. In short, things Hungarian were both revered and promoted within the household. At the same time, however, the House of Habsburg-Teschen was an integral part of both the high aristocracy and the ruling house; moreover, being of the dynasty, it was inherently Austrian in the most fundamental way.[40] Not only did Friedrich and the emperor share the same great-grandfather (Leopold II), but the archduke was the highest-ranking Habsburg other than the emperor himself in the army, which was one-third of the triad that upheld the dynasty. Archduke Friedrich also possessed the third-largest court in the realm, and hence he and his family lived within the highly structured environment, with scant separation between public and private life, that was part and parcel of being one of the chiefs of the dynasty.[41] The family whiled away time in the prescribed aristocratic lifestyle in its city palaces, the Albertina in Vienna and the Grassalkovich Palace in Pressburg (Bratislava), or on one of its country estates, Halbthurn in eastern Hungary, for example, forever surrounded by the requisite entourage and locked, so to speak, in the preordained boredom of their gilded cages far from the hurly-burly and mundanity of daily life for the overwhelming majority of Franz Joseph's subjects. Moreover, the peculiar mixture of the culture of the archaic with that of the modern that Friedrich and his family experienced must have left them with a perspective ill suited to accurately divining the realities of the unfolding modern world.[42]

Legally being Austrian meant holding citizenship in the Dual Monarchy. But, in terms of national identity, being Austrian was a state of mind, an attitude stemming from emotionally embracing a perspective within the context of an idea resting in history. The Austrian idea was an abstraction built around the Habsburg dynasty as political heir to the Christian-Roman imperial tradition, which in modern times received tangibility, and hence legitimacy, through the institutions, liturgy, and ceremony of the Habsburg court in tandem with that of the Roman Catholic Church. Further, in modern times the Austrian idea was a perspective built around a concept of loyalty to throne and altar that was irrelevant to perceptions of political identity stemming out of a secular materialist culture as well as out of an ethno-national political one. Because the Austrian idea was an inherently pan-European, multinational, and multicultural perspective, it could be fully comprehended only within the parameters of the supranational state. Loyalty was given to he who was emperor and king, not in a personal sense, although a cult of personality did threaten to envelop Franz Joseph toward the end of his reign, but in the sense of the *Kaiser und König* being the court's chief liturgical prop, giving continuity to her present by visibly linking it with Austria's past.

In an era of waxing nationalism unleashed through the twin forces of capital and industry, the centripetal forces generated out of the traditions focusing around the imperial court were insufficient to overcome the centrifugal ones generated by popular concepts of cultural nationalism, and the stability of the old order was threatened by the emergence of the new. Because many existing communities of privilege benefited, or at least perceived benefits, from the traditional state synthesis, they attempted to infuse the old state with new life. The likes of Baron von Beck tried to uphold the old *Gesamtstaat* by expressing the Austrian idea not only in a German or Magyar idiom, but with a new nuance, one that attempted to give equal value to all of old Austria's newly self-conscious national cultures. An approach like Beck's, however, required a certain restraint, a willingness of each ethno-cultural part to equally respect its counterparts.

Similarly, as will be discussed in the next chapter, this new nuance for an ancient idea recruited *Baukunst mit Kunst*—architecture fused with high art—so that the Austrian idea might receive from high art an infusion, made tangible with bricks and mortar, of its intellectual power and so create an outer reality that touched human emotions, thereby opening up Austria's inhabitants to both the legitimacy and immutability of the Austrian idea. This alliance between art and architecture, however, called for the participation of the capitalist classes as well, adding still another dimension to the prescription of the Austrian idea. The end result, however, was a very different Austrian idea than the one envisioned by Baron von Beck.

Notes

1. See Ritchie Robertson and Edward Timms, eds., *The Habsburg Legacy: National Identity in Historical Perspective, Austrian Studies V* (Edinburgh: Edinburgh University Press, 1994). See also George V. Strong, "The Austrian Idea: An Idea of Nationhood in the Kingdom and Realms of the Emperor Franz Joseph I," *Journal of the History of European Ideas*, vol. 5, no. 3 (1984), pp. 293–305.

2. Technically, being Austrian meant being a citizen of the hereditary lands ruled from the *Reichsrat* in Vienna. This rather tortuous terminology for convenience's sake was referred to as the crown lands or the Austrian crown lands.

3. The Hungarian lands being those belonging to the Crown of St. Stephen.

4. Robert Musil, *The Man Without Qualities* (New York: Capricorn, 1965), pp. 198–199.

5. See Josef Schneider, *Kaiser Franz Joseph I und sein Hof* (Vienna: Leonhardt Verlag, 1920), pp. 191ff. This concept was demonstrated when, for example, Prince Rohan wrote to the Vertrauenmannen of German Bohemia, in the course of the outbreak of violence due to the controversy over the Badeni language ordinances, that the Prince wished from them "unshakable loyalty to our dynasty [*Herrscherhaus*], to our Austrian fatherland and to the German population in Bohemia." See Ernst Rutkowski, ed., *Briefe und Dokumente zur Geschichte der österreichischen-ungarischen Monarchie unter besonderer Berucksichtigiund des bömisch-märischen Raumes,* Teil I: "Der Verfassungstrauer Grossgrundbesitz, 1880–1899" (Vienna: R. Oldenbourg, 1983), pp. 321–322.

6. See Richard S. Geehr, *Karl Lueger: Mayor of Fin de Siècle Vienna* (Detroit: Wayne State University Press, 1990).

7. On the evolution of the army, see Scott W. Lackey, *The Rebirth of the Habsburg Army: Friedrich Beck and the Rise of the General Staff* (Westport, CT: Greenwood Press, 1995). On social development of the officer corps, see especially Istvan Deák, *Beyond Nationalism: A Social and Political History of the Habsburg Officer Corps* (New York: Oxford University Press, 1990).

8. See Robert A. Kann, *Dynasty, Politics and Culture: Selected Essays,* ed. Stanley B.

Winters (Boulder, CO: Social Science Monographs, 1991), especially "The Social Prestige of the Officer Corps in the Habsburg Empire from the Eighteenth Century to 1918," p. 246. On the army in general see Istvan Deák, *Beyond Nationalism: A Social and Political History of the Habsburg Officer Corps,* and Gunther E. Rothenberg, *The Army of Francis Joseph* (West Lafayette, IN: Purdue University Press, 1976).

9. Because these political processes applied to the navy as well, insights to the same are given by Lawrence Sondhaus, *The Naval Policy of Austria-Hungary, 1867–1918: Navalism, Industrial Development and the Politics of Dualism* (West Lafayette, IN: Purdue University Press, 1994), especially pp. 77–115.

10. Quoted in Friedrich Weissensteiner, *Franz Ferdinand: Der verhindererte Herrscher, Zum 70. Jahrestag von Sarajevo* (Vienna: Österreicher Bundesverlag, 1983), p. 204. Two years later, on the same subject but also showing a deep alienation toward elements within Austria's unfolding bourgeois society, the heir to the throne wrote Franz Joseph that "I consider it my holiest duty to warn Your Majesty that the mood of the army is not good and that the officer corps is being eaten away. The officers are paid as badly as the most inferior bureaucrat . . . the aim of many is to unite and work together to rob the army of its elán and the officer corps of its capacity . . . this work is being carried out by Hungarians, Freemasons and Socialists" (ibid., p. 206). And again, "The government is in the hands of Jews, Freemasons, socialists and Hungarians and all of these wish to corrupt and render the army dissatisfied." (ibid.).

11. Johann Christoph Allmayer-Beck, *Ministerpräsident Baron Beck: Ein Staatsmann des Alten Österreich* (Vienna: R. Oldenbourg 1965), p. 80. In 1932, Joseph Roth colorfully described the transformation of perspective taking place at the turn of the century when he wrote:

After every return from Vienna, or any other part of society in which he kicked his heels so familiarly . . . Count [Chojnicki] would give an ominous lecture. . . . "The Monarchy is bound to end. The minute the Emperor is dead, we shall splinter into a hundred fragments. The Balkans will be more powerful than we are. Each nation will set up its own dirty little government, even the Jews will proclaim a king in Palestine. Vienna's begun to stink of the sweat of democrats, I can't stand the Ringstrasse anymore. The workers all wave red flags and don't want to work anymore. The mayor of Vienna is a pious shopkeeper. Even the parsons are going red, they've started preaching in Czech in the churches. At the Burgtheater all the performances are filthy Jewish plays. And every week another Hungarian water-closet manufacturer is made a baron. I tell you gentlemen, if we don't start shooting pretty soon, it'll be the end. You just wait and see what's coming to us."

See Joseph Roth, *Radetzky March* (Berlin: Gustav Kiepenheuer Verlag, 1932). I have used the English translation by Eva Tucker (Woodstock, NY: Overlook Press, 1983, p. 129).

12. Certainly no better example of the result when high-flown political theory falls into the hands of a member of the alienated masses is Adolf Hitler's *Mein Kampf.* See especially the first three chapters of the work in the annotated edition (New York: Reynal and Hitchcock, 1940), pp. 3–162.

13. See H. Birkhan, "Popular and Elite Culture Interlacing in the Middle Ages" *Journal for the History of European Ideas,* vol. 10, no. 1 (1989).

14. Alfons Clary-Aldringen, *Geschichten eines alten Österreichers: Mit einem Vorwort Golo Mann* (Frankfurt am Main: Ullstein, 1977), pp. 14–18. In Bohemia, one

displayed the black and yellow flag to demonstrate solidarity with the Austrian idea. But very often the white and red flag of Czech solidarity was displayed within Austria as well. Forbidden by the police for display were the black, red, and yellow flag of Bohemian German nationalists, followers of Schönerer's and Wolf's *"Los vom Rom"* movement and the blue, white, and red tricolor of pan-Slavism. See Erwein Lobkowicz, *Erinnerungen an die Monarchie* (Vienna: Amalthea Verlag, 1989), p. 105.

15. Clary-Aldringen, *Geschichten eines alten Österreichers*, p. 142.

16. Ibid., pp. 142–143.

17. Allmayer-Beck, *Ministerpräsident Baron Beck,* pp. 10–16.

18. Ibid., p. 13. But the Josephistic idea still held up to the end of old Austria. For example, Generaloberst Friedrich Count Beck-Rzikowsky (no relation to the Becks above), originally a bourgeois from south Germany and one of the creators of Franz Joseph's modern army, always maintained that Austria's destiny was to subsume, mostly peacefully, the emerging Balkan nations out of the declining Porte so as to end up on the Aegean Sea. See Lackey, The *Rebirth of the Habsburg Army,* especially pp. 59–77.

19. See Allmayer-Beck, *Ministerpräsident Baron Beck.*

20. Albert Alexander Vinzenz, Freiherr von Margutti, *Vom alten Kaiser: persönliche Errinnerungen an Franz Joseph I, Kaiser von Österreich und apostolischen König von Ungarn* (Leipzig: Leonhardt, 1921), pp. 261–262.

21. Clary-Aldringen, *Geschichten des Altens Österreicher,* p. 143. Clary was not alone in this regard. Even as late as August 1918, at a birthday celebration for Kaiser Karl, Archduke Friedrich gave a sincere toast that Austria was "indivisible and inseparable—so has it always been and so will it always be . . . [for] no one, even the darkest pessimist, did not in the slightest conceive how near it was to the end." Erwein Lobkowicz, *Erinnerungen an die Monarchie,* p. 331.

22. Lobkowicz, *Erinnerungen an die Monarchie,* pp. 337–339.

23. Clary-Aldringen, *Geschichten des altens Österreicher,* pp. 158–159.

24. Ibid.

25. Archives of the Institute for Social History, Amsterdam, box labeled "F. Adler," folder L-M.

26. Evidently the barrister, Zweig, also ultimately agreed with Alder et al. Although Laufer infers his Jewish background, the outcome of the case cannot be passed off as anti-Semitism, if for no other reason than of the fact that both Adler and Ellenbogen had Jewish backgrounds, as probably did Zweig. However, the tone of the documents surrounding Laufer's case implies that Laufer was dismissed because of class. That is, the postal clerk belonged to, as old Austria would have it, the *Publikum* and consequently was fated to bow before the force of history. Archives of the Institute for Social History, Amsterdam, box labeled "F. Adler."

27. For a general statement on European nationalism, see Carlton J.H. Hayes, *Contemporary Europe Since 1870* (New York: Macmillan, 1958), especially p. 124, and his *A Generation of Materialism: 1871–1900* (New York: Harper and Row, 1941), especially pp. 15–18ff. A less structured view is given by Eric J. Hobsbawm, *Nations and Nationalism Since 1780: Programme, Myth, Reality* (Cambridge: Cambridge University Press, 1990). See also Gordon A. Craig, "The Kaiser and the Kritik," *New York Review of Books,* January 18, 1988, wherein the author suggests it was the instincts of nationalism rather than causes such as economic distress that brought about the rise of Adolf Hitler in Germany. See also Robert W. Seton-Watson, *Masaryk in England* (Cambridge: Cambridge University Press, 1943), pp. 117–118, where, quoting Thomas G. Masaryk, nationalism is described as being structural in modern European political culture and tied to recently unleashed popular democratic forces not likely to be subsumed by structures dependent on perspectives arising out of earlier political culture.

28. Quoted in Hitler, *Mein Kampf*, p. 595.

29. Musil, *The Man Without Qualities*, p. 239.

30. Quoted in Ernst Trost, *Kaiser Franz Joseph I von Gottes Gnaden Kaiser von Österreich apostolischer König von Ungarn* (Vienna: Fritz Molden, 1980), p. 37.

31. Ernst Trost, *Kaiser Franz Joseph I*. For more on this von Hofmannsthal–von Andrian exchange, see Jacques Le Rider, "Hugo von Hofmannsthal and the Austrian Idea of Central Europe," in Ritchie Robertson and Edward Timms, eds., *The Habsburg Legacy: National Identity in Historical Perspective* (Edinburgh: Edinburgh University Press, 1994), especially pp. 128ff.

32. See, for example, Karl Renner, *Die Nation als Rechtsidee* (Vienna: Ignaz Brand, 1914). See also Otto Bauer, *Nationalitätenfrage und Sozialdemokratie* (Vienna: Volksbuchhandlung, 1907), and his "Die Bedingungen der Nationalen Assimilation," *Der Kampf* VI (1912), pp. 246–263.

33. See R. Rocker, *Nationalism and Culture* (Los Angeles: Rocker Publications Committee 1937), especially pp. 1–240.

34. Erwein Lobkowicz, *Erinnerungen an die Monarchie*, pp. 337, 353.

35. Quoted in Seton-Watson, *Masaryk in England*, pp. 117–118.

36. See, Ernst Rutkowski, ed., *Briefe und Dokumente zur Geschichte der österreichischen-ungarischen Monarchie unter besonderer Berucksichtigung des bömisch-mährischen Raumes*. Teil I: "Der Verfassungstreue Grossgrundbesitz, 1880–1899," pp. 321–322.

37. See the very good summary of the impact of the Industrial Revolution on old Austria's political culture in Allmeyer-Beck, *Ministerpräsident Baron von Beck*, especially pp. 71–74.

38. Technically, Habsburg Ungarisch-Altenburg-Teschen.

39. These were certain estates on the present Austrian-Hungarian border as well as at Teschen on the Austrian-Prussian border. Actually, the dukedom of Teschen was the only land belonging to Emperor Joseph II in his own right; nevertheless, at his mother's behest, he willingly gave it over to his sister and her husband, Albert of Saxony. See Derek Beales, *Joseph II: In the Shadow of Maria Theresa, 1741–1780* (Cambridge: Cambridge University Press, 1987), p. 153.

40. All family members descended from the male children of Maria Theresa and Franz of Lorraine were considered members of the dynasty and, like Archduke Friedrich of Habsburg-Teschen and his male issue, subject to Habsburg *Hausrecht* and hence to the dictates of the chief of the House of Habsburg-Lorraine, the emperor and king of Austria-Hungary.

41. After the courts *(Hofstaaten)* of the emperor and the heir to the throne, Archduke Franz Ferdinand.

42. See Vilmos Heiszler, Margit Szakács, and Károly Vörös, *Ein Photoalbum aus dem Hause Habsburg: Friedrich von Habsburg und seine Familie* (Vienna: Böhlau Verlag, 1989).

✧ 5 ✧

Socialism, Nationalism, and National Socialism: Social Democracy's Struggle with National Identity in Austria-Hungary

National socialism, given the experience of Germany during the period 1933–1945, has been so fused with the history of the Third Reich that it means, in contemporary parlance, Hitler, thereby encompassing all the baleful baggage carried by this abhorrent name. The fact that the term "national socialism" was embraced by diverse groups even before the First World War, endeavoring to strengthen progress toward socialism by linking it to rising popular political perspectives such as nationalism, has gone by the boards because, understandably, today no group wants to share a podium with the likes of Adolf Hitler. Nevertheless, the strength of both nationalism and socialism prior to the great war was such that it was only natural that these two currents find one another and link together across a broad spectrum of political consciousness. It is understandable too that Austria's Marxist socialists also allied themselves, either implicitly or explicitly, with nationalism. Therefore it is both appropriate and necessary in any discussion of political culture in old Austria to examine the links forged between socialism, social democracy, and nationalism in Austria-Hungary and the ramifications of those links.

In 1899, at its party conference, the Austrian Social Democratic Workers' Party unveiled a somewhat convoluted nationality proposal, the Brünner Program, by which it would reconcile the Austrian crown lands with its nations.[1] Central to this program was the party's call to "replace the historic [Austrian] crown lands with nationality-demarcated and self-administered entities whose legal basis would rest on national chambers created by means of a general, equal, and direct election."[2] Hence, whatever else this proposal implied, it attempted to co-opt the idea of nation and use it to destroy Austria's historic *Länder* so as to make possible the state's restructuring in a manner that would withstand escalating nationality conflict. In other words, socialism would preserve the state from disintegration under the press of nationalism by means of that same nationalism.

The original 1899 Brünner Program, its basic principle unaltered, was reworded in 1912 so as to further address nationality conflict in Austria as it had developed during the intervening years, explaining in more detail exactly how the party would accommodate those national minorities that existed as aliens scattered within the "nationally demarcated . . . territories." This accommodation was to be achieved "by [coalescing] a given minority administratively [as against territorially] within its ethnic group *[Verein]* so that it could carry out its cultural affairs within its own national union and hence possess the completest national autonomy." In this way, the party promised, there would be guaranteed cultural equality for national minorities existing within another nation's territory, physically isolated from their own national core territory.[3]

By its Brünner Program, the party thereby expressed its intention to work to establish a framework in which old Austria might finally be constitutionally recast into a functional, democratic, and egalitarian state by first eliminating ethno-cultural conflict. The party's plan rested on the presupposition that nations residing within the Austrian crown lands could be guaranteed their cultural and civil existence, thereby defusing ethno-culturally generated differences threatening the state. The party further suggested that this program could be set in motion quickly by means of a new constitution. But such a constitution, warned the party, must grant special privilege to no nation; specifically, establish no state language *(Staatssprache)* but merely a language for mediation *(Vermittungssprache)*.[4]

It must be stressed that the Brünner Program did not envision recasting the Austrian realm on the basis of its historic states. Moreover, despite the fact that its proposed restructuring would give the German Austrians the largest bloc of territory within the crown lands, the party insisted that its nationality program looked to remove German culture from its historic role as the primary idiom of Austrian culture and hence strip from its German-speaking people their perception that theirs was the preeminent nation. In every sense of the word, then, the socialists' nationality program was radical. Not only would the historic states that made up the Habsburg realm exist no more, but Austria's German nation would be deprived of its sense of identity, stripped of its pride of mission to carry Catholic German baroque culture down into the bowels of central Europe. Thereby, in the name of recognizing the drive of her so-called subject nations for cultural-national equality, the national socialism articulated by Austrian Marxism would jettison five hundred years of Austria's political cultural evolution, along with the concomitant accumulation of special interests that had been invested over time in the evolving status quo. That the party felt forced to pursue such an insurrectionist agenda was not, strictly speaking, related to its social ideology. Rather, the party's conviction (or at least that of its leadership, ensconced in Vienna) was that the preservation of all of Austria-Hungary was in the vital interest of her working class, given that the Dual Monarchy was the most economically equiponderant in all of Europe. The Brünner Program was the means by which the party sought to preserve the state amidst the overwhelming demand among Austria's non-Germans for national equality. But it is also on this point that the party's program seemed caught up in contradiction. Beyond

the fact that the program drove away many would-be German Austrian supporters, it appeared flawed by the paradox that its declared intent to remove German
as Austria's predominant cultural idiom flew in the face of the fact that, because
the Austrian crown lands would be restructured on the basis of the majority
nationality resident in a given territory, the end result, whether intentional or not,
would put the largest territorial bloc in the hands of the German Austrians.
Thereby, not only did the party squander some of its support among German
Austrians, but at the same time its non-German critics viewed the program as
returning to German Austrians that political leverage that had in fact been slipping away from them as actual demographic evolution came to favor Austria's
Slavic populations.[5] Indeed, critics of a German-dominated Austria viewed in the
party's Brünner program a premeditated ploy to both continue and strengthen
German cultural domination of Cisleitha, and what was worse, all under the
pretext of seeking cultural equality among Austria's nations.

Initially, however, and despite sharp criticism of its nationality program, the
party's leadership was euphoric because of its conviction that at last it had found a
formula whereby the crown lands would be harmoniously divided according to the
ethnic groupings that predominated in a given territory. Ethnic minorities no longer
would have to be swallowed up, for they would be identified and administratively
linked with their fellow nationals, residing in a territory in which they predominated.
Thereby a minority nation could conduct its cultural affairs not in forced concert
with the ethnic majority within whose territory it lived, but with its ethnic kin. In
other words, the party felt it had found the means for Austria's social assembly,
while its critics viewed it as a formula for the Dual Monarchy's social disassembly.

At first glance the proposed division might appear to call for the recasting of
the state along simple territorial-national lines. But given the reality of Austria's
ethnic demography, most of the delineated national territories actually would
contain minorities that would operate as cultural outsiders in the territorial unit in
which they resided. However, social democracy took consolation in the fact that
these dichotomies would be harmonized at the next stately level, the suprastate
level, where each nation would give its allegiance to Austria, acting as a common
umbrella for all of her nations.

Social democracy's nationality program made no provision sanctioning the
Habsburg dynasty as a rallying point for Austria's nations. And certainly the
party wanted no truck with aristocracy. Unofficially, however, while much of the
party's leadership viewed the current dynastic organization as both too privileged and exploitative, many socialists were not unwilling to retain the emperor
as Austria's standard-bearer. In truth, many among the party's Viennese leadership privately were emotionally committed to the maintenance of the dynasty,
both because they recognized the utility of the Austrian state's historic linkage
with it and because they were somewhat besotted by the glitter of the Habsburg
court.[6] In any event, the name *Austria* would refer to a state that embraced all the
nationalities living within it. Thereby the socialists would make real the often

stated (but perhaps too often less deeply felt) idea that Austria's nations needed to cultivate "an understanding as to the admirable qualities and characteristics of the various ethnic groups and by coming to realize their reciprocity and dependence on one another . . . come to recognize those feelings of solidarity that bind all our peoples to the Austrian fatherland."[7] Beyond the removal of the bone of cultural discord among the nations, socialism hoped not only to put to rest the struggle for ethno-cultural recognition among Austria's peoples, but further to ensure that each nation would rest content within the parameters of the historic, supranational crown lands. If the proletariat no longer could be divided along the lines of nationality by a bourgeois leadership, it might then stand fully behind the supranationally oriented Austrian Social Democratic Workers' Party and give it needed political leverage with which to recast all of capitalistic, aristocratic Austria-Hungary into a social democratic state founded on economic democracy.

It is said that the road to hell is paved with good intentions. And good intentions, in turn, come from those of goodwill who would reform the world in a just and rational way so as to make a break from the wicked past. It was in this context that Marxist socialism sought to build a new order for the Austrian state. But its critics appeared not to recognize these good intentions and were quick to point out that by insisting that there be a clean break with the past, Austro-Marxism failed to appreciate that the nationality question might better be resolved within the evolutionary framework of Austria's historic *Länder*. These critics suggested that in its obsession to reform, the party was dispensing with a major avenue, hallowed by tradition and experience, by which the nations might be reconciled to history and, through Clio, to the present Austrian state as a whole. So, for example, the socialist nationality program would have it that there would be no Bohemia and hence no more Bohemians. Rather, there would exist only Germans and Czechs in the territory of what once had been the historic Bohemian crown. And so too it would follow that there would be no attempt to resolve the current Czech-German cultural struggle taking place in Bohemia within the framework of the Crown of St. Wenceslas; rather, Czechs and Germans were to be reconciled to one another only within the larger, historically somewhat nebulous Austrian crown lands. The German majority currently resident in southern Bohemia and Moravia would be fused with territory belonging to German majorities living in the archdukedoms of Upper and Lower Austria and in Vorarlberg, Tyrol, Styria, and Carinthia, creating a single large German territorial bloc in Austria in place of seven (six excluding Bohemia) ancient states possessing their own variations of political culture. Further, the Brünner Program called for Czech minorities residing in southern Bohemia and Moravia, for purposes of their cultural affairs, to be linked administratively with their national kin to the north so as to form a single, if smaller, Czech territorial bloc focused around the Czech-speaking territories in upper central Bohemia and Moravia.[8] In other words, Austria, instead of being made up of a series of multiethnic *Länder* validated through history, would consist only of amorphous blocs of nations, and presumably—if Marxist ideas of economic democracy should take root—class-less nations at that. Little wonder that many Austrians saw in social democracy's program a demonic and destructive device, devastating to the Austrian peoples and their cultures. No wonder too that even Marxist socialists who identified with Austria's non-German nations were highly suspicious of what they saw as the motives of the Vienna leadership.

To remain with the example of Bohemia, the dynamics describing the rise of nationalism had caused two nations, German and Czech, to overlook the fact that historically both were involved in Bohemia's creation. Approaching the dispute objectively, each unjustly had laid exclusive claim to the kingdom.[9] But, by the same token, neither the Germans nor the Czechs were in dispute over Austria as a whole; rather, the dispute was over a part of Austria, over national ownership of the ancient Bohemian state that, in turn, had become a part of the greater realm of Austria through the accidents of historical evolution. The socialists, however, while willing to submit to the necessity of granting each nation its cultural identity within a constitutional framework embracing the Austrian state as a whole, were unwilling, out of a series of benignly made but false assumptions, to recognize them within Austria's existing stately parts. Further, the party was unwilling to argue that the kingdom of Bohemia should be granted to both Czech- and German-speaking Bohemians together.[10]

The Brünner Program, therefore, generated criticism from two chief sources. One source was those who could not conceive of an Austria except as constituted by her historic parts, a collection of individual *Länder* that each had a political culture of its own and had fused its population to a common destiny, in turn receiving a civil identity permitting each of them unique visibility within the state as a whole.[11] The other source of criticism came from those driven by cultural chauvinism that had rendered them unwilling to share their state with other nations brought into it through the forces of history. But it is also understandable, given the irreconcilability of these two positions, why the party's leadership attempted to surmount fractious debate by simply seeking to abolish the historic *Länder* and reconstruct the state solely on the basis of ethnic nationalism. But by embracing not only national socialism but German national socialism and offering no amelioration to those seeking to preserve the traditional *Länder,* the party also fused two powerful streams to create an opposition so strong that it threatened to outweigh any elements of possible resolution contained in its nationality program. Worse still, this program served to intensify the centrifugal elements contained in the nationality debate itself, and thereby its good intentions threatened social disassembly for all of Austria. Besotted by the issue of nationalism, the party had failed to see that the struggle among Austria's nations was not a single fight for the state but a series of individual struggles for Austria's component parts.[12]

The German Austrian socialist deputy Engelbert Pernerstorfer clumsily attempted to reconcile the implicit contradiction in the Brünner Program between socialist internationalism and national socialism by playing on the words *nationalism* and *internationalism* so as to demonstrate that "nationalism is the prerequisite for internationalism, for if there exists no nation, then, naturally, there can be no international relations among nations. [Moreover,] he who stands under the banner of internationalism stands with nationalism in the highest form."[13] With seemingly premeditated rancor, Pernerstorfer pulled at Czech sensitivities, declaring, "It is necessary to be clear on the concept of nationalism. Our ... comrades understand nationalism as being very much opposed to internationalism; that is false. Rather ... the concept of internationalism opposes only objectionable concepts of nationalism. ... The nationalism of the Czech people is a neurosis to which they are oddly subjected. ... We Germans have nothing to fear; we cannot perish. Our existence is very clear."[14]

Writing from Reichenbach in northwest Bohemia, an infuriated Josef Strasser rebutted Pernerstorfer's rather slick explanation. Strasser set off the distinction to be drawn between national socialism and international socialism when he reminded the German Austrian deputy that "the Communist Manifesto tells us— 'proletariat of all lands unite.' All workers belong together—equally—whether they be German or French, Catholic or Protestant, man or woman, qualified or unqualified. ... This truth is often misunderstood. Is [Pernerstorfer] to be interpreted that workers have opposite interests as a group than they do as individuals? ... All workers have ... class interests in common."[15] This is not to say that German Austrians such as Pernerstorfer were not well-intentioned. Pernerstorfer was attempting to face up to the apparent barricade set against socialism by the spirit of nationalism that seemed to be welling up all across Austria. Moreover, while it is true that he confronted this nationalism with distortion, it was a distortion that originated in Marxist doctrine; that is, an ideological abstraction that would have nationalism as a device conceived by the bourgeoisie to divide the proletariat against itself so as to weaken any political leverage socialism might derive through the unity of the working class. From a Marxist socialist perspective, settling the Czech-German struggle within the context of the Bohemian crown would keep the issue of nationality alive within Bohemia, and so the working class would continue to be divided, nation against nation, in the crown lands as a whole, depriving the party of the political cohesiveness necessary to drive political culture in the direction of working-class solidarity. Indeed, the party leadership insisted that it did not seek national socialism but rather looked to restructure Austria along cultural national lines merely as a tactic in laying those foundations that would bring humanity to a higher level of existence. So, for example, at the burial service of Viktor Adler in November of 1918, Ludo Moritz Hartmann insisted before Adler's mourners that the party's founder "was ... a man of culture. He saw nations as merely a human cultural form. He desired the brotherhood of man. He considered socialism as merely a means toward [the achieving] of this aim. He would link the growing power of the proletarian international to the heights of human culture."[16]

One might argue, however, that Viktor Adler did not fully comprehend the instinctual passions generated by territorial national self-consciousness. By focusing on cultural rather than territorial-cultural questions of nationalism, he (and through him Austro-Marxism) failed to confront the real issue, which was the struggle among national groups over specific turf. As a consequence, even many within the party's rank and file did not take a profound view of the party's stand on nationalism. Indeed, some saw in the program no more than a ploy for establishing, once and for all, German cultural hegemony throughout Austria. The Czech Marxist Anton Němec, for example, bitterly complained that the German Austrian socialist leadership in Vienna "has opted for [German] national assimilation . . . [and] has concluded a . . . compact that they are the best, most reliable of Germans and are the defenders of the German character of Austria."[17] But it must be admitted that here Němec was not without grounds for his suspicions. For example, the very same Ludo Hartmann who in 1918 lauded Viktor Adler's humanity may have forgotten that in 1910 Adler had promoted a kind of national socialism by writing of the need to stamp out Czech national aspirations through the forced use of German in Bohemia's public schools. Thereby Hartmann, himself of German Bohemian origin and a historian of classical antiquity at the University of Vienna, implied that socialism sanctioned a kind of forced Germanization of the Czech population: "The assimilation of a national minority into the majority of the population is a natural necessity. . . . [Social democracy] should not step in to check or otherwise stop this natural social process. . . . We must teach national minorities that it is their eventual destiny to assume . . . the speech of the majority."[18]

Declarations such as those by Pernerstorfer and Hartmann worried Viktor Adler. Clinging to the hope that economic prosperity would, of itself, eventually promote the integration of nationalities, Adler cautioned, "We must wait until [nationalist] separatism dies out. A wall between ourselves and the Czech proletariat must not be built from the inside. . . . The power of the working-class movement faces a crisis which in itself is not a crisis yet. . . . We must work toward unity."[19]

And indeed, Adler's views did have the support of other German Bohemian socialists. For example, the German Bohemian socialist Josef Seliger set himself against the likes of Hartmann and Pernerstorfer when he clearly demonstrated his commitment to international socialism, or at least to cultural equality in Bohemia between Czechs and Germans, by warning that "to force the Czech minority . . . to accept the German language . . . would create a gulf of hatred between the Czech worker and ourselves which no power could overcome. Therefore . . . [we must] hold true to the concept of the international and of class struggle."[20]

It was, however, the Hartmanns and Pernerstorfers, not the Strassers and Seligers, that dominated the German Austrian socialist debate over the Czech-German struggle for the Bohemian crown. Viktor Adler's detached and elevated position seemed at best to offer lukewarm support to the Strassers and Seligers and a slap on the wrist to the others, but no more. The position taken by the party's founder on this debate, when viewed through the prism provided by the Brünner Program, seemed to at least superficially validate Czech socialists' complaints of German national bias on Adler's part; further, Adler's perceived stance only too easily could be construed to be that of the entire party leadership in Vienna.[21]

It was certainly true that personally Adler, and indeed his parents' generation, were self-consciously German. In addition, it was a well-known fact that the Adler family had Jewish origins. Moreover, his father had been brought up in Moravia but settled in Prague. And it was from Prague that his father, now a successful industrialist, had taken his family to live in Vienna. Once there, the Adlers participated fully in the lifestyle of the capital's haute bourgeoisie; young Adler was encouraged to enter the ranks of German high culture by becoming a member of the professions *(Berufadlen)*. Toward this end, Viktor took a degree in medicine and went on to study psychiatry.[22] In short, taking his father's lead, young Viktor became German by choice. Further, his becoming German obviously was related to the family's move from Prague to Vienna, for unlike in the Bohemian capital, one could be wholeheartedly, unselfconsciously German in Vienna. The fact that Viktor saw himself as German and not Czech surely explains the tenuousness, if not outright ambivalence, of his support of the Strassers and Seligers in his party. At the same time Adler's views do not necessarily support opinions like Němec's.

While later generations came to think of Adler and his descendants as Jewish (out of considerations of race rather than religion), Adler's father, as was very often the case among Viennese of that socioeconomic ilk, had renounced Judaism and brought his family to join the Christian evangelical church. The issue of Adler's Jewishness sheds light on why the Adlers embraced the German, among Austria's nations, and why Viktor and his likes within the party's leadership unwittingly may have played social democracy on a German fiddle.

The Dual Monarchy's Jewish subjects often supported a Germanized Austria because they hoped that it would carry what they viewed as the liberating and humanizing culture of the likes of Goethe and Schiller deep into central Europe, bringing tolerance and freedom into the Jewish ghettos throughout central and south-central Europe under the benign auspices of the House of Austria. It is likely, at least deep down, that the experience of the Adler family may have led Viktor to sense that the Jews would reap both freedom and assimilation through the establishment of a German Austrian emancipation culture, not only in the Dual Monarchy, but throughout all of central Europe; certainly Adler's own experience justified this perception.[23]

Joachim Schoenfeld, writing of his childhood in an Austrian Galician shtetl, echoes Adler's view of the benign rule of Austria, as far as her Jews were concerned, from the viewpoint of a more modest social stratum. In addition, the author's recollections preserve the flavor of the difficult nuances governing intranational relations in rural areas of central Europe before the First World War.

Schoenfeld, who was persecuted later under the Polish and Nazi regimes, recalls that "Austrian Jews were patriots. They loved their Kaiser Franz Joseph whom they nicknamed Froyim Yossed."

> In 1908 . . . Franz Joseph passed through our city on the way to Czernowitz, on the occasion of the so-called kaiser maneuver. . . . The streets of the city and especially the shtetl were lined on both sides with people . . . waving black-yellow flags. When the emperor . . . saw the representatives of the Jewish community holding torahs and waiting to greet him he got out of his carriage, approached the group, and shook hands with the rabbi, who said the appropriate blessing when meeting the emperor. The kaiser asked the rabbi to repeat in German what he had said in Hebrew. The rabbi did so, much to the great pleasure of the emperor. The kaiser then exchanged words with some other members of the Jewish delegation. This event was later discussed with much satisfaction. . . . "Our kaiser" didn't stop to talk to the priest but did stop when he saw the *"hadras ponim"* (the "majestic face") of the rabbi with the [Torah].[24]

In contrast to the Germanophile perspective of the likes of Viktor Adler, there were many conservatives in old Austria who, although opposed to social democracy's nationality program, nevertheless were aware that a settlement to the nationality question required the dethroning of German cultural preeminence. But they meant to face this issue on its own terms, meaning that nationality had to be confronted within the framework of Austria's historic *Länder* rather than solely in terms of her nations. Czech and German Bohemians, for example, were to be forced to settle their dispute within the framework of the Bohemian crown so as to bring about breathing space on territorial-cultural issues within which both nations might develop and eventually grow to cooperate in sharing the *Land* between them. Such cooperation, in turn, was necessary if Bohemians were to become good Austrians. To give one example, Prince Karl von Schwarzenberg, sometimes a member of the Bohemian state parliament as well as of the Austrian parliament and *Obmann* (chief) of Mirovic and Mühlhausen, deplored the failure of Emperor Franz Joseph to have himself crowned king of Bohemia. Further, Schwarzenberg actively supported an autonomous Bohemia within Austria, tied to it by both dynastic and federative principles as a proper reflection of its historical evolution. Indeed, while the prince saw the issue of nationalism through a sort of feudal perspective natural to the conservative big landowners in Bohemia, nevertheless he also viewed it as a mistake when other members of his social class aligned themselves, if only out of expediency, with Czech nationalist parties because he feared deepening the Czech-German split at the expense of the general welfare in Bohemia and, by extension, Austria-Hungary as a whole.[25] Such a split, of course, would destroy the traditional property rights enjoyed by these Austrian landowners.

The Vienna socialist leadership, on the other hand, remained with the national socialist solution because they questioned whether it was feasible to arrive at a nationality settlement state by state. They believed that such a tactic would result not in cultural parity but, as for example in the case of Bohemia, independent statehood with the total exclusion of either Czech or German culture. Hence the party took as its priority the preservation of the state and declined to pursue the sort of formula envisioned by Schwarzenberg.

Justice also requires the reminder that a plan for the restructuring and preservation of Austria had to be fabricated within the framework of the perception that the realms of the Hohenzollerns and Romanovs were more or less permanent institutions, along with the rest of Europe's stately constellations. Few could have foreseen, even in 1912 or 1913, that an apparently permanent and fundamental international order would disappear in the conflagration that would begin during early August of 1914.

Even Karl von Schwarzenberg himself eventually came to view the chances of achieving a settlement in Bohemia on the basis of Czech-German parity as small when, in 1889, elections for the provincial parliament brought about the rise of the seemingly uncompromising, chauvinist Young Czechs at the expense of the less ideologically vehement old Czech movement. Worse, in Schwarzenberg's view, was that the rise of the Young Czechs also brought that of equally chauvinist German Bohemian radicals, led by the anti-Czech, anti-Semitic, pan-Germanist Georg von Schönerer. This latter group of ideologues wanted to solve the Czech-German struggle by forcibly tearing the province from Austria, joining it with the German *Reich,* and silencing the Czechs under an overwhelmingly German regime.[26] The old Czech movement, under the able but restrained leadership of Dr. Franz Ladislaus Rieger, who was the bearer of the views of Dr. Frantisek Palacky, had promoted a program agreeable to the common Bohemian people, both Czech and German. But by 1899, a thoroughly alarmed Schwarzenberg feared—rightly, as it turned out—that this policy of national co-dominion had been fatally weakened.[27]

In contrast to the pragmatism of Schwarzenberg, the antihistorical nationalist socialist approach contained within the Brünner Program appears as no more than something of a political abstraction, an intellectual product of a leadership that lived in the cocoon of the rarefied circles of Vienna's intelligentsia, within the comfortable socioeconomic confines of Vienna's haute bourgeoisie. And as ideological abstractions often are, the Brünner Program was suffused with generalities. For example, it never presented a precise demarcation between national business that might be pursued within a homogeneous national union and that which must be pursued within constitutional and civil parameters because of its general impact on the state as a whole. This confusion laid the party open to accusations that in reality it was seeking a sort of Josephistic state and that it thereby was an ally of the dynasty and, ipso facto, an opponent of truly democratic (and socialist) reform.[28] Czech socialists, for example, chastised the German Austrian leadership in Vienna because our German comrades always report the solution of nationality problems from the standpoint of [their] power. They wish to apply force to the political decisions of the Czech worker. . . . They crown themselves as the founders of. . . socialism and therefore, the Czech worker must dutifully subject himself to German social democracy. . . . Do German [Austrian] social democrats propose to do what the whole Austrian capitalistic government with its entire legal, military and bureaucratic systems has been unable to do?[29]

The concern about German domination on the part of Czech socialists surely stemmed from the knowledge that, given the lack of definition as to precisely what constituted national business as apart from the business of the *Land,* the German Bohemians, while a minority in terms of their numbers, were economically more powerful than their Czech-speaking compatriots. Therefore, could not the German Bohemians use their economic leverage to blunt the Czech Bohemians' pursuit of cultural equality? This fear also caused the Czech socialists to demand from their comrades in Vienna a "community *(Gemeinsamkeit)* with our German companions, not a common party *(Gesamtpartei).* We are willing to cooperate on the basis of equality with our German companions, but not at the price that they dictate to us. We are willing to demonstrate our socialist principles in the form of community, [but] live our own life as we must live it [and] not the life foreign to the Czech worker . . . that we not . . . carry forth our war against capitalism in a position subordinate to German [cultural] interests."[30]

The German Austrian leadership simply could not fathom what they saw as parochial views by Czech nationalist socialists. Belonging to the Viennese haute bourgeoisie, rooted in German high culture while at the same time committed to the abstractions of Marxist internationalism, the Vienna leadership simply was not open to the pleas of their Czech comrades, whom, when all was said and done, they saw as reflecting an inferior, provincial culture that had the obligation to accept the higher German culture. However, being a part of the German Austrian bourgeoisie signified more than a certain economic perspective, for it perceived itself as existing within a dynamic, forward-looking, and commanding Austrian cultural community. Members of this community tended to patronize other cultural groups, whom they perceived as not sharing their general and uplifting experience. Austria's working classes—to say nothing of members of the subject nations residing in the Dual Monarchy's provincial cities—could not be expected to comprehend the superior values emanating from an experience they did not share. These silver-spoon social democrats not only saw international Marxism as the proper vehicle on which to drive society toward the industrialist nirvana but also saw such a vehicle most clearly in a German idiom. They were not the least inclined to listen to the protests from other Marxist cultural communities, and not the least shy in correcting these for the error of their ways. At bottom, then, these Marxist scions of Vienna's haute bourgeoisie were men of their era and milieu, cultural chauvinists of a sort, though not in a narrow political or economic sense. Little wonder, then, that they desired a state using their language, the German language, and focused around their German cultural-national icons. Hence, it is not surprising that these German Austrian Socialists found themselves uncomprehendingly in an intellectual crossfire between their nationalist feelings, generated at the instinctual level, and their adherence at the intellectual level, to the abstraction of international proletarian class struggle in pursuit of supranatural solidarity. In a word, they were Austrian national socialists in spite of their commitment to the socialist international. More than one among them would have agreed with this Hegelian play of words:

> The Marxist who would substitute opposition between factory owner and worker for civil peace is a thing of the past. Who would not understand that this Marxist antithesis results in the synthesis that the worker and the factory owner have common interests outside of capital just as do the north and south ends of a [steel] rod because both together are carried within the same piece of steel? . . . The Marxist can't reduce the complexity of society with its thousandfold variations to . . . factory owner and worker.[31]

The dichotomy between nationalist feeling and the abstract goal of proletarian supranational solidarity posed no immediate problem for Marxists operating in what were already more or less functioning nation-states such as France or Germany. French and German bourgeois Marxists, if the oxymoron be excused, already enjoyed the fruits of their chauvinistic impulses. In addition, believing that in all probability there would be no changes in the existing European state system, and perhaps somewhat driven by envy toward the existing possessing classes in their nation-states, they could wax lyrical over the need for change, over the need to deconstruct the existing material order of things in favor of the less advantaged. And in all probability they included themselves among the disadvantaged—if not materially so, at least in the sense that they perceived themselves as not socially accepted by their social betters in the existing order.

The problem for the German Austrian leadership was complicated by the fact that they already lived in a supranational entity that might be, if appropriately restructured, a prototype for the Marxist international. But at the same time its members were culturally driven by the values of bourgeois culture while at the same time intellectually committed to an ideological abstraction. The conflict here was between a matter of the mind and a matter of the heart, of sentiment, of feeling, of instinct. Hence these German Austrians lived, thought, and wrote within contradiction. Their writings as well as their squabbling among themselves, Czech against German and so on, reflects the real tensions derived from living within contradiction. As Robert Musil summed up the circumstance: "One acted . . . differently from the way one thought . . . or thought differently from the way one acted."[32] Musil, at least, understood why the writings of the German Austrian socialists not only provoked conflict with non–German Austrian socialists, but often were convoluted and, over time, lacking in consistency.[33]

A perusal of the German Austrian socialist monthly *Der Kampf* demonstrates the confusion between those agendas driven by ideological abstraction and the individual subconscious driven by instinct. So, for example, the socialist Juraj Demetrovič, writing in the journal, perhaps confusing enemy ruling class with enemy ruling nation, passionately urged

> that Croat social democracy generally . . . come forward and create the conditions for the free development of the proletariat,—a common struggle to lead along with the bourgeoisie against reactionary power. However, this is only part of the battle for freedom and progress. The broader agenda calls for the preparation of the worker for a solution to the south Slav question. It must be our aim as Socialists and democrats not to continue with our colonial position imposed by our enemy ruling class. In the interest of the development and advancement of our national rights, for [preparation] of future battles in the interest of the masses of working people . . . it is only natural that social democracy work for the unity of all south Slavs and for the constitution of the south Slav nation.[34]

Beyond general Marxist ideology, the socialists' antihistoric, suprastate stance, written into the party's Brünner Program, appears to have its roots in several specific sources connected with the evolution of socialist national policy in Austria. One of these sources were the views of the Social Democratic deputy Karl Renner that state and cultural identification were two different things and could be separated in such a way that an individual might hold, so to speak, two passports, one representing one's state and the other one's cultural nation.[35] This tactic would allow that same individual to reside not only in the state as a whole in the civil sense, but in a territory within it not belonging to his nation and still permit him participation in the conduct of his national business as if he were residing in a nation-state. In other words, Renner's idea proposed to deal with an individual's cultural national identification without losing his support for the state as a whole. It was through views like that of Renner's that some in the party came to view the necessity of separating cultural territory from political territory as envisioned in the Brünner Program.

Renner's ideas on restructuring failed to convince opponents of the German Austrian leadership within the party of his sincere commitment to true internationalist social democracy. For his part, Renner in fact was pan-Austrian. His opponents therefore can be excused if they worried that his ideas aimed not so much at the destruction of old Austria as a means for her reconstruction, but at the preservation of her essentially German orientation. For example, in reacting to the barrage of protest in foreign capitals over the annexation of Bosnia-Herzegovina in 1908, Renner, only halfheartedly condemning the annexation, robustly maintained:

> Western publicists overlook that today Austria possesses the most pronounced democratic political parties [including] a social democratic one having 89

deputies [in parliament]. . . . Austria has a franchise . . . as broad as that of England's, is less bureaucratic than even France, her administration of social justice arises out of a greater social *esprit* than . . . in Germany. . . [or] England. . . . [Further,] Austria has neither incorporated nor politically enslaved a single central European nation. . . . Austria must be held up today as an international, as a conglomerate of peoples existing between the Alps, Carpathians and Balkans, that guarantees the peaceful development of Europe.[36]

Another source for German Austrian socialism's approach to the nationality question lay in the works of the socialist political writer Otto Bauer.[37] Bauer was convinced that national assimilation, at least among the working classes, would come of its own accord as soon as the multinational suprastate demonstrated that it could and would grant genuine economic benefit, regardless of nationality, to the broad elements of its population. Bauer articulated the confidence shared by many in his party that Austria could be recast if first made economically practicable, and thus made to work to the benefit of all of her inhabitants. Bauer's optimism is implicit in the very fact of the Brünner Program itself.[38]

Otto Bauer, at least before the First World War, appears to have stood with the revisionist Marxist wing of the international. With regard to politics in Austria, he was desirous of walking the well-trodden line between active cooperation with the political status quo and intransigent opposition to it. But again, opponents of the leadership in Vienna might be excused for wondering if Bauer's position sprang from his commitment to achieving true international socialism or served merely as a cover for his allegiance to the existing German-oriented bourgeois state.[39] Despite criticism, Bauer upheld the long-range perspective contained within his thesis. Perhaps viewing the future as too easy a thing to achieve, he stoutly held that

old Marxist learning does not suit us today, and particularly in a time of political uncertainty though with economic upswing. . . . Through cooperation [with the petit bourgeois and peasant parties] the workers under social democracy have achieved a great deal. Working hours have been shortened, wages have increased, and protective laws have been instituted by the possessing classes in hopes of taking the wind out of the sails of social democracy. . . . This has strengthened social democracy, and must, as economic development increases industrial development, continue to do so. . . . The worker someday will be in the majority classes and the democratic institutions then will turn the power of the state over to the worker and the aim of social democracy will have been achieved.[40]

The idea of recasting Austria into a sort of United States of nations also appears to have come in part from outside of the party. Perhaps the most seminal idea of this sort came from one of Franz Joseph's Hungarian subjects, the Rumanian-Transylvanian Aurel Popovici, who in 1901 published *Die Vereinge Staaten des Grossösterreich*, in which the author, somewhat oversimplifying the snares posed by the Dual Monarchy's ethnic distribution, sketched out a plan for the recasting of the state internally .along the lines of nationality.[41] Like the Brünner Program, Popovici to some extent also ignored the historic states from which Austria-Hungary had evolved; in this sense, he laid stress on an agenda of both nationalism and Josephism. Popovici was a nationalist, but not at the same time a Marxist socialist. Neither could Popovici really be called an Austrian patriot in the strict Josephistic sense, for in 1892 he was the sponsor of a demand that called for the creation out of Transylvania of an autonomous Austro-Rumanian state in which Franz Joseph would take the title of grand duke of the Rumanians. However, the subtext of his argument clearly demonstrates that Popovici wanted more; he wanted to detach Hungarian Transylvania from Hungary and join it with the Rumanian state to create a greater Rumania. But, of course, it took a world war before Popovici's nationalist dream came into being.[42]

Both Austrian politics as a whole and the struggle between state and nation remain best witnessed in the Bohemian forum. Just as the Austrian government in Vienna found it futile to divide cultural influence in Bohemia between Czechs and Germans, so too did the Vienna social democratic leadership find it futile to search for a way whereby Czech and German socialists might operate under the common umbrella of Austro-Marxism, under the so-called *Gesamtpartei.*The Vienna leadership, while willing to grant to Czech socialists the right to determine policy for purely Czech problems, nevertheless demanded that the *Gesamtpartei* be headed from Vienna. The Czechs, for their part, viewed such recognition as meaning that in practice they would lose control of their own Czech cultural affairs, and accused the leadership in Vienna of planning it to be exactly that way. And so during the years 1908–1911, before the Czech socialists did in fact break from Vienna, accusations flew back and forth between Vienna and Prague in which the supernationalism of the former contested with the chauvinism of the latter. In a word, neither group could act like supranational, self-conscious international bodies because each was driven by chauvinist sentiments rendering the one irreconcilable to the other. For example, Otto Bauer, viewing the dispute from the pinnacle of German superiority, could have won over few of his Czech comrades when he lectured to them that

> the history of the common party *[Gesamtpartei]* has shown us how deeply is the autonomy of the national section of Austrian social democracy rooted in the mother soil of Austrian social democracy. Our common party was never a unified organization. Nor was it a narrow federation [Bund] of the worker's party of a particular nation. Indeed, [the common party] cannot today, or in the near future, be otherwise. Clearly this lecture will bring no pleasure to many of our comrades. But, in the name of national autonomy, the Czechs . . . have torn apart the trade union movement and have greatly undermined the common party. [These actions] have brought much evil to the working classes . . . and danger to our comrades.[43]

Later in 1918, in the midst of the flotsam from old Austria, which then was clogging the political currents of central Europe, Friedrich Austerlitz, the editor of the renowned Vienna socialist daily *Die Arbeiter Zeitung,* gamely admitted the existence of that same flotsam. But he was unable to completely tear himself from the traditional and leading cultural role exercised by German Austria in south-central Europe.

> It appears that the Czechs, at last, have achieved their nation-state. However, [German] Bohemia is to go with a revolutionized Austria and not with the Czech state. . . . The declaration of independence of the German Austrian state was a historical necessity but perhaps, given the right conditions, a union between the Austrian and Hungarian peoples might possibly be reconstructed. One based on democracy rather than on chauvinism. Social democracy would construct such a state and alter the form and content of the state so as to forge a social community that would replace the now worn out and destroyed state organization.[44]

One may conclude that the appearance of the Austrian Habsburg state was a historical accident, a fluke born out of a chance constellation of circumstances. But shortly before the curtain came down on old Austria's final act, at least some came to realize that these same chance circumstances had produced a vibrant culture manifest across the whole spectrum of the arts. In addition, there was recognition that Austria made economic sense in that the realm possessed the means to advance modernism through capital and industry and thereby bring prosperity and well-being to a good many of the state's citizens—citizens who in themselves represented a cultural and ethnic diversity that found a civil identity under the Habsburg stately umbrella. In a word, the Dual Monarchy, for all of its internal contradictions, was politically rational in that the state promised to provide a framework in which the small nations of south-central Europe might develop while being free of the threat of conquest not only from one another, but also from Russia, the Ottoman Empire, and Germany. And finally, many were captivated by the beautiful imperial and royal court and the complex social infrastructure that maintained it, secretly (if not openly) reveling in their link to the ancient Catholic House of Habsburg and its baroque ceremonial, taking pride in their beautiful if erratic empress and admiring their much-tried noble old emperor.

But on all these fronts, the positive attributes proved not sufficient. If the splendor of the court and aristocracy evoked admiration, these also aroused envy. The forces of modernism, while promising utility in the lives of Austria's urban masses, also aroused cultural antagonism, which came to be expressed in racism, thereby generating what has been called integral nationalism. It was this nationalism that produced those centrifugal forces that threatened the stability of the whole. And last, Vienna could not avoid being caught up in the vortex of Europe's international relations. Given the strong currents produced by these tensions, the positive elements of Austria could not offset the negative ones. Austria's foundations ultimately proved too shallow, too ephemeral. And so old Austria collapsed, demonstrating that in the final instance, human institutions cannot live divorced from the roots of the circumstances that brought them about in the first instance.

If the socialist leadership was bourgeois, it also was Viennese, self-consciously German, and haut bourgeois. This was the social element that brought Austrian cultural development to a high point of development and thereby demonstrated the positive benefits to be gained by supranational political organization. And those who created this Austria valued her, for they understood the potential worth of their creation. To realize that potential, however, required that the old Austrian state be preserved. And so the Viktor Adlers, Karl Renners, and Otto Bauers joined with the Karl Schwarzenbergs, the Karl Luegars, and even the emperor himself in devising plans for her salvation. History attests that these ideas were insufficient, no match for the hatreds unleashed once the masses were politically empowered and inflamed by the sirens of popular political culture tied to the engine of modernism through capital, industry, and their concomitants. But perhaps the Austrian experience does demonstrate that the state, as against the nation-state, is a positive and rational abstraction of the human political imagination and cannot always operate in tandem with the visceral forces generated out of human instinct. If this is the lesson to be drawn from the Austrian experience, history then underscores that human beings have little alternative but first to live with themselves, so as to live with one another. Only then can one hope that viscera born of instinct does not always have to trump reason.

Notes

1. The Brünner Program did not apply to Hungary but only to all or part of the six rooted nations (and thereby the territories in which they had taken root) that lived scattered within the Austrian crown lands; that is, scattered within the hereditary lands of the House of Austria. These were Germans, Italians, Czechs, Poles, Ruthenes, and Slovenes. The Croats, Magyars, Slovaks, Serbs, and Rumanians occupied the lands belonging to the Crown of St. Stephen; that is, Hungary. Jews would not be counted among any of these even if one assumed that they were a nation, because they were perceived as possessing no territory of their own: that is, they were not viewed as one of the rooted nations sharing possession of Austria-Hungary.

2. See DÖSDAP, *Was Will die Sozialdemokratie?* (Vienna: Volksbuchhandlung, 1912), p. 27.

3. For example, Prague, at that time a center of nationality strife between its Czech majority and its economically dominant but numerically inferior Germans, was a case in point. The social democrats would have Prague be Czech but guarantee her Germans complete cultural autonomy by linking them administratively with territory determined to be German.

4. *Was Will die Sozialdemokratie?* The original articulation of the Brünner Program in 1899 was somewhat vague as to the specific handling of minorities within different speech territories contenting itself only with the statement "In place of the historic crown

lands, national administrations be established as a result of elections based on universal suffrage, the right of nationality minorities be protected by law [, and] all autonomous areas be united in a federation which will be composed of autonomous nation states" See Klaus Berchtold, *Österreichische Parteiprogramme: 1866–1966* (Vienna: Verlag für Geschichte und Politik, 1967), pp. 144–145.

5. See Adam Wandruszka and Peter Urbanitch, eds., *Die Habsburger Monarchie, 1848–1918*, 3 vols. (Vienna: Verlag der Österreichischen Akademie der Wissenschaften, 1975).

6. See Friederich Austerlitz, "Der Kaiser," *Der Kampf* IV (1911), pp. 145–153.

7. Crown Prince Rudolph of Habsburg, ed., *Die österreich-ungarische Monarchie in Wort und Bild*, 11 volumes. I: Abtheilung: "Naturgeschichte Theil" (Vienna: Druck und Verlag der K.K. Hof-und Staatsdruckerei, 1887), pp. 5–6.

8. Involved here was a question of preponderance, German as against Czech, in Bohemia and Moravia. Civil rights per se were not involved because of the already existing Laws on the Rights of Citizens (one of a series of five laws popularly known as the December Constitution, concomitant with the 1867 *Ausgleich*). For example, Article 19 of the Laws on the Rights of Citizens stipulated that "all nationalities have the right to cultivate their mother tongue and to have educational facilities in it." See Karen J. Freeze, "The Progressive Youth in the 1890s: Children of the December Constitution" in Hans Lemberg et al., *Bildungsgeschichte, Bevölkerungsgeschichte, Gesellschaftsgeschichte in den Böhmischen Ländern in Europa*, (Vienna: Verlag für Geschichte und Politik, 1988), p. 279.

9. See the especially interesting collection of published documents well illustrating this point: Errnst Rutkowski, ed., *Briefe und Doukmente zur Geschichte der österreichisch-ungarischen Monarchie unter besonderer Berücksichtigung der bömisch-mährischen Raumes. Teil I and II: "Der Verfassungstreue Grossgrundbesitz 1880–1899/1900–1904"* (Vienna: R. Oldenbourg, 1983).

10. Of course there were those long active in attempting to achieve a modus vivendi between Czechs and Germans in Bohemia, who wondered if the Bohemian question was ever to be given resolution in terms of Bohemia. In writing to Max Egon Prince zu Fürstenberg, for example, Count Oswald Thun stated, "I am a real pessimist when it comes to the business of Bohemia. I know the land up and down and know that its digestive process *[Eingeweiden]* is not good. Fire and water can't be reconciled; strongly [articulated] special interests cannot stand next to one another; these special interests are in direct conflict with the fundamental ideals involving states' rights." (Rutkowski, ed., *Briefe und Dokumente*, II, p. 640).

11. That is, in the sense of the opening lines of the *Volkshymn:* "Gott erhalte unser Kaiser, Gott beschutze unser Land." (God uphold our emperor, God protect our land.)

12. See, for example, David S. Luft, *Robert Musil and the Crisis of European Culture: 1880–1942* (Berkeley: University of California Press, 1980), wherein the author winds up his monograph with an interesting analysis of the relationship between cultural nationalism and territory (he calls the territory in question national redoubts) claimed by those same ethnic (national) groups.

13. Engelbert Pernerstorfer, "Kurzen Wort zur Frage des Socialismus und Nationalismus," *Der Kampf* V (1911–1912), pp. 56–57.

14. Ibid., p. 57.

15. Josef Strasser, "Nationalismus und Sozialismus," *Der Kampf* V (1911–1912), pp. 109–110.

16. Ludo Hartmann, "Viktor Adler," *Der Kampf* XI (January-December, 1918), pp. 773–776.

17. Anton Němec, "Die Pfiffigkeit der deutschen Sozialdemokratie," *Der Kampf* V (1911–1912), pp. 112–113.

18. Ludo M. Hartmann, "Zur Frage der nationalen Minoritätsschulen," *Der Kampf* II (1909–1910), pp. 59–63.

19. Viktor Adler, "Die Separatische Krise," *Der Kampf* IV (1910–1911), pp. 531–532.

20. Quoted in Otto Bauer, "Die Minoritäten, wie Sie enstehen und wie Sie erwachen," *Der Kampf* II (1908–1909).

21. For example, applied to Otto Bauer, Friedrich Austerlitz, Max Adler, and so on; that is, social democrats of Jewish background, but viewing themselves as German while at the same time active in defining the position of the party's leadership on various social issues.

22. In this fashion Viktor had associations with Sigmund Freud; indeed, Freud's now famous flat on Vienna's Berggasse was purchased by the latter from the Adler family. For more on Viktor Adler, see Julius Braunthal, *Viktor und Friedrich Adler: Zwei Generationen Arbeiterbewegung* (Vienna: Wienervolksbuchhandlung, 1964). See also Mark E. Blum, *The Austro-Marxists, 1890–1918: A Psychobiographical Study* (Lexington: University of Kentucky Press, 1985). On more concerning the relationship between Viktor Adler and Sigmund Freud, see William J. McGrath, *Freud's Discovery of Psychoanalysis: The Politics of Hysteria* (Ithaca: Cornell University Press, 1986).

23. Steven Beller, "Patriotism and The National Identity of Habsburg Jewry, 1866–1914," a paper presented before the German Studies Association, October 2, 1992. See also this author's *Vienna and the Jews, 1867–1938: A Cultural History* (Cambridge: Cambridge University Press, 1989). See also William O. McCagg, *A History of the Habsburg Jews: 1670–1918* (Bloomington: Indiana University Press, 1989). The writer Karl Kraus demonstrated similar sentiments regarding the gala parade in connection with the celebration of the sixtieth year of Franz Joseph's rule in Austria, which took place in 1908. The parade featured historical representatives of Austria's nations in traditional costume with a view toward celebrating the idea that the Austrian state provided an umbrella under which her various nations enjoyed its individual development and hence underscored the Austrian idea that the state existed as a fatherland (as against *Heimat*) for each and, in return, enjoyed the loyalty of each. And so the Viennese witnessed a colorful spectacle. Kraus's reaction, however, was "Einheutsgedanke der Hasslichkeit zu einer Verstandigung fuhren konne." See Elizabeth Grossegger, *Der Kaiser Huldigungs Festzug* (Vienna: Österreichischen Akademie der Wisschaften, 1922), especially p. 296. For a discussion as to how these expectations fared within academe, especially in Prague, see Robert Luft, "Politische Professoren on Boehmen, 1861–1914," in Lemberg et al., *Bildungsgeschichte, Bevölkerungsgeschichte, Gesellschaftsgeschichte,* especially pp. 300–301.

24. Joachim Schoenfeld, *Shtetl Memories: Jews in Galicia Under Austria and in the Reborn Poland: 1898–1939* (Hoboken, NJ: KTAV Publishing House, 1985), pp. xx–xxi.

25. Memoirs of Prince Karl von Schwarzenberg in Vienna, Austrian State Archives, N.P.A. (01/la), Karton 448, f. 120.

26. See Andrew Gladding Whiteside, *The Socialism of Fools: Georg von Schönerer and Austrian Pan-Germanism* (Berkeley: University of California Press, 1975).

27. Schwarzenberg, Austrian State Archives, ibid.

28. See Redaktionen (editors), "Eine Antwort des Právo Lidu," *Der Kampf* IV (1910–1911), pp. 534–547.

29. Ibid.

30. Němec, "Die Pfiffirgkeit der deutschen Sozialdemokratie."

31. Karl Renner, "Zur Krise des Sozialismus," *Der Kampf* XI (1915), pp. 87–88.

32. Robert Musil, *The Man Without Qualities* (New York: Capricorn, 1965), pp. 33–34.

33. Otto Bauer certainly was conscious of this ambivalence when he wrote, "[Social

democracy] stands upon a new threshold where now in the west the struggle [for socialism] is between class and the power of the state and where, in the east, the struggle is between the nations and the organization of the . . . state. Austria stands in the middle between east and west . . . we would join in with the proletarians in the west in their struggle with political power and, we would join in with the peoples in the east in their fight for the right of national self-determination." See Otto Bauer, "Der Weg zur Macht," *Der Kampf* VII (1908–1909), p. 343.

34. See Juraj Demetrovič, "Die Entwicklung der Südslawischen Frage," *Der Kampf* V (1911–1912), pp. 549–550.

35. Karl Renner, later first chancellor of the first Austrian Republic and first president of the second, was, during the bulk of his activity before the First World War, a social democrat deputy in the Austrian parliament *(Abgeordnetenhaus)*. Renner, hailing from a German-speaking background in Moravia, also was a political writer on behalf of social democracy and a member of the leadership of the Vienna-based German Austrian Social Democratic Workers' Party. In 1903, he wrote a controversial proposal calling for the recasting of Austria along the lines of nationality and permitting an individual to carry a self-selected national identity with him no matter where he might reside in the Austrian state. Renner's advocacy of this *Persönlichprinzip* rendered him one of the leading, if controversial, political philosophers belonging to Austrian social democracy. See Rudolf Springer [Karl Renner], *Grundlagen und Entwicklungsziele der österreichische-ungarischen Monarchie* (Vienna: Franz Deuticke, 1906); Renner put forth these ideas under his own name at a later date. See Karl Renner, *Österreichs Erneuerung* (Vienna: Volksbuchhandlung, 1916).

36. Karl Renner, "Sympathien und Antipathien," *Der Kampf* VII (1908–1909), pp. 164–169.

37. Otto Bauer, later second foreign minister of the first Austrian republic (following Viktor Adler, who died within days of taking office), was a political writer and member of the German Austrian party leadership. After 1917, he generally spoke for the party's left wing. In 1906, he published his watershed work on the nationality problem in Austria, *Die österreichischen Sozialdemokratie und die Nationalitätenfrage* (Vienna: Volksbuchhandlung, 1906). A shorter, updated summary of Bauer's views on the nationality question in Austria can be read in his "Die Bedingungen der Nationalen Assimilation," *Der Kampf* V (1912), pp. 246–263.

38. It must be admitted, however, that over time Bauer came to fear that capitalism would unwittingly succeed in undermining Europe's stately order before the broader processes of economic prosperity would effect ethnic assimilation. So, for example, he once decried that "the development of capitalism is against us. Capitalism penetrates the lands to the east . . . it shatters the orderly foundation of entire states, it renders the territory in the east as an object of struggle among capitalist states" (Otto Bauer, "Österreich-Ungarn und Italien," *Der Kampf* IV [1910–1911], 251). . . . He also noted, "Nationalism is on the march. . . . the [social democratic] party has won recent elections . . . necessitating that the parties of the bourgeoisie react by trying to woo the worker away from his task . . . through the instrument of nationalism. Hence, the *nationalen Schützverein* and the *nationalen Jungmannschaften* are promoted by the bourgeois press. . . . So everywhere . . . the German nationalist and the social democrat oppose one another, ... Class struggle has degenerated into personal enmity" (Otto Bauer, "Krieg oder Friede," *Der Kampf* IV [1910–1911], 7. See also his "Die Bedingungen der Nationalen Assimilation," p. 248, where Bauer explains, "Capitalists, in pursuit of cheap labor through the hiring of the ethnically underprivileged, often furthered [national] division when, for example, a factory is built outside of a German village [in Bohemia] and houses for the workers [are placed] by the village gate, and the enterprise is staffed by

Czech [speaking] workers who then find little need to travel outside of Czech circles and thus, are not assimilated, and their children are assimilated, if at all, only with difficulty."

39. See criticism leveled at Bauer by Siegfried Schab in "Obstruction und Sozialdemokratie," *Der Kampf* VII (1913–1914), pp. 78ff.

40. Otto Bauer, "Die Grundfrage unsere Tatik," *Der Kampf* VII (1913–1914), pp. 49ff.

41. See Aurel C. Popovici, *Die Vereinigten Staaten von Grossösterreich* (Leipzig: B. Elischer Nachfolger, 1906).

42. See Aurel C. Popovici, *Die Rumanienfrage in Transylvanien und in Ungarn: Antwort der Rumanien Studeten der Transylvanien und Ungarn* (Vienna and Antwerp: Jos. Theunis, 1892).

43. See Otto Bauer, "Der Gesamtpartei," *Der Kampf* VI (1910), pp. 5ff.

44. Friedrich Austerlitz, "Der Deutsch-Österreische Staat," *Der Kampf* XI (1918), pp. 713–718.

✧ **6** ✧

The Final Transformation: The Impact of Bourgeois *Kunst* and *Kapital* on the Austrian Idea

Most formidable of the popular mass political movements rising to the support of the Austrian idea was Christian Socialism. This popular political synthesis advocating socialism with God—in contrast to Marxist socialism's atheism—also stood, somewhat paradoxically, for a traditional Austrian state supported by the twin pillars of throne and altar. Its driving force derived from a number of currents: monarchist, Catholic pietist, and German racist traditionalist, to name the most important. Its intellectual underpinnings involved a plethora of disparate German Austrians, Habsburg loyalists all, such as Baron Karl Vogelsang and Prince Alois (von and zu) Liechtenstein, Catholic priests such as the Bohemian Ambros Opitz, and grassroots politicians such as Ignaz Mandl and Karl Luegar.[1]

Perhaps, however, it was not Mandl but Karl Luegar, popular and controversial mayor of Vienna from 1899 to 1910, who gave Christian Socialism its reputation as a volatile, potentially violent mass political movement.[2] Like many other emotive mass political movements, Christian Socialism pursued the politics of scapegoatism, whereby it designated victims so as to gather in followers by preaching to them what elements in society were to blame for their discontents. Foremost among the weapons belonging to the arsenal of this politics of victimization was Christian Socialism's use of what Luegar called political anti-Semitism, which Luegar wielded as a weapon to attack the tenets of economic liberalism structural to the perspective of much of the Austrian *haute bourgeoisie*. Further, the lethal twist in this strategy rested on the truism that a goodly proportion of this same *haute bourgeoisie* was, or at least had been in some sense or other, Jewish.[3] In the same fashion, but by playing anti-Semitism as a counterpoint to Catholicism, Christian Socialism rallied Catholic pietism in support of the Habsburg dynasty. All the while Luegar and his followers buttressed these attacks on the unfolding industrial capitalist world by promoting a kind of pragmatic, home-grown variety of socialism sponsored by the city government. In a sense the political circus generated by scapegoatism was balanced by the bread of socialism. But it must be admitted that Christian Socialism patently did improve the lot of Vienna's masses. It did so, however, at a high price, for while these tactics cemented the loyalty of many Viennese to the Christian Socialists, they were also won over to its violent rhetoric as it was molded by the hands of demagogues of the likes of Karl Luegar. Thereby the mayor of Vienna created in himself not only a prototype of those political incendiaries that bedeviled central Europe in the twentieth century, but also a mass political movement that threatened as much as it cajoled the political order of things. Consequently, it was for negative reasons that neither the mayor nor his movement could be ignored by the imperial and royal government.[4]

For his part, Emperor Franz Joseph disliked Luegar's demagoguery and especially the anti-Semitic hue of his variety of Christian Socialism. But, by the same token, the emperor did come to see, albeit unhappily, that the integrity of Austria in modern times did in fact depend on the sanction of her population. However, the old emperor sidestepped rather than confronted the specifics of rampant race-oriented chauvinism, preferring to think that if his government delivered a well-administered, economically viable state, its people would sanction a more or less traditional Austria. And it was for this reason that the emperor, again unhappily, eventually conceded, in 1907, the granting of universal manhood suffrage in the Austrian crown lands for the electing of its parliament on the basis of one man one vote.[5] To this extent, the politics of the likes of Karl Luegar did help to convince the emperor of the necessity of engaging the *Publikum* (general public) on the political field of battle.[6] But Franz Joseph also saw in Luegar all those elements that caused the old monarch to fundamentally distrust the masses, their political icons, and their participation in the political decision-making process of state.

During the first decade of the twentieth century, however, many among Austria's upright citizens were drawn toward the rhetoric surrounding Luegar's sanguine brand of Christian Socialism. Luegar's draw operated even among the aristocracy, who felt compelled to protect their interests (if not always wholeheartedly) within the political slipping and sliding of things. For example, the brother-in-law to the heir to the throne, Count Joraslav Thun, wrote to Archduke Franz Ferdinand in 1905 that he was

> a Dualist. What else can one be if one keeps one's eyes fixed on high and lofty goals without becoming a visionary for all that! How splendid it sounds: Catholic Austria! It almost casts a bright glow on the horizon! And how wonderful it would be if the foremost prince of this country succeeded in raising the banner around which all right thinking people could congregate to give new strength to Austria's reawakening to its old splendor, an Austria that God once created as the bulwark for Christianity.[7]

Thun's letter to the archduke was a private one that may have reflected more his viscera than his reason, but the sentiments were honest. And Franz Ferdinand's reply to his brother-in-law was no less honest, though perhaps not reflective of what might have been his actual policy once he was at the helm of the Austrian ship of state. The archduke once told Count Thun that he was "unable to understand how 'our venerable Monarchy' could have fallen into the hands of a Jewish editor." The archduke went on to castigate "the Jews, the Hungarians, the Freemasons, and the Social Democrats," among others, for promoting elections reform. "The emperor's government," complained the archduke, "should be firmly anchored on the nobility, the clergy, Christian Bürgers . . . and peasants."[8]

Archduke and count were not alone among old Austria's elites in the use, albeit in private, of Luegar-style rhetoric in support of the *Gesamtstaat* so as to uphold the aristocrats' version of the Austrian idea. And while it is true that such gentlemen, especially considering their background and upbringing, probably were not inclined toward really sanguine political action, the choice of their private words well illustrates the link between the somber nuances detected in the rise of the mass political movements and the retreat of the Austrian idea from the higher principled ground of past times. In the hands of an older generation of elites, such as Franz Joseph's, the Austrian idea lacked those elements of narrow pan-Germanism, religious fanaticism, and anti-Semitism that, when in the hands of the younger generation of Franz Ferdinand's ilk, looked, perhaps unknowingly, toward the future, toward both the implosion and the bloodletting that swept central Europe in the course of the twentieth century. The rhetoric of archduke and count can be viewed as a harbinger of the chilling events—murder, fascism, and finally genocide—that commenced with the First World War.

Indeed, for their part, many among the older elites, again motivated by instincts of economic and social survival, came to accept that a certain degree of mingling with the bourgeoisie, especially in the economic sphere, was essential. But the process that actually took place was commingling rather than true assimilation. Moreover, this meeting was played out mostly within narrow social confines—theater, charity affairs, and the like—whereby the bourgeoisie absorbed the imprint of their social betters but only with regard to externals having to do with lifestyle, never in accordance with the fundamental spirit of those processes by which the bourgeoisie financially maintained itself.[9] Unlike the aristocracy, it was the bourgeoisie that drew its keep from the innovations coming out of technology, which it had harnessed to society through its hold over capital.[10] Thereby the bourgeoisie, and especially those involved in industry, came to possess leverage over the emerging modern Austria. Nevertheless, this leverage permitted them only limited political influence, because the socially hidebound aristocracy eschewed that degree of assimilation that would have enabled them to really share in the newfound bounty derived from modern ways. Indeed, true assimilation—a real degree of integration between the old and new—would have helped in furthering the cohesion of Austria by bringing about a kind of partnership that might have reinvigorated the state.

For one thing, these older elites could neither share nor give up their lifestyle, which was based on land. The income derived from land, of course, could not keep pace with that derived from industry and capital.[11] So proceeded the rise of the new classes and the demise of the old elites. There was no merging of the groups in this process. Rather, one rose from obscurity and the other sank into it. In this way the substance of the Austrian synthesis was transformed. For the most part this transformation was silent and unseen, but the end result was a broad cultural and social revolution, commencing with the Austrian *Grunderzeit* (ca. 1866–1873), favoring as well as driven by the bourgeoisie. This transformation took place rapidly. Given the industrial bourgeoisie's near-absolute control of industry and capital, came to possess the financial means by which it subsumed the aristocracy on the cultural plane. Hence, the aristocratic culture of the eighteenth century gave way to the secular values belonging to the rising bourgeoisie of the nineteenth.[12] Joseph Roth, the novelist whose origins lay in Austro-Galicia, wrote poetically about the subtlety of this transformation. And while he wrote after the fact, in the same vein as the historian, Roth's artist's pen captures an atmosphere fraught with tension between the old and the new. In this exchange, one of his characters, Count Chojnicki, says:

> ". . . The Fatherland no longer exists."
> "I don't understand!" said Herr von Trotta.
> "I assumed you wouldn't understand. . . . Naturally . . . in literal terms, it still exists. We still have an army . . . and officials . . . but the monarchy is disintegrating while still alive; it is doomed! . . . This era no longer wants us! This era wants to create independent nation-states! People no longer believe in God. The new religion is nationalism. Nations no longer go to church. They go to national associations. Monarchy, our monarchy, is founded on piety, on the faith that God chose the Habsburgs to rule over so and so many Christian nations. Our kaiser is the secular brother of the Pope, he is His Imperial and Royal Apostolic Majesty; no other is as apostolic, no other majesty in Europe is as dependent on the grace of God and on the faith of the nations in the grace of God. The German Kaiser still rules even when God abandons him; perhaps by the grace of the nation. The emperor of Austria-Hungary must not be abandoned by God. But God *has* abandoned him!"[13]

The internal stresses and strains within the state, however, were not always obvious, especially if one was apolitical and tended to focus only on the externals of stately life. Such a perception would have seen Austria's great centers of entrepreneurial and cultural activity, cities like Budapest, Cracow, Prague, and Vienna, not as beacons of decline but as dynamic places, full of creation, energy, and speed. It was, for example, the music critic Max Graf, growing up in Vienna during what turned out to be the final days of the Dual Monarchy, who once remarked that he for one did not in the least look back darkly on his salad days, for he "had no idea during [Vienna's]. . . brilliant period before the First World War that this epoch was to be the end . . . and still less . . . suspected that the Habsburg Monarchy was destined to decline. . . . We enjoyed the splendid city [of Vienna] which was so elegantly beautiful, and never thought that the light which shown over it could ever be that of a colorful sunset."[14]

If Max Graf confused Vienna's brilliant cultural life and the kaleidoscopic plumage of Franz Joseph's *Hofstaat* for the substance of stately well-being, he was not alone. Stefan Zweig attested that, while growing up in Vienna, he too loved the capital and "[her] broad and beautiful . . . streets . . . the powerful splendor of the public buildings, and . . . the material luxury. . . . One saw the modernization of everything as the wealth spread out and was assimilated. Everywhere there were new theaters, libraries, museums, and conveniences such as bathrooms and telephones. More to the point, the lower middle classes had penetrated the narrow circle of privilege and below them, since work time had been shortened, the proletariat was propelled a little bit upwards and took a bit of joy in the pleasures of life."[15]

And certainly, because their city truly had become a metropolis, Viennese such as Zweig were at ease with one another amidst a babel of tongues and a cultural potpourri. Vienna, in the aggregate, was rich, and her wealth glossed over the cultural divisiveness that lurked behind her luxuriant opulence and played itself out within the parliament building on the Franzenring.[16] Indeed, beyond Vienna's status as metropolis, the capital was a world unto herself, apparently both beneficiary and embodiment of the Austrian idea, of those fruits that flowed in from the provinces of the realm of the Habsburgs. And that realm as a whole was one of the richest, most self-sufficient, and economically well balanced in Europe. However, unlike the denizens of the capital, those in the provinces perhaps understood that they enjoyed less than the whole in the sense that while Vienna might be Austria, Austria was not Vienna. The whole was supranational; the parts Czech, German, Magyar, Pole, Slovene, Croat, and Italian. In hindsight, the glitter and glow of magical Vienna seemed not to have flowed sufficiently eastward to penetrate beyond the Marchfeld, to hug the banks of the Danube, or to travel westward over the Kalenberg and along the Wachau. The question, then, was: In the time of sunset, by what means might have Vienna's *élan,* the very epitome of the Austrian idea, suffused the monarchy as a whole with the glow that appeared to so brilliantly illuminate life in the Habsburgs' capital?

The sociocultural dynamics pushing the bourgeoisie to the fore has its iconography in the cityscape created within the zone of Vienna's Ringstrasse. This area of the capital was developed after 1860 and hence reflects a series of perceptions of various sociopolitical attributes that evolved during the era of the advent of industrial capitalism. Hence, the Ringstrasse today stands as a tangible and tactile demonstration of the transformation of human perceptions and values that took hold during the period 1860–1914. This cityscape reflects the evolution of social and political priorities as these were formed within the period of the rise and domination of Austria's industrial bourgeoisie.[17]

In the period before 1848, there was a tendency to build in Vienna's city center luxurious residences relatively small in size when compared to the nineteenth-century mansions that replaced them. These earlier buildings, of course, were built for Austria's aristocracy, for her court nobility *(Hofadel)* as well as for members of the high bureaucracy *(Beamtadel)*. However, during the period commencing with *Grunderzeit,* building lots within the Ringstrasse zone became too expensive even for housing the privileged classes in single units. Hence, as the proverbial entrepreneurial bourgeoisie *(Betriebadel)* appeared on the scene, it became the convention to combine a grandiose dwelling under the same majestic roof with other units of varying scale so as to fit the resources of the new middle classes. Sometimes, too, in order to increase the rental income, a discreet commercial venture quietly occupied the ground-floor spaces. These units shared not only a common roof but also a common facade (set in some historical style then current). Thereby these apartment buildings assumed an outer cloak (often in a historical style drawn from the prototypes of the true aristocratic seventeenth-century palaces found in Vienna's inner city) that gave public expression to the owner's image of who he was, or perhaps who he wished to be.[18] What were in fact deceptively grand dwellings also were iconographic representations of the course of the bourgeoisie. Moreover, the manner in which the interior living spaces were divided also underscored the self-perceptions and social aspirations of both owner and renters. Most often, of course, this aspiration was to be identified with the elite that presumably articulated Austria. These combinations of grand mansions (occupying the so-called *belle étage*), lesser ones, middle-class apartments, and commercial establishments together constituted what was called a "noble rental palace" *(Nobelzinspalais)*.

The sensibility behind edifices was different from that of the aristocrats who had built in Vienna's city center in earlier times. The new builders, taking mundane fiscal matters under consideration, sought to recoup some of the outlay by building what they wanted for themselves in a manner that at the same time would produce substantial income. In addition, because these buildings served as backdrop to the Hofburg, their luxurious and outwardly grandiose idiom interjected a certain hyperbole into the pomp and pageantry of court ceremony. Thereby the bourgeoisie unknowingly impressed its stamp even on the very inner sanctum of old Austria. Moreover, these buildings demonstrated not assimilation but amalgamation of new values with the old, achieving their effect by displaying an unstable and entrepreneurial blend of show with consumerism. In a word, the tenor and substance of Vienna's *Nobelzinspalais* loudly, even rudely, proclaimed the arrival of the bourgeoisie.[19] The Ringstrasse zone stands as an iconographic representation of the failure of the new social classes to assimilate with the old, thereby representing in sand and stone the gulf that separated the aristocracy from the bourgeoisie in old Austria.

Any city is like a multihued mosaic in that it reflects the perspective of its creators. Like a mosaic, which encapsulates its message in stone, changing nuances of attitude over time can be detected in a given cityscape, which, because it consists of ideas rendered tangible through the efforts of a variety of its denizens, architects and builders alike, collectively speaks for the multitude living within its spaces in different epochs. Just as an individual artist may be understood through his creations, the character and perspective of a society, in all of its manifestations, may be understood through an analysis of the architecture it creates as a backdrop to its civic life. The Vienna of Franz Joseph can be viewed as a cognitive map iconographically manifesting value as well as a record of the passing of time. In addition, this Vienna was a paean to a cultural elite, which, like all cultural elites, sought to perpetuate itself by controlling human behavior through the manipulation of human responses.[20] So the pre-1918 architecture of this city reflects, as well might be expected in the chief political-administrative city of the Dual Monarchy, the Austrian idea in tangible form, a collective expression of ideology in the bricks and mortar put up to house the dynasty, the institutions of modern democratic capitalism, and the cultural locales belonging to the emergent industrial bourgeoisie.

Events in 1848, the year when tumult in the streets of Vienna and Prague as well as anti-Habsburg national movements in Italy and Hungary pushed the young Franz Joseph to the throne, were driven in great part by the enormous changes concomitant with the beginnings of the Industrial Revolution, then poised to sweep across central Europe. One result of this, through political trial and error, was the emergence of what might be called modern liberal capitalism as the economic modus operandi within the political institutions of a parliamentary state. A physical transformation of the capital both accompanied and reflected the changing cultural-political attitudes in Austria. Hence, the sparkling baroque city awash with a certain yearning captured especially on the canvases of Canaletto gave way to the pastels of Biedermeier lovingly recorded by the likes of Peter Fendi and Rudolf von Alt to, by 1900, the rapacious reality of the city as metropolis. The bulk of this transformation took place within a single adult life span, most dramatically in the planning and execution of the Ringstrasse zone during the reign of Emperor Franz Joseph. Hence, through the accidents of time and place, the Ringstrasse came to be that final cognitive map on which to trace the iconography that tells of both the transformation and the cultural character of the newly emergent socioeconomic structure of Franz Joseph's Austria-Hungary.[21]

On December 20, 1857, the first step was taken toward freeing Biedermeier Vienna of her fortifications and thereby opening the way to the creation of the nineteenth-century ambience that the Austrian capital retains to this day. Although there had been much talk and more than a few abortive first steps toward the reconstruction of the city prior to 1857, much of the initiative, reflecting a barely perceived momentum pressing for the creation of modern Vienna, was due to Emperor Franz Joseph and his energetic minister of the interior, Alexander von Bach.[22] The emperor's initial handwritten order, ostensibly to his minister, not only decreed that fortress Vienna must break out of her walls but went on to outline how the reconstruction of the city should proceed. And so it was that, as the emperor bade, the fortress walls came down, the deep moat before them was filed with their debris, and the inner, aristocratic city was linked by means of a broad pastoral glacis with Vienna's increasingly bourgeois suburbs. At the same time began the Ringstrasse zone's orderly architectural reconstruction.

But the end result was not as Franz Joseph originally had ordered. Instead of his vision of a garrison city that might hold back future outbreaks like those that had taken place in 1848, pressures emanating out of the ongoing Industrial Revolution, and especially commercial factors reflecting the socioeconomic changes brought about by it triumphed over the dynasty's concerns for its internal security. The final outcome thus reflected an entirely new urban social iconography grounded on bourgeois liberal capitalism.[23]

Austria's defeat in 1859 by waxing Italian nationalism allied to a resurgent France under Napoleon III forced Franz Joseph and his ministers to reexamine Austria's internal political structuring. As a result, the synthesis of 1850, a neo-absolutism founded on an authoritarian dynastic centralism, finally was written off as a means for holding the ramshackle state together. The vigor and the drive of the industrial bourgeoisie was to be tapped instead. So it was that the Austrian ship of state—somewhat halfheartedly, to be sure—headed into more liberal waters, which required the restructuring of its governing apparatus. The final result of the new approach was the so-called February Patent of 1861, which, whatever its ideological contradictions, formed the constitutional basis of Austria's parliamentary government until her final collapse in 1918.[24] And so too the kinds of politically prophylactic buildings called for by the emperor prior to his defeat in Italy gave way to those that reflected more broadly based, grass-roots perspectives. Barracks designed for the use of the imperial bodyguard and for an expanded police gave way to a resplendent Vienna focused around buildings for a parliament, ministry of justice, a university, and—perhaps most significant—a stock exchange. These new buildings were a stylistic representation of their institutional functions according to the bourgeois perspective of both those same institutions and of itself. Finally, these buildings were placed in relation to one another so that the totality of the completed Ringstrasse reflected that order of institutional priorities perceived as proper in the consciousness of the society that built them.

So, for example, various proposals roughed out between 1857 and 1859 for development of a parade ground along the Franzenring underwent a complete metamorphosis. An authoritarian government had seen no necessity for putting this parcel of land, despite its value having increased manyfold in an era of feverish speculation, to purposes other than the accommodation of large military spectacles and splendid new quarters for the army and various units of the palace guard.[25] Gradually, however, the dynamics crystallized by the February Patent resulted in this land being used to house what might be called temples reflecting bourgeois values and perspective. A parliament building, a city hall, a national theater, and a university replaced what originally had been intended for military and police use.[26] In addition, each of these temples, iconographically speaking, was given an exterior skin in the style thought appropriate to its intended role. For example, the architect Theophil Hansen selected a high-flown neo-classical style for his parliament building. In doing so, Hansen was only following those well-trodden paths back to the ancient classical world traversed, indeed to some extent created, by the imagination of scholars such as J. J. Winckelmann and Hans Mommsen; that is, Hansen desired to invest his parliament building with the spirit of the vaunted democracy of classical Athens and the ambience associated with the ringing Ciceronian oratory of the Roman republic. Thereby the building came to be (if hyperbolically so) an alter ego in stone, the image the emergent bourgeoisie had of itself. Later, to make an even stronger statement as to both the priority and primacy of the function of Hansen's building, Karl Kundermann placed wisdom in the guise of Pallas Athene on a spectacular watery throne at the parliament building's ceremonial entrance.[27]

Just as the neo-classical motif was intended to underscore the commitment of Austria's industrial bourgeoisie to democratic, if not popular, political processes, Friedrich von Schmidt expressed the same sentiment by choosing the Gothic temper of the Teutonic high Renaissance for his city hall, thereby joining the ideal of civic self-government to a hackneyed view of the mercantile glory associated with the Hanseatic and Rhineland cities where supposedly manufacture and trade once had flourished unimpeded by dynasty and its attendant warrior-class aristocracy. Under the press of similar perceptions, it was only natural too that the architect Heinrich Ferstel, while attempting to concretize his definition of learning, would associate academic enterprise with the humanism of the Italian Renaissance, especially as it was then being articulated by the Swiss German historian Jakob Burckhardt, and therefore gave his university building its sunny style reminiscent of fifteenth-century Florence.[28] The result was an Aula cloaked in the raiment of the humanities and linked to political reason by its being placed in proximity to the parliament, the city hall, and the new theater.

As for the neo-baroque theater, built by the architects Gottfried Semper and Karl von Hasenauer between 1874 and 1888, it gave expression to the pride taken by the Viennese in their renowned court theater, founded and built in rococo style on Vienna's Michaelerplatz in 1776 by Emperor Joseph II. By the mid-nineteenth century, and indeed just as that emperor had intended, Joseph II's theater had become the primary stage in the German-speaking world.[29] Moreover, there was universal applause for the marriage of German theater and the grandiloquence of Italian humanism represented in this new cynosure, for whereas the eighteenth-century aristocracy had identified its stage with the rococo period, Austria's nineteenth-century bourgeoisie wished it to harken back to the Renaissance in Italy.

By 1888, four buildings—city hall, parliament, theater, and university—stood facing one another across a square set on the Franzenring. Each was cloaked in an idiom expressing its creator's perception of its function, but as that role was perceived within the collective imagination of its builders—that is, in the minds of articulate bourgeois liberal capitalists. The eclectic impression of the whole, while perhaps meant to reflect the Austrian idea, in fact disassembled that idea, for the individuality of the four buildings made it impossible to achieve the visual unity that might have reflected the harmony contained in the Austrian idea. The buildings' only relationship to one another is demonstrated visually by the fact that all four buildings face that same great ribbon of pavement that unites and harmonizes the variety in Vienna focused around it—perhaps just as the Austrian idea was meant to gather Austria's diversity under the umbrella of the state. However, the overall impression is one not of harmony but of disassembly, for the Ringstrasse was an insufficient instrument to pull the whole together— perhaps in the same way that the state increasingly seemed unable to contain the centrifugal forces at loose within it. The essayist and critic Friedrich Löhr unintentionally caught this point when he said of the Ringstrasse zone:

> Who'll buy Classical—Gothic—German or Italian Renaissance? And all of it—what more could you ask—neatly displayed; for this is the architectural old clothes market of the Imperial capital city of Vienna. Now, in an old clothes market everybody grabs what he particularly wants. So I stand in front of a building. I know quite well it is the Imperial Parliament. Anyone who does not know this already is certainly not going to guess it; it is a house built in the style of a Greek temple. Imposing columns soar upwards; it is surrounded by friezes above which there are pediments. I go in, and a guide attaches himself to me, not without need, for I immediately fall into serious intellectual difficulties, not to say confusion.[30]

Nonetheless, on the assumption that the present is illuminated by knowledge of the past, the four buildings were cloaked in historical styles in which the culturally articulate intended to express their conviction of the utility of a political synthesis propelled by enterprise and technology. So four temples dedicated to the bourgeois perspective arose on what formerly had been intended for a military parade ground dedicated to the neo-absolutist Austrian idea. The visual impact of the square itself comes not from the tangible and tactile but from the iconography of the ideological assumptions that inspired it. This iconography proclaimed the advent of Austria's industrial bourgeoisie as both mediator and articulator of Austria.[31] While the material remains of Austria in transformation are still clearly visible to the eye, the idea of Austria as it had been has evaporated into nothingness.

The late-nineteenth-century Vienna of bourgeois inspiration stood in contrast to a more traditional view of the Austrian idea held by others among Franz Joseph's subjects. They would have had the old capital on the Danube recall that, first and above all, Austrians were Europeans. Austria's civic backdrop therefore should contain those cultural components that existed throughout Europe as a whole, and not merely reflect the multicultural diversity of the current state.

From this perspective, bricks and mortar should be used to underscore Austria's legitimacy in history by hailing Vienna as the residence of the Christian Roman emperor. To those espousing Austria in the tenor of *Austriae est imperare orbi universo,* the Ringstrasse zone should be made to visually demonstrate what to them was Austria's mission to carry Christian European civilization deep into the central and eastern spaces of the continent. By having Vienna reflect her true place in Europe's past, the capital thereby would symbolize Austria's present and future grounded on the Habsburg state, which had evolved out of old Europe's Christian Roman Empire.

A variant on this use of architecture as an advocate for the supranational, pan-European idea is illustrated by the arguments put forth at the turn of the century for reviving the baroque as the proper Austrian style in place of the historical eclecticism invoked by the likes of Theophil Hansen or Heinrich Ferstel. Proponents of the neo-baroque saw in it an idiom for underscoring the Catholic foundations of the monarchy and thereby the empire's common religious makeup (Catholicism was the faith of the overwhelming majority of Franz Joseph's subjects). In addition, its advocates saw the neo-baroque style as an highly emotive one that would bring to life the memory of Austria's rich past:

> If the baroque is allowed to again rise up it will emerge . . . full of vitality. . . . How unfortunate it is that the genius of Art doesn't renew the spirit of the days of Leopold, Karl VI, and the great Theresa. If only there were a revival of the splendid style of baroque Austria. . . . This original and unique style gave Austria a sense of herself rather than pandering to the instincts of the people at the expense of harmony.[32]

Partisans of the neo-baroque were especially anxious that this style be used in the construction of two museums, of natural history and of art, to form, along with the rococo royal stables to the southwest, a great imperial forum in the heart of the capital. These twin neo-baroque structures, built to display to the public imperial collections hitherto rarely seen outside privileged circles, flanked, overpowered even, the old Heldentor, the ceremonial entrance to the imperial citadel. Plans also called for placing a monument between the two museums, in the center of the proposed square (now the Maria Theresiaplatz), facing the imperial palace, for here was a fitting place for pursuing an Austrian politics of art.

Proposals for the reconstruction of the Burgplatz by Gottfried Semper and Karl von Hasenauer, among others, met with determined opposition either because these called for some design other than baroque or because there was too much that was deemed parochial, French, or Italian in the suggested style. Especially with regard to the Burgplatz did the politics of the neo-baroque have the support of the heir to the throne, Archduke Franz Ferdinand. The archduke, who never was timid in expressing his views, initially had been drawn into the matter of construction along the Ringstrasse due to his position, since 1905, as *Protektor* of the General Commission for Monuments. Restless by nature and holding

ideas that represented a somewhat unstable blend of conservatism and progres-
sivism, Franz Ferdinand was an indefatigable builder and restorer of buildings
outside Vienna. In 1906, as overseer of the building committee for the new
imperial palace, the archduke was given an added opportunity to leave his stamp
on his house's capital and residence city.[33]

Franz Ferdinand had little use for the modern unless it was for a railway
station or for some similarly utilitarian structure assigned to the outer rim of the
expanding city. In Vienna's center, however, where older, historical buildings
associated with the dynasty were to be found, the archduke energetically insisted
upon using the prevailing architectural idiom. In the case of the Burgring, given
that the Leopold-era wing of the imperial Hofburg faced it, he viewed that idiom
as baroque. Moreover, Franz Ferdinand opposed the idea of shielding or otherwise hiding from view older historical buildings, even if by contemporary standards they were less than beautiful. His reasoning was obvious enough: If the
Austrian idea focused on dynasty, then its continuity between past and present as
revealed in historical architecture must be left intact. Hence, the present
Heldenplatz owes not only its neo-baroque coloration but its unfinished state to
the active intervention of the archducal heir to the throne, the latter due to the
archduke's insistence that any restructuring of the Burgring leaves the seventeenth-century Leopoldinischer Trakt in view. Given Franz Ferdinand's stone-
walling on this issue, discussion of the northeast quadrant of the vast space was
still going on when, on June 28, 1914, the archduke's assassination unwittingly
brought Austria to the point of her overwhelming fate. The unfinished square
therefore stands today as an astonishing monument to the grandiose tragedy that
began with the assassination at Sarajevo.[34]

Still another manifestation of the retreat of aristocratic culture is seen in the
growth and spread of popular theater, and not only that of the stage but of the
opera and concert hall as well. Prior to the nineteenth century, concerts, opera,
dramatic theater, and the like were held for the most part only within the mansions of noblemen, and the gilded doors to these rooms were opened only by
invitation. In this fashion, popular national culture and the high German culture
of the ruling aristocratic elites operated in two separate and distinct spheres.[35]
But by the end of the nineteenth century, every significant provincial town
within the Dual Monarchy was the proud possessor of these public gathering
places wherein diverse strands of society met, even if there was little more than
formal acknowledgment among them. And, of course, the same was more true of
those in the Austrian capital—the court theater and opera as well as that of the
building belonging to the *Musikverein* (the Friends of the Society of Music), to
mention an obvious few, institutions that came to be regarded as monumental
symbols of Vienna's new position as metropolis.

All of these buildings were tangible evidence not only of the rise of the
bourgeoisie, but also of the ascendancy of its culture over that of the aristocracy.
The rising power of the bourgeoisie had spilled over into the cultural arena;

cultural articulation no longer was contained solely within the walls of the aristo-cratic salons. Inevitably, the aristocracy and the bourgeoisie came to comingle, but only briefly, in public places of the empire. But this amalgamation forced aristocratic culture to give way to the power and overwhelming numbers of the bourgeoisie. In the process, aristocratic culture gave way to the primary of the bourgeoisie.[36] And so too metropolitan Vienna now stood at the center of the bourgeois Austrian synthesis, an iconographic representation of a new perception of the new Austria.

The impact of one of Franz Joseph's Jewish subjects, Baron Friedrich von Schey, on Vienna's cityscape, is not untypical of the culmination of the often spectacular commercial successes of the capital's upwardly mobile bourgeois families, whose actual roots lay obscured in the uncharted social vastness of Austrian Transleitha.[37] The son of a well-to-do merchant, young Schey studied at Vienna's Polytechnic Institute before apprenticing with the banking house of Wertheimstein. The Wertheimsteins, already a part of the capital's brilliant so-cial-cultural life at midcentury, and not least because of their generous patronage of Austrian letters, proved a valuable entrée for Schey into the great world of high finance.[38] In 1839, now well armed with the knowledge of that world's byzantine ways, Schey became a partner in banking with his brother-in-law, Joseph Landauer, who had a spectacular career in finance in his own right. In 1855, after the death of Landauer, Schey established his own banking house with the capital he had accumulated as a result of his successful speculations during the risky but opportunistic era of *Grunderzeit*. Schey then used his considerable resources to promote a number of enterprises, which included woolen mills, machine manufacture, and not least the construction of a railroad, commencing at Vienna's Elizabethbahnhof, linking Austria with western Europe.[39] Eventually Schey, ennobled in 1869, emulated aristocratic society by acquiring vast country estates, including a most splendid one in Hungary at Karomla. He also built a grand *Nobelzinspalais* in the very shadow of the imperial Hofburg, overlooking the Kaisergarten. It was from this vast pile on the Opernring that Baron von Schey played a significant cultural role of his own as patron to the arts.[40]

In this manner Vienna's Ringstrasse became "the most beautiful street in the imperial city . . . [its] palaces generally adorned alike . . . and belonging to mil-lionaires made up of the 'chosen people,' for only a few are in the possession of the suppressed Christians. . . . Regarding the overly decorated Theater Wiens . . . its interiors are crammed with boxes and stalls belonging to entrepreneurs, jour-nalists and other Jews."[41] Indeed, initially at least, perhaps one of the chief beneficiaries (and benefactors as well) of the evolution and rise of bourgeois civilization in old Austria were the Habsburgs' Jewish subjects. Possessing only precarious standing and uncertain security until the emancipation—and, even after this deliverance, still uncertain of their security until the acquisition of civil liberty between the years 1848 and 1860—the Jews left scant imprint on the surface mosaic of the Habsburg state until well into the second half of the nineteenth century. But Jews had been present in the Habsburg realm for a very long time. Before the dawn of Austria's industrial era, however, they had for the most part been confined to the ghetto in towns scattered throughout the monarchy; Jews were outsiders who, while rooted in their religious community, were strangers and barred by law from participation in the local traditional life. Therefore, Jews seldom became an integral cultural part of the nations among which they lived. Little wonder, then, when granted the right by the imperial government to travel freely and participate in the life of the Austrian state on terms of civic equality, Jews seized the opportunity and left their provincial ghettoes for the great urban and cosmopolitan centers coalescing in the empire; Prague, Budapest, Vienna. Moreover, the boom-and-bust urban atmosphere, linked with Austria's *Grunderzeit,* could only mean opportunity, for those who would serve the demands resulting from the spreading industrialization for these centers presented both a focus and release for the pent-up talents of the heretofore repressed outsider.[42] Vienna especially provided an auspicious setting, for there "the Jew encountered . . . an easygoing people, inclined toward conciliation, and under whose apparent laxity of form lay buried an identical deep instinct for cultural and aesthetic values which was so important to the Jews themselves. And . . . they found [in Vienna] a personal task . . . to carry on . . . the glory and fame of [the city's] culture."[43] So, for example, even though it was with some reservation, the aristocratic society matron Princess Eleonore Schwarzenberg (née von und zu Liechtenstein) invited Jewish bourgeois *arrivistes* to her much-cherished charity ball that took place in her mansion on the Neuermarkt. To be sure, once present, they tended to be ignored by the great lady. Nevertheless, no one, and obviously not Princess Eleonore herself, doubted for a moment the real influence of the likes of Anselm von Rothschild in the real world of everyday Austria.[44]

Given the opportunity provided by the emancipation of the Jews in the Austrian crown lands, perhaps it was not an entirely random accident that the father of the author and playwright Arthur Schnitzler took his leave of rural Hungary to try his chances amidst the glamour of Vienna. In any event, the rise of the Schnitzler family in the Austrian capital from misty origins on the Hungarian *puszta* also was not untypical of many of Vienna's well-known families, Jewish and non-Jewish alike. Schnitzler remembered his father only after he already had become a successful laryngologist who counted among his patients a litany of the famous associated with Vienna's brilliant world of theater and opera and who brought to the Schnitzlers a prosperous income enabling the family to live in one of the more splendid *Mietpalais* on Vienna's opulent Ringstrasse. But the elder Schnitzler's origins had been humble enough, and his rise into the solid upper reaches of Austria's professional classes well demonstrates the possibilities for social and economic advancement in old Austria in the wake of the liberal and capitalistic tides unloosened in 1860 by the establishment of the February Patent. Born in the provincial Hungarian town of Gross-Kaniza (Nagykaniza) to Josef Zimmerman, a poor, illiterate carpenter, and his wife, Rosalie (née Klein), the author's father, Johann, changed the family name to Schnitzler not long before he set off to study at the University of Budapest. Earning his keep by tutoring the daughters of a prominent Budapest bookseller, young Johann Schnitzler fell in love with one of his charming young charges but was unsuccessful in his pursuit. Subsequently—although not necessarily as a direct result of his failure in matters of the heart—Schnitzler went west to Vienna, where he not only finished his medical studies but also met and married the Jewish woman who, in time, became the mother of Arthur Schnitzler along with his younger brother and sister.[45]

Louise Schnitzler (née Markbrieter) also signaled by her existence that rise of Austria's Jews into the bourgeoisie that went hand in hand with the waxing of industrial society. Louise was the granddaughter of a Viennese court jeweler whose forebears had come to the capital during the eighteenth century to serve as artisans to the increasingly wealthy and cosmopolitan court of the German Habsburgs. As perhaps was implicit in their position, the Markbrieters soon were absorbed by and became wedded to the sophisticated cultural life of the capital while at the same time the family orbited up into the emerging industrial bourgeoisie. By the last half of the nineteenth century, during which time young Arthur Schnitzler arrived on the scene, the Markbrieters long had been at ease in Vienna's musical and theater salons. Indeed, Louise's grandfather Philipp Markbrieter even had acquired that subtle and somewhat soft patina of decadence that so often is said to have been concomitant with the overblown ambience of fin de siècle Vienna.[46] While a practicing physician of some talent, Philipp Markbrieter nevertheless had allowed himself to be sunk in gambling debts and was saved from ultimate financial ignominy only by the periodic intervention of family and friends.

It is not inappropriate to take note of Stefan Zweig's recollection that what prevailed in Europe before the ascent of nationalism and has since been lost was the Viennese outlook of "live and let live." The writer, perhaps too nostalgically, recalled: "Rich and poor, Czechs and Germans, Jews and Christians, lived peaceably together in spite of occasional chafing, and even the political and social movements were free of ... terrible hatred. ... In old Austria they still strove chivalrously, they abused each other in the news and in the parliament, but at the conclusion of their Ciceronian tirades the selfsame representatives sat down together in friendship with a glass of beer or a cup of coffee, and called each other *du*."[47]

Writing in 1903, Arthur Schnitzler addressed the shifting nuances in the social atmosphere through the perspective of his character Baron Georg von Wergenthin. Schnitzler's fictional centerpiece is amiable, privileged, educated, and a talented young man. In short, young Wergenthin appears to be the impeccable German Austrian. But self-centeredly sensuous and irresponsible, Wergenthin also is gripped by an enervating ennui that undermines his giftedness and cleverness. His male companions (as against his female lovers), although untitled, otherwise are like him with a single rarely spoken exception: They are Jews. In fact, Wergenthin and his friends, in this case both male and female, were patterned after the youthful Schnitzler and his circle, who the author describes as having had "the upbringing characteristic for a liberal regime: good will, a tendency to affection, sentimentality directed toward oneself: respect for superficial values, no actual feeling for truth, no actual comprehension of discretion [and where] mediocre qualities were described as virtues."[48]

Georg falls into a discussion with two of his Jewish friends over whether they really could be Austrian or whether, as then was being advocated by the Zionist Theodor Herzl, the Jews should depart from Europe in order to found anew their homeland in Palestine. The discussion, which takes place in the lovely spring-tinted setting in the fabled Wienerwald, turns into a heated exchange between Wergenthin's two companions. One of the discussants, Heinrich Bermann, protests to the other, a dedicated Zionist, that it was madness to ask that he leave Austria for Palestine, for he

> regarded Zionism as the worst affliction that ever burst upon the Jews. . . .
> National feeling and religion, those had always been the words which had
> embittered him with their wanton, yes malignant ambiguity. Fatherland. . . .
> Why, that was nothing more than a fiction, a political idea floating in the air,
> changeable, intangible. It was only the home, not the fatherland, which had
> real significance.[49]

Wergenthin holds his tongue. But as he takes in the sharp exchange between his two companions, both of whom he esteems, he becomes uncomfortable, above all because the two men are not Jews or Austrians but his friends. Yet later, when Georg is quietly cogitating alone on why he held back from telling his companions how he felt about them, cogitating free of that embarrassment derived from having been present but silent before the discussants, Wergenthin discovers that his true reaction is both startling and unforeseen. He was silent because

> he realized . . . that during the whole time he had not been able to shake off a
> kind of guilty consciousness of having not been free during his whole life from
> a certain hostility toward foreigners . . . not justified by his own personal
> experience. . . . This thought aroused an increasing malaise within him which
> he could not properly analyze . . . the dull realization that clean relations could
> not flourish even between clean men in an atmosphere of folly, injustice and
> disingenuousness.[50]

Even as early as 1903, Schnitzler was all too prescient. The author set his three gifted and urban characters amidst a stately and romantic setting and gave them that languid cadence peculiar to old Austria's favored classes. Thereby Schnitzler presented the reader with a civilized tale of humanity and sensitivity; but his story also is the history of decline as well. Even Schnitzler seems to have had little idea as to how rapid and how steep that decline would be, no thought perhaps that decay would quickly overtake those lingering qualities of humanity that were so much a part of Georg von Wergenthin's Austrian Empire. For even as Schnitzler set forth his tale, other young men, young men not favored by fortune, were gathering in that bile that one day would fuel the twentieth-century Holocaust. Yet, even in 1903, Schnitzler could write:

> "But supposing the medieval stakes were to be lighted again."
> "In that case," retorted Heinrich, "I hereby solemnly bind myself to take your advice implicitly."
> "Oh," objected Georg, "those times certainly will not come again."
> Both the others were unable to help laughing at Georg being kind enough to reassure them in that way about their future, in the name, as Heinrich observed, of the whole of Christendom.[51]

Indeed, it was barely two decades following Arthur Schnitzler's childhood that Austria's Jews were pained by the proclamation of the so-called Waidhofen Manifesto, issued in 1896. This declaration, put forth by the Waidhofen Association of Militant German Student Organizations in Austria *(Waidhofener Verband der Wehrhaften Vereine Deutscher Studenten in der Ostmark),* was a scruffy piece of anti-Semitism that proclaimed:

> With all due respect to the fact that such a profound moral and psychic difference prevails between Gentiles and Jews, and that our racial character has already suffered so much from Jewish abuse, and in view of the massive proof that the Jewish student has given us of his dishonorableness and character deficiency, and since he is totally lacking in honor according to our German understanding of the word, the German militant student organization meeting today has come to the resolution *henceforth not to give a Jew satisfaction, with any type of weapon whatsoever, since he is not worthy of the same.*[52]

This outbreak of anti-Semitism must have hit hard, for during the seventies not a few Jewish students at the University of Vienna, undoubtedly viewing themselves as German, unselfconsciously joined with their fellow German Austrians in founding a reading society, the Deutsche Studenten Lesenverein, dedicated not to the Austrian idea but to promoting a union between those Austrian lands occupied by the German nation and the vibrant German *Reich* of the Hohenzollerns. This reading society was a radical departure from similar clubs once founded by their fathers when, as students, the latter devoted their youthful energies toward achieving a free and democratic society for all of Austria. Unlike in the fifties, the emphasis among much of the educated young in the seventies was placed on nation. Perhaps they were following the calls they saw as coming from the likes of Schopenhauer, Nietszche, and Richard Wagner. In any event, these German Austrians, Jew and Gentile alike, had united their wills in *Deutschtum* (Germandom), pulling away from the Austrian idea, away from the hope of national conciliation within the supranational parameters of Habsburg Danubia.[53] Such actions set the stage on which, twenty years later, appeared the likes of the Waidhofen Manifesto. Indeed, by the nineties, the growth of the nation-state idea caused a shaking out of the Jews from the reading society. By then, the *Lesenverein* already had attracted many members imbued with anti-Semitism, who were to play a primary and lugubrious role in the last days of the Dual Monarchy.[54]

The rising tide of anti-Semitism, however, cannot be seen as a result of official favor by those who clung to the older Austrian idea. No less a personage than the emperor himself, while quite inclined to distinguish between Jew and Gentile in daily social discourse, made the distinction without its having a significance other than recording the fact itself. Moreover, the monarch would not tolerate anti-Semitism about him. So, for example, Franz Joseph uncharacteristically refused his empress's request for a lady-in-waiting because in her the emperor detected anti-Semitic views. And so too he wrote to Elizabeth: "I received a letter from [Archduchess Marie] Valerie the day before yesterday and an enclosed letter from old Princess Arenburg, born Auersperg, to Valerie and the Baroness Vecsey in Salzburg in which [Karl] Luegar and his party are warmly and urgently recommended to me. Anti-Semitism is an uncommonly diffused sickness even among the highest circles, and their agitation is unbelievable. The foundation [of the aristocracy] is sound, but [its] excrescence is awful."[55] In point of fact, however, the dynasty unwittingly had contributed to the decline of the Austrian idea. Despite its unique pan-European origins, the House of Habsburg-Lorraine early on had come to consider itself a German dynasty; therefore, unless its chief were to self-consciously call popular attention to its supranational evolution, the House of Habsburg would be too fragile to serve as a focus for the Austrian idea. But Franz Joseph especially was given to viewing himself personally as a German prince. Moreover, it was as a German prince that he assumed the throne of his forebears at Olmütz on December 2, 1848; further, it was as a German prince that the emperor stood at the head of those counterrevolutionary forces that put an end to the delicate democratic perspectives then blossoming forth out of Biedermeier culture in the Kremsier assembly.

Franz Joseph placed no primary significance on his German veneer or on its cultural primacy within his court.[56] For the same reason, the emperor saw few reasons, other than tactical ones, for earnestly pursuing the demands of the Magyars or Czechs on their own terms. But by the same token, Franz Joseph could not fully comprehend the impact of his *Deutschtum* (Germandom) on ethno-cultural nationalism because his dynastic identity blinded him to the strength of popular nationalist political culture, a strength that would need to be co-opted if he was to preserve the preeminence of both his house and the Austrian idea. Therefore, Franz Joseph did not perceive that the dynasty required a supranational, not a multinational, character if it was to be serviceable in the pursuit of the Austrian idea. Too often, the Austrian idea was used merely as a means for strengthening the House of Habsburg and not as an end to be served by it.[57]

A nationalistic political culture is always implicit in any community living within a society that identifies itself on the basis of some tangible manifestation—language or religion, for example—that it sees as implying ethnic solidarity. If this process of communal identification becomes too pronounced, then a centrifugal force is created that, if it becomes too strong, will overcome the centripetal ones created by society as a whole, destroying the cohesion of that same society. The tension between the forces of social assembly and disassembly, therefore, are always present in a multicultural state structure. The question then arises of when, and how, the centrifugal forces become so strong to counter the centripetal ones and bring about the state's disassembly. In old Austria this question is answered by observing the growth and spread of capital and industry within a single generation. The concomitant secular society, or at least forces that articulated it, destroyed the primacy of the dynastic, Catholic consciousness as a unifying factor that might transcend ethnic communities residing within the state and bring them together within a single sociopolitical identity. The spread of capital and industry, and its impact on society, is nowhere better seen than in that secular and extravagant material culture of the Vienna Ringstrasse as it had evolved by the end of the nineteenth century. The political reaction to these same forces is nowhere better observed than in the creation of the Christian Socialist party, which acted as a sort of counterpoint to that other, more cosmopolitan reaction, social democracy. The very exclusivity with which Luegar's party cloaked the dynasty transformed the House of Austria, against the conscious will of its patriarch, into a narrowly based Roman Catholic and German institution, hence producing a final mutation of the Austrian idea that no longer could hold sway over Austria's non-German and non-Catholic subjects. At the same time, the demographic effects of the initially unconscious mixing of self-perceived national communities, because of the demands of capitalistic enterprise, rendered the nations conscious of one another, but antagonistically so. And so too industrial capital enterprise set off a plethora of turf battles such as that between Germans and Czechs, which bedeviled Bohemia, or between Magyars and Rumanians, which threw Transylvania into turmoil. And finally, the pressure of capital situated some national communities as scapegoats, perceived as responsible for the misfortunes of a given community. In short, seismic changes in the ways a society labored activated and then made explicit those centrifugal forces of cultural nationalism always implicit in old Austria. And with this the state commenced to pull apart.

If circumstances are right, centripetal forces of society can, and do, prevail. If, however, conditions are ripe for the unleashing of centrifugal forces, then these can overcome the centripetal ones to threaten society, if not utterly destroy it. This is not to say that multinational communities inevitably must submit to their inherent centrifugal natures. Wise and foresighted leadership might make all the difference. Foresighted leadership, however, must be self-conscious and self-sacrificing. Unfortunately, self-sacrifice rarely seems to be an attribute of political leadership and hence, rarely an attribute of political culture. Perhaps if the Dual Monarchy had avoided the cataclysm of the First World War, Austria-Hungary might have muddled through the unwanted social restructuring brought about by the advent of modernism. But she did not, and so historians must deal not with what might have been but with events as they happened.

Notes

1. See John Boyer, *Political Radicalism in Late Imperial Vienna* (Chicago: University of Chicago Press, 1981).
2. Ignatz Mandl was a cousin of the playwright Arthur Schnitzler, and, like Schnitzler, he was Jewish. However, just what it meant to be Jewish as this related to being German or Austrian was not yet clear. Racial anti-Semitism, as the twentieth century had to endure it, was still to come. In his memoirs, Schnitzler remarks with regard to a political partnership between Mandl and Karl Luegar, that Mandl

> was active, without any justification whatsoever, as an anti-corruptionist, and so to begin with formed, together with Dr. Luegar, what might be termed a party of their own. Soon they were joined by other rather questionable ethicists, and the anti-corruption party soon developed into the anti-Semitic wing of the city administration, not because more corrupt elements were to be found among the Jewish population . . . but because it seemed more easily explicable to the masses. . . . Although [Luegar] understood so well how to exploit the lowest instincts of the masses . . . to further his own ends, at heart . . . he was no more anti-Semitic than he had been in the days when he played tarot at the home of Dr. Ferdinand Mandl, with his brother Ignatz and other Jews.

See Arthur Schnitzler, *My Youth in Vienna,* trans. Catharine Hutter (New York: Holt, Rinehart and Winston, 1970), especially pp. 119–120.
3. See Robert Wistrich, "The Modernization of Viennese Jewry," in Jacob Katz, ed., *Toward Modernity: The European Jewish Model* (New Brunswick, NJ: Transaction Books, 1987).
4. On Karl Luegar, see Richard S. Geehr, *Karl Luegar: Mayor of Fin de Siècle Vienna* (Detroit: Wayne State University Press, 1990). Also see Boyer, *Political Radicalism in Late Imperial Vienna.* Helpful in understanding the increasingly ambivalent position of Jewry in society is Robert Westrich, *Socialism and the Jews: The Dilemmas of Assimilation in Germany and Austria* (Rutherford, NJ: Fairleigh Dickinson University Press, 1982). Although it is fiction, Arthur Schnitzler's *The Road to the Open* (Berkeley: University of California Press, 1994), is most helpful in describing the landscape of Jewish ambivalence.
5. See William Alexander Jenks, *The Austrian Elections Reform of 1907* (New York: Columbia University Press, 1950).
6. Johann Christoph Allmayer-Beck, *Ministerpräsident Baron Beck: Ein Staatsmann des alten Österreich* (Munich: R. Oldenbourhg, 1956), pp. 223ff.
7. Quoted in Robert A. Kann, *Dynasty, Politics and Culture: Selected Essays,* ed. Stanley B. Winters (Boulder, CO: Social Science Monographs, 1991), p. 169. Jaroslav Thun was the younger brother of the sometimes Bohemian *Staathalter* (as well as sometimes Austrian minister-president) Count Franz von Thun-Hohenstein. The younger

Thun's friendship with the archduke primarily was due to the fact that he was married to a sister of Franz-Ferdinand's wife. See also Friedrich Wiessensteiner, *Franz Ferdinand: Der Werhinderte Herrscher* (Vienna: Österreichischer Bundesverlag, 1983), especially pp. 185–186.

8. Robert A. Kann, *Dynasty, Politics and Culture: Selected Essays* (Boulder, CO: Social Science Monographs, 1991). p. 170.

9. This point, however, must not be overdrawn. For example, some of the great families did possess lands that, beyond agricultural uses, had valuable mineral deposits. Such families—branches of the Schwarzenburgs, Larisches, and even some of the Habsburgs—made use of hired hands to develop and exploit these resources in the modern sense. Thereby these same families, while no doubt retaining their aristocratic veneer, were in effect as capitalistically motivated as some of the notable bourgeois parvenus among them. See, for example, the introduction to Adolph Schwarzenberg, *Prince Felix zu Schwarzenberg, Prime Minister of Austria: 1848–1852* (New York: Columbia University Press, 1946).

10. Works dealing with the social structure of the Dual Monarchy are legion. See especially Elizabeth Lichtenberger, *Wirtschaftfunktion und Sozialstruktur der Wiener Ringstrasse* (Vienna: Hermann Böhlaus, 1970), especially pp. 49ff; Erich Alban Berg, *Als der Adler noch Zwei Köpfe hatte: Ein Florilegium: 1858–1918* (Vienna: Styria Verlag, 1980), especially pp. 65–79, 106–123; Hermann Swistun and Heinrich Baltazzi-Scharschmid, *Die Familien Baltazzi-Vetsera im kaiserlichen Wien* (Vienna: Hermann Böhlaus, 1980), especially pp. 11–33, 248ff; Hilde Spiel, ed., *Wien: Spektrum einer Stadt* (Munich: Biederstein Verlag, 1971), passim; Reinhard Petermann, *Wien im Zeitalter Kaiser Franz Joseph I*, 3rd edition (Vienna: Verlag R. Lechner, 1913). Also very useful is the catalogue printed in connection with the *Ausstellung* held at Schloss Grafenegg from May 9 to October 26, 1987, entitled *Das Zeitalter kaiser Franz Josephs, 2 Teil, Glanz und Elend: Katalog und Beiträge 1880–1916*, (Vienna: NÖ Landesregierung, 1987).

11. See Alois Mosser, "Die Wirtschaft im Habsburgerreich," in Schloss Grafenegg, *Das Zeilteralter Kaiser Franz Josephs: Glanz und Elend, 1880–1916,* I (Beiträge), pp. 4–19.

12. For the political dimension of this process, see Lothar Hoebelt, "Parliamentary Politics in a Multinational Setting: Late Imperial Austria," University of Minnesota, Center for Austrian Studies Working Paper, March 1992. For the cultural manifestations of this transformation, see Carl E. Schorske, *Fin-de-Siècle Vienna: Politics and Culture* (New York: Alfred E. Knopf, 1980), pp. 46–52. For a somewhat different interpretation than Professor Schorske's, see James Shedel, *Art and Society: The New Art Movement in Vienna* (Palo Alto, CA: Society for the Promotion of Science and Scholarship, 1981). See also the description of society during this period in Gunther Martin, *Als Victorianer in Wien: Erinnerungen des britischen Diplomaten Sir Horace Rumbold* (Vienna: Österreichischer Bundesverlag, 1984).

13. Joseph Roth, *Radetzky March,* trans. Joachim Neugroschel (Woodstock, NY: The Overlook Press, 1995), pp. 161–162.

14. Max Graf, *Legend of a Music City* (New York: Philosophical Library, 1945), p. 65.

15. Stefan Zweig, *The World of Yesterday: An Autobiography by Stefan Zweig,* trans. Harry Zohn (Lincoln: University of Nebraska Press, 1965), pp. 24–25.

16. Today the former Franzenring is named the Dr. Karl Renner Ring.

17. Klaus Eggert and Johanna Fiegl, *Der Wohnbau der Wiener Ringstrasse in Historismus, 1855–1896,* vol. VII in Renate Wagner-Rieger, ed., *Die Wiener Ringstrasse: Bild einer Epoche: die Erweiterung der inneren Stadt Wien unter Kaiser Franz Joseph,* 10 volumes (Vienna: H. Böhlaus Nachf., 1969).

18. See Kurt Mollik, Hermann Reining, and Rudolf Wurzer, *Plannung und Ver-*

wirklichung der Wiener Ringstrassezone, vol. III of Renate Wagner-Rieger, ed., *Die Wiener Ringstrasse: Bild einer Epoche: die Erweiterung der inneren Stadt Wien unter Kaiser Franz Joseph.* See also John P. Spielman, *The City and the Crown: Vienna and the Imperial Court, 1660–1740* (West Lafayette, IN: Purdue University Press, 1993).

19. Elizabeth Lichtenberger, *Wirtschaft und Sozialstruktur der Wiener Ringstrasse,* volume VI in Renate Wagner-Rieger, ed., *Die Wiener Ringstrasse, Bild einer Epoche: die Erweiterung der inneren Stadt Wien unter Kaiser Franz Joseph.* See also volume V of the same series by Franz Baltzarek, Alfred Hoffmann, and Hannes Stekl, *Wirtschaft und Gesellschaft der Wiener Stadterweiterung,* pp. 255ff.

20. Renate Wagner-Rieger, ed., *Die Wiener Ringstrasse,* Ibid. See especially volume II in the series by Elizabeth Springer, *Geschichte und Kulturleben der Wiener Ringstrasse,* pp. 456ff. See also George V. Strong, "Baukunst and Politics: The Vienna Ringstrasse, 1863–1918)," *Journal of the History of European Ideas,* 5 (1986).

21. Springer, *Geschichte* 1.

22. Mollik, Reining, and Wurzer, *Plannung und Verwicklichung der Wiener Ringstrassezone,* pp. 443ff., 456ff.

23. Ibid., pp. 456ff.

24. Ibid., especially pp. 104–109.

25. Springer, *Geschichte und Kulturleben,* pp. 159ff.

26. Kart Mollik, Reining, and Wurzer, *Plannung und Verwicklichung,* pp. 153, 162ff.

27. Maria Potzl-Malikova, *Die Plastik der Ringstrasse,* volume IX/2 of Renate Wagner Rieger, ed., *Die Wiener Ringstrasse: Bild einer Epoche,* pp. 44ff.

28. Springer, *Geschichte und Kulturleben,* pp. 63–67, 169–170, 180–188.

29. See Derek Beales, *Joseph II.* vol. I: *In the Shadow of Maria Theresa, 1741–1780* (Cambridge: Cambridge University Press, 1987), pp. 230–238, especially p. 233.

30. Quoted in Kurt Blaukopf, *Mahler: A Documentary Study* (London: Thames and Hudson, 1976), p. 173.

31. Strong, *Baukunst und Politics.*

32. Springer, *Geschichte und Kulturleben,* pp. 424–425.

33. See Springer, *Geschichte und Kulturleben,* pp. 427ff. For a detailed description regarding the evolution specifically of the Vienna Hofburg, see Moriz Dreger, *Baugeschichte der K.u.K. Hofburg in Wien bis zum XIX Jahrhundert* (Vienna: Anton Schroll, 1914).

34. Springer, *Geschichte und Kulturleben,* pp. 596–598. See also Pozal-Malikova, *Die Plastik der Ringstrasse,* pp. 99ff.

35. See Ann Tizia Leitich, *Vienna Gloriosa: Weltstadt des Barock* (Vienna: Wilhelm Andermann, 1947), especially pp. 61–78. An excellent overview of the evolution of the court theaters, and especially the court opera, is found in Henry-Louis de la Grange, *Gustav Mahler: The Years of Challente, 1897–1904,* vol. 2 (New York: Oxford University Press, 1924), pp. 1–36. (Note: The original work in French, published by Fayard between the years 1979 and 1984, consists of three volumes. Oxford University Press currently is at work to bring out translations of the other two volumes.)

36. Reinhard E. Petermann, *Wien in Zeitalter Kaiser Franz Josephs* I, 3rd edition (Vienna: Verlag R. Lechner), pp. 68–69. See also Volkmar Braunbehrens, *Mozart in Vienna: 1781–1791,* trans. Timothy Bell (New York: Harper, 1986), especially pp. 142–163, 293–304, 372–380.

37. In 1880, the count of Jews in Vienna's population (by attribution) was 75,588, or 10.06 percent of the city's total population. This figure is more instructive regarding the interaction between the growth and spread of industrial and capital as this is linked to Jewish emancipation when one recalls that the the total number of Jews living in the capital (again by attribution) in 1857 was 6,217, which amounted to only 2.16 percent of

the total population. By 1890, the total Jewish population in Vienna amounted to 118,495 and by 1910, the figure stood at 127,318. This last figure represented only 8.6 percent of the city's total population, but this was because in 1910 the city had annexed some of the suburban territories surrounding it thereby changing, if only temporarily, the demographic mix. See Wolfdieter Bihl, "Die Volker des Reich: Die Juden," in Adam Wandruszka and Peter Urbanitsch, eds., *Die Habsburgermonarchie: 1848–1918,* 3 volumes (Vienna: Verlag der Österreichischen Akadamie der Wissenschaften 1980), vol. III, part 2, p. 884.

38. The family, for example, was patron of one of Austria's most noted literati of the first half of the nineteenth century, Franz Grillparzer.

39. Today, Vienna's Westbahnhof, rebuilt in its present state after its destruction during the Second World War.

40. Eggert and Fiegl, *Wohnbau,* pp. 294–295.

41. Springer, *Geschichte und Kulturleben,* pp. 618–619.

42. Bihl, "Die Volker." See also Peter G.J. Pulzer, *The Rise of Political Anti-Semitism in Germany and Austria Before the First World War* (New York: Wiley, 1964) and William O. McCagg, *A History of the Habsburg Jews, 1670–1918* (Bloomington: Indiana University Press, 1989), especially pp. 181–222. Some scholars want to say that to a very large extent Vienna's bourgeois culture was Jewish. See Stephen Beller, *Vienna and the Jews: 1867–1938: A Cultural History* (Cambridge: Cambridge University Press, 1989), and Robert S. Wistrich, *The Jews of Vienna in the Age of Franz Joseph* (Oxford: Oxford University Press, 1988). Jews did dominate certain segments of bourgeois endeavor out of proportion to their numbers in Vienna's overall demographic mix. Stefan Zweig claimed that the Jews in Vienna constituted a sort of professional elite dedicated to the "glory of the fame of Viennese culture"; see Stefan Zweig, *Die Welt von Gestern: Errinerungen eines Europers* (Berlin: Fischer, 1968), p. 24. So, for example, out of Vienna's 681 lawyers *(Anwalte)* listed in the year 1890, 394 counted themselves as Jewish. Moreover, 310 of the capital's 360 higher-ranked barristers *(Advokatursanwalte)* were Jews. Almost half the medical faculty at the University of Vienna was Jewish. In the arts, Peter Goldmark, Gustav Mahler, and Arnold Schoenberg garnered world renown as composers of music while Oscar Strauss and Leo Fall carried on the tradition set by Vienna's waltz kings. Jewish names such as Hofmannsthal, Schnitzler, Beer-Hofmann, Altenberg, and Zweig dominated in literature. In journalism, the Jewish names of Moritz Szeps and Moritz Benedikt absolutely overwhelmed in the public consciousness numerous gentile names engaged in that same enterprise. See Karl Eder, *Die Liberalismus im Altösterreich* (Munich: R. Oldenbourg, 1965), pp. 225 and passim. The author of this work feels that to say that Viennese bourgeois culture was Jewish overstates the case. Rather, the bourgeois framework served as a home for those from all walks of life, and from diverse ethnic backgrounds, who wished to (and could) leave their past behind them and start, as it were, anew in the secular social culture of industry and capitalism. The Jews, very literate but having no rooted society to give up, were psychologically well placed to embrace the new with enthusiasm. Hence, the numbers cited above. But they did not consciously interject their culture into their activities (if, of course, they brought their values with them from their Jewish backgrounds). But experience transforms values; this first generation of entrepreneurs had new experiences, the same as their fellow bourgeois in general, and hence new perceptions and values.

43. Zweig, *Die Welt von Gestern,* pp. 20–21.

44. Swistun and Baltazzi-Scharschmid, *Die Familien Baltazzi-Vetsera im kaiserlichen Wien,* pp. 108–109.

45. Schnitzler, *My Youth In Vienna,* pp. 4–10.

46. Schorske, *Fin-de-Siècle Vienna,* pp. 3–23, 322ff.

47. Zweig, *Die Welt von Gestern,* pp. 11–12. A less rosy but not essentially different

picture is presented in George Clare, *Last Waltz in Vienna: The Rise and Destruction of a Family* (New York: Holt, Rinehart and Winston, 1982).

48. Schnitzler, *My Youth in Vienna,* p. 4.

49. Arthur Schnitzler, *Weg ins Freie* (Berlin: Fischer Verlag, 1920), pp. 128ff.

50. Ibid., pp. 141–142.

51. Arthur Schnitzler, *The Road to the Open,* trans. Horace Samuel (New York: Alfred A. Knopf, 1923), p. 113.

52. Quoted in Schnitzler, *My Youth in Vienna,* p. 269. See also Clare, *Last Waltz in Vienna,* pp. 29ff.

53. See Fritz Stern, *The Politics of Cultural Despair: A Study in the Rise of the Germanic Ideology* (Berkeley: University of California Press, 1961).

54. On these reading clubs, see William J. McGrath, *Dionysian Art and Populist Politics in Austria* (New Haven: Yale University Press, 1974).

55. Georg Nositz-Rieneck, ed., *Briefe Kaiser Franz Josephs an Kaiserin Elizabeth,* 2 volumes (Vienna: Verlag Herold, 1966), vol. II, p. 111. This perception is verified by Alexander Novotony in his "Der Monarch und seine Ratgeber," in Wandruszka and Urbanitsch, eds., *Die Habsburger Monarchie, vol.* III, part 2, pp. 63–64.

56. See Robert A. Kann, "The Dynasty and the Imperial Idea," in *Dynasty, Politics and Culture: Selected Essays,* pp. 43ff.

57. See Allmayer-Beck, *Ministerpräsident Baron Beck,* pp. 66–67, and Kann, "The Dynasty and the Imperial Idea," pp. 43ff.

✧ 7 ✧

Into the Abyss: The First World War

It is not easy to comprehend how Austria-Hungary, that most fragile of states, came to be party to the unleashing of the hounds of war. But about one thing there is certainty: When Vienna unsheathed the sword in August of 1914, the end result was not only war but revolution. By the same token, it cannot be said that by avoiding war the Dual Monarchy would have escaped dissolution; peace, however, greatly would have increased the odds for its survival. Knowing full well the implications for Austria of the centrifugal nationality forces within, why did her leadership risk everything in its response to the murders of the heir to the throne and his wife at Sarajevo?

One explanation for the monarchy's handling of the crisis arising out of Sarajevo is that the leadership panicked precisely because it was fully aware of the implications of the nationality strife for Austria and, moreover, because it knew that its enemies understood these implications as well. Hence, at the moment of the murders, no muted response appeared possible; rather, what was required was a hard line so as to underscore Austria-Hungary's determination to live and even to exist as one of Europe's great powers. In this sense, it might be said that upon perceiving the abyss yawning before it, the Austrian government leaped into it.[1]

Franz Joseph and his inner circle of advisors—for the most part elderly scions of Europe's medieval warrior class, imbued with an antimodern bias, and especially with a sort of martial spirit that passed for chivalry—did perceive the instrument of their undoing in the crisis. Accepting the challenge with fear and trepidation, because they faced the heaviest of odds, they girded themselves to do battle, for they preferred a quick and noble death to a lingering and dishonorable one.[2] The end result was a historic cataclysmic event that brought the politically ramshackle realm of the Habsburgs to the ground. But of course much else as well went down in the debacle.[3]

In fairness it should be noted that blood spilled in the course of political terrorism still shocked in 1914; hence, the assassination of the heir to the throne and his wife by Gavrilo Princip filled the orderly civilization of that era with horror.[4] It was shortly after ten in the morning when, in a holiday mood, a gaily decked-out crowd in Sarajevo lined the Appel-Quai leading from the local commandant's headquarters, the Konak, to the Cumurga Bridge in hopes of catching a glimpse of their future emperor. All present knew that the imperial and royal party would make its way along this route as it went to the city hall to take part in the prescribed ceremonial festivities. It was a simpler era, and excitement was palpable as three shiny, flag-bedecked automobiles led by the black-and-gold banner of the double eagle appeared moving slowly amid cheers of *"Zivio!"* Local worthies—the mayor, members of the city council, and prominent clergy—sat in the first car. The second carried the archduke and his wife, Field Marshal Count Oskar Potiorek, the military governor of the province, and an aide to Franz Ferdinand, Count Franz Harrach. In the third, colorful in their dress uniforms, sat various other members of the archduke's entourage.[5]

Amid the sportive crowd set to enjoy the pageantry on that sparkling June day, the imperial party appeared relaxed and in the best of humor; as always, Franz Ferdinand's consort, Sophie, Duchess of Hohenburg, displayed her sincere and infectious smile to all and sundry. It was then that there followed a series of entirely unexpected events that in hindsight should have been not only foreseen but also not allowed either to have happened or to have led to a catastrophe of unheard-of proportions.

> A bouquet of flowers flew over the car carrying the heir to the throne and landed on its folded-back roof. Everything disappeared behind a screen of fine smoke. . . . The automobile came to a halt, and the heir to the throne climbed out of the car. His first question was directed to his wife: Had she seen what had happened? She answered with a no while dabbing a speck of blood from her neck with her handkerchief, the result of a small fragment from the bomb having hit her. . . . Everyone then took their places and the caravan continued on to the city hall without further incident.[6]

Relief that the bomb had not done more damage was audible among the crowd, a circumstance no doubt heartening to Franz Ferdinand and the officers in his company. However, one member of the military governor's staff had been hurt. But Lieutenant Colonel Merizzi's head wound was slight, and in any event, the doctors in the local hospital quickly ministered to him. Clearly, although dangerous and disturbing, the attack had been a failure.

The day's fortunes, however, soon took a sinister and final turn. A few hours later, Archduke Franz Ferdinand determined that he would visit Colonel Merizzi at the district hospital before returning to the Konak. Hence, the archduke would travel northwest into the city's unguarded interior prior to recrossing the little river that bisected it, the Miljaka, on his way back to his headquarters. This intention caused considerable consternation among the officials present, and especially to Count Potiorek, who was responsible for security. The military governor mentioned the possibility of another attempt on the archduke's life. But Franz Ferdinand, his usual irascible humor not improved by the events of that morning, was not to be deflected, and especially in view of the fact that the perpetrators of the bomb attack had been apprehended; the odds appeared against another attempt on the same day.

Although Potiorek, if given his wishes, would have preferred to wrap the remainder of Franz Ferdinand's visit in caution, the archduke had his way. That the archduke thought differently from the unwilling Potiorek reflected the mores of the former, for according to the code of that caste into which Franz Ferdinand had been born, the archduke viewed it as his duty to visit the wounded lieutenant colonel. In addition, Franz Ferdinand may have been propelled by a certain sense of fatalism that was joined to an ennui born of resignation. The last empress and queen of Austria-Hungary, Zita of Bourbon-Parma, tells of a dinner with her husband's aunt and uncle taken *en famille* in Vienna's Belvedere Palace. Upon the Duchess of Hohenburg's leaving the room to attend to bedding down her children, Franz Ferdinand turned to Zita and her husband, Archduke Karl, to say:

> "I must tell you something. . . . I soon will be murdered." The archduke spoke with absolute clarity. There was no room for misunderstanding. We both looked at Franz Ferdinand in horror and astonishment. Finally Archduke Karl responded as much as possible without at the same time creating a breach by saying that he thought what he had heard absurd. "But Uncle, that can't be possible!" And generally, "Who would do such a thing?" Just after Karl had finished [speaking,] the heir to the throne answered with a curious authority, saying to us both, "Don't contradict me! I know it with absolute certainty. In a few months I will be murdered. . . . I am fortunate that everything is in readiness at Artstetten . . . even the crypt . . . who knows how soon it will be needed." "But Franz," his wife [who had returned to the room] interjected, "are you on that topic again?"[7]

In any event, a visit to the district hospital at Sarajevo required a drastic change in the archduke's schedule for the remainder of the day. In addition, this visit meant wide and unavoidable public exposure of the high-born visitor, because the hospital was approachable only through a series of narrow, winding streets. In hasty deference to security, for the officials in charge of these matters were beside themselves with worry, it was decided that the automobile caravan would proceed with the utmost speed from city hall first to the hospital and then from there southward back to the safety of the Konak. And so it was that the imperial and royal pair set off on a fateful trip. Both royals were present because the duchess, a good and faithful wife, insisted that she accompany her husband on his foray to the northwest precincts of the city.

The remainder of the sad tale is history. Through an oversight stemming from the confusion of the morning, the driver of the archduke's car was not told of the impending visit to the bedside of the wounded Colonel Merizzi. Perhaps because he too was concerned for the archduke's safety, the chauffeur drove at breakneck speed from the city hall southward directly toward the Konak, toward the safety promised by the commandant's headquarters. He directed the car along Franz Joseph Strasse and was commencing his turn southward into the Rudolphgasse so as to cross the Miljaka a little way down at the Roman Bridge. As the driver headed the car onto the bridge, still only a short block from the city hall, Potiorek barked out orders for correcting the course. In response to this command, the driver brought the car to a complete stop so as to reverse and head northwestward in the direction of the hospital. Standing on the corner where the Franz Joseph Strasse and the Rudolphgasse intersected—two streets named for the two men perhaps most identified in the popular mind with the last and final drift of Austria's dynasty—stood Gavrilo Princip:

> Three shots rang out.
> One hit the archduke, the second the duchess, the third was aimed at and should have hit the military governor.
> But it missed.
> Their Highnesses sank back into the automobile, the tunics of the generals turned red with the blood of the heir to the throne, who had been hit on his neck in the jugular. . . .
> A shriek of horror rose up from and spread through the crowd. The car changed course and spurted over the Roman Bridge toward the Konak. Those present found themselves at the watch for the dead and dying. . . . The archduke was breathing still when he was brought in and laid out on a sofa on the ground floor of the building. But . . . he died.[8]

It remained to send the news of the misfortune to Vienna, but the catastrophe emanating out of this tragedy already was irreversible. As Franz Ferdinand slipped into death, Europe commenced her slide toward the Great War.[9]

Franz Joseph, for his part, had always entertained serious reservations about the archducal couple because he considered their marriage a *mésalliance* that undermined the future stability of the imperial house. The emperor's attitude had thereby resulted in both political and personal estrangement between the Hofburg and Belvedere. Perhaps because he bore in mind the unhappy history of the dynasty during the fifteenth century, when the issue of muddied succession almost undid his house, Franz Joseph feared that the children born of the heir to the throne's morganatic marriage, although barred by law from the succession but nevertheless growing up within the shadow of their father's throne, would become the focus of *Learian*–like plots against the legitimate heir; moreover, given the nationality strife coursing through Austria-Hungary, the possible effects of such plots appeared all the greater.[10]

The old monarch blamed his weakness for what he saw as the unhappy potential of Franz Ferdinand's marriage. As emperor, patriarch, and chief magistrate of the House of Habsburg, Franz Joseph might have forbidden the marriage, but, pressed by the archduke and by Empress Elizabeth as well, the emperor decided against an exercise of *force majeure*. Instead, he contented himself, although much against his better judgment, with the formal stipulation that his dynastic heir should inherit the throne within the constraints of a morganatic marriage. Nevertheless, the issue continuously vexed Franz Joseph, who himself always placed his duty to Austria first above everything.[11] These reservations of the emperor's gave rise to a number of near-apocryphal tales, for example one told by the former governor of Lower Austria that when

> the horrible news of the murder came from Sarajevo, the emperor was staying at [Bad] Ischl. His nearest neighbor [of requisite rank] in Gmunden, the Duke of Cumberland, threw himself into his automobile and went to the emperor in order to be the first to offer condolences. It happened that on the next day, I came to Gmunden because of a prior invitation from the duke. I had scarcely entered his castle when the duke came to my room to tell me what had happened at Ischl. . . . He had found the emperor very composed; it had been a shock to him [but] nevertheless [Franz Joseph] spoke of the deed in a matter-of-fact way. But eventually he said that he took consolation in that the heir to the throne and his wife would have been an embarrassment for the dynasty.[12]

Certain reservations toward his heir notwithstanding,[13] the inherent impulses of Franz Joseph's very being seemed to have driven the old emperor to conclude that he could not permit the murders to pass without his meting out retribution. Further, the punishment must have its source from within his sovereign authority. A lesser reaction—for example, one framed within and circumscribed by the parameters of the usual diplomacy—only would have signified, to Franz Joseph's mind, that Serbia had struck a decisive blow against the inviolability of the dynastic principle in Austria-Hungary. Thereby, Belgrade would have succeeded in undermining the bedrock upon which the cohesion and stability of the Dual Monarchy rested. Although, from hindsight, the emperor's perspective was founded on what might even then be considered outworn dynastic principles, Franz Joseph's reaction cannot be understood as one grounded solely in his own narrow self-interest. Rather, the old gentleman in the Hofburg firmly believed that if it were demonstrated that his house could be regarded as something less than sacrosanct, then the Dual Monarchy would have lost the vital substance of its cohesion, the very core of its rationale for existence, and so Austria-Hungary would fall apart.[14]

Other considerations, however, ones related to the power position of Austria-Hungary in south-central Europe and hence closely but indirectly related to the dynastic idea per se, also must have played a central role in the emperor's decision. Indeed, perhaps as early as the autumn of 1913, Franz Joseph had concluded that a point of no return had been reached with Serbia as far as the Balkan peninsula was concerned. The estrangement, always present between Vienna and Belgrade, became more explicit in 1903 with the overthrow of the Obrenovič dynasty by the Karageorgevičs by means of a bloody palace coup. Propelling the Karageorgevičs was a near-fanatical commitment to creating a Greater Serbia; that is, a state focused around Belgrade but incorporating all the Balkan south Slavs. The Karageorgevič Greater Serbia idea ran counter to what might be called the de facto smaller Serbia idea implicit in the Obrenovič policy of living with the existing Austro-Hungarian state.[15] This turning point, however, seems to have become much sharper in 1913 because of Serbia's occupation of Montenegro in the course of the Second Balkan War. Occupation of Montenegro gave Serbia access to the Adriatic and hence the potential to challenge Austrian naval domination of the Adriatic and so threaten free access in and out of the monarchy's chief entrepôts, Trieste and Fiume.[16] Perhaps more ominous in the emperor's view was the possibility that Belgrade, given her long record of anti-Austrian tactics and now her possession of a window on the Adriatic, might link her interests against the Dual Monarchy with those of Italy's so as to create, beyond the current irredentist south Slav threat, an Italian irredentist one as well. Beyond the possible Italian connection, of course, was the always overriding consideration that Serbia, wittingly or unwittingly, might be both vehicle and pawn in Russia's hands through which St. Petersburg might obtain, if not Istanbul proper, at least a strategic window on the southeastern coast of the Adriatic. Franz Joseph feared that a Russian-Serb connection would weaken Austrian-Hungary not only by bottling up the Dual Monarchy at the mouth of the Adriatic but also by generating increasing irredentist pressures via the pan-Slavic idea. It went without saying that should the combination of these circumstances come to pass, the end result would undermine the *raison d'être* of the Dual Monarchy and hence of the House of Habsburg as well.[17] And so for all these reasons, Franz Joseph, who for so long had held back the aggressive forces alive beneath the surface glitter of his realm, perhaps reluctantly had concluded, and this well before the July crisis of 1914, that war between Vienna and Belgrade was inevitable.

With what intensity Franz Joseph may have held to his views, however, is difficult to document before the last week of July 1914, because of the emperor's habit of not setting his views in writing and never discussing with one minister affairs pertaining to the business of another. Moreover, the public's general tendency to trust the old emperor's instincts because of their confidence that he very much desired peace, combined with the parliament being prorogued during the crisis summer of 1914, may have blunted Franz Joseph's perception of the harsh reality that ultimately it was he who was responsible for decisions taken by his government in matters of war and peace.[18]

The idea of the necessity of settling accounts with Serbia was widely shared by, among others, Franz Joseph's chief of (military) staff, Field Marshal Conrad von Hötzendorf, as well as a number of the statesmen and politicians surrounding the government in the Hofburg. Added to the calamitous ether during that summer of 1914 was that usual mixture of irresolution and shortsighted ambition common among many of these same elements, who, either because they feared coming down on the wrong side or because they saw a way to advance their careers through a victorious war with Serbia, failed to encourage their elderly monarch to take a tactic ensuring that the crisis would be peacefully surmounted. Perhaps primary among the irresolute was the foreign minister, Count Leopold Berchtold.[19] However, other luminaries of varying political stripes also played out their dolorous roles, including aristocrats such as Count Alexander Hoyos, who carried on negotiations in Berlin for the Vienna government, and diplomats such as Baron Stephen Burian von Rajec and Alexander von Muslin, who continually urged a hard line on the emperor, as did deputies such as Joseph Redlich and Joseph Barenreiter. This role also should include Minister-President Count Karl Stürgkh as well as the former minister-president Baron Max Vladimir von Beck along with the minister of defense, Alexander Krobatin.[20]

The official actors in the Dual Monarchy, not least the emperor himself, in dealing with the July 1914 crisis seemed only too cognizant that war with Serbia must inevitably pull in Russia, and with it France, on the side of Belgrade. Such an escalation also inevitably would drag the German Empire into hostilities on the side of Austria-Hungary. Emperor Wilhelm II, for example, more than once had reminded Vienna of his loyalty with words like those spoken in 1889 to Austria's ambassador in Berlin: "In any event His Majesty Kaiser Franz Joseph is also a Prussian field marshal. He only has to give the orders and my army will obey."[21] Certainly, by the end of July 1914, the views of both Wilhelm II and Franz Joseph that the Central Powers knowingly were pursuing a European war, not a localized one, are confirmed by an exchange of telegrams that took place on July 31, in which the Austrian emperor informed his ally in Berlin:

> The official report from my ambassador in St. Petersburg (Count Szögyeny) reports that the emperor of Russia has ordered the mobilization of all his military districts on my borders. Count Szögyeny has reported to me that you have already told Emperor Nicholas in a most explicit way that the initiating of Russian preparations will place the entire responsibility for a world war on his shoulders. I, being conscious of my difficult responsibility for the future of my realm, have ordered the mobilization of my entire armed forces. . . . The recent bolstering of Serbia by Russia's intervention must have the most serious of consequences for my lands and therefore I maintain that such intervention is unacceptable.[22]

Wilhelm replied to Vienna at once, telling Franz Joseph:

> Today, on my command, I have initiated the mobilization of my common army and my navy so that it will take place in the shortest time possible. I reckon the second of August as the first day of full mobilization, and I am prepared, in fulfillment of *my* duty to our alliance, to immediately begin war against Russia and France.[23]

Prior to the summer of 1914, telling opposition to any war that must involve Russia apparently came only from Archduke Franz Ferdinand, who, in turn, found only lukewarm support for these views from members of his shadow government.[24] Franz Ferdinand's opposition, however, did not chiefly spring out of humanitarian concerns. Rather, what the heir to the throne feared most was that a war that paired off Austria against Russia would bring with it the threat of overarching revolution in both states and hence the collapse of the monarchical dynastic order as the political foundation for central and eastern Europe. In addition, Franz Ferdinand recognized the need for some sort of restructuring of the Dual Monarchy, not through a federation of nationalities but by military force, which must call for some form of dictatorship.[25] Such restructuring, because it was bound to generate opposition despite its having apparently widespread support among the aristocracy and elements of the haute bourgeoisie who were panicking in the face of the rising tide of popular nationalism, certainly could not have been carried out in the face of all-out war.[26] Hence, it well might have been that the primary effect of Franz Ferdinand's assassination was that it made a European war more certain than it had been up till July 1914.[27] If Great Britain had not joined the Entente powers, such a war, of course, while it would have been a European one involving much of the world, would not have been a world war in the sense of the one that broke out on August 4, 1914. But apparently Vienna did not foresee that relations between London and Berlin had come to such a bellicose pass. And there is considerable evidence that at least Germany's ambassador to Vienna, Heinrich von Tscherschky und Bogendorff, feared a weakening of the British perception of Germany if Berlin did not support Austria-Hungary in a European war with Serbia. Thereby, it was in part to keep a war from breaking out between Berlin and an emboldened London that Tscherschky put pressure on Vienna by telling the Ballhaus:

> Austria must know what she has to do, we have no advice to give. She must decide whether she is going to remain a great power or not. If she cannot pull herself together and make a decision . . . she throws away her great-power status and . . . Germany will be compelled to [rethink] whether to adhere to her present policy or to take another tactic. You have long known that you can count on us in an emergency.[28]

Added to other pressures for a decision for war against Serbia, then, was that Germany apparently demanded such a policy from her ally. To decide otherwise was to leave the Habsburg Dual Monarchy bereft of powerful friends while surrounded by states determined to detach its Slavic subjects. At the same time, this anti-Austrian pan-Slavism coincided with a rising crescendo of socioeconomically driven centrifugal nationality pressures. And so the Austrian leadership took that leap into the abyss that yawned before it. One Viennese journalist, looking backward from 1915, saw the issue as being one where the old emperor should be condemned, even if he was desperate and unwitting, for the fabrication of "imperial Austria's policy of catastrophe."[29] But of course it is also true that hindsight, unlike foresight, is unclouded by panic.

In all events, during the summer of 1914, Franz Joseph and his ministers did not steer the Austrian ship of state away from the turbulence that, in the end, proved to be the approach to war. The multiplicity of elements from which history is made—great events intersecting with sincerely held but outworn attitudes grounded on an archaic political perspective held by assorted individual actors—had converged on a point of weakness in a given time and place to produce a cataclysm. No wonder that the usual mundane mechanisms of European diplomacy, which too often reflected very different interests and perspectives than those realities describing the Dual Monarchy, hardly was up to the task of preventing war.

In the summer of 1914, therefore, there was no repeat of Franz Joseph's moderating influence evident, for example, during the First Balkan War of 1912, when it was the emperor's will that had prevented the intervention of the Dual Monarchy into the political spasms of its Balkan neighbors. Gone too were the moments when the emperor had rejected the pleas of his chief of staff, Conrad von Hötzendorf, for a preventive war against Italy by abruptly closing the subject with the words, "My policy is a policy of peace . . . my foreign minister carries out my policy in that sense."[30]

The words of Franz Joseph's manifesto of war, sorrowing words grandiloquently expressing the archaic Weltanschauung the emperor brought to bear on the assassination of princes, explained to his subjects that

> it has been . . . my deepest desire to devote the years still granted to me by the grace of God to works of peace and spare my people from the harsh exigencies of war. The councils of Providence have decided otherwise. The machinations of a hate-filled opponent have compelled me, in order to defend my monarchy, its credibility, and power position, after long years of peace, to unsheathe the sword. . . . In this hour I am entirely conscious of all the consequences of my decision and of my responsibilities before the Almighty. I have examined and reflected on everything. With quiet conscience I go the way which duty dictates.[31]

The emperor's declaration of war came as a shock to many, for generally there had been no public perception of urgency in Austria-Hungary at the moment of the assassination in Sarajevo, no sense of emergency or of fateful events in the making during the long, brilliant summer days of July. To be sure, the murders nearly universally were regarded as heinous, and it was diplomatically a humiliating business as well, more of the sort of political misfortune to which poor Austria seemed prone and which necessitated that the public push aside happy thoughts.

True, the bodies of the dead archducal couple had to be brought home in state and then properly respected in Vienna before being carried on to Artstetten for burial. All of this disagreeable business had to be surrounded by suitable pomp, and this too was a matter of squabbling among court officials, all thereby bringing home that the venerable ancient realm of the Habsburgs had been dealt one more blow, one more insult that had to pass more or less unrequited; a nasty business. But the ill wind from Sarajevo generally was not thought to imply any action of greater magnitude, nothing more than unease and wearisome unpleasantness. Nothing relating to *raison d'état* seemed involved, nothing having to do with the jockeying among the great powers, nothing whether there be war or no. Quite the contrary, "it soon was apparent that the initial anger over the assassination had no staying power. Music soon again was heard in the evenings. . . . people laughed and made playful small talk with one another and trusted that the old kaiser's diplomats would find a means by which Belgrade would be held in check."[32]

The dead were duly received in Vienna, where they were eulogized, consecrated, and then carted off to Artstetten to be interred in the little crypt beneath the simple castle chapel there; ceremoniously brought out of Sarajevo to the Dalmatian coast, the bodies had been borne northward along the Adriatic coast on the imperial dreadnought *Viribus Unitis* to Austria's sea link with the world, Trieste. Once in the harbor of the Istrian seaport, the coffins were loaded onto a huge barge decked out for a funeral and brought, accompanied by vessels from the imperial and royal navy, flags at half-mast, to shore. Some older observers were chilled by the thought that almost the very same obsequy had been enacted forty-three years earlier when, in 1867, Admiral Tegetthof had brought the body of Archduke Maximilian, second brother of Franz Joseph and martyred emperor of Mexico, home from Queretaro. How many more such ceremonies could the old *Hofstaat* withstand before it crumbled under the press of modernism?[33]

All loyal Austrians were agreed that Franz Ferdinand had been a worthy man and that his duchess had been a charming, cheerful, winsome consort to the archduke. The archduke had been both socially and religiously conservative— perhaps too much so, for the archduke's general outlook seems to have had a baroque tenor to it that was fundamentally in conflict with the unfolding dynamics that were to define the twentieth century. But he also had been a hardworking man who took his inherited responsibilities seriously. Because he was somewhat ungainly and not especially personable, he had tended toward a quick temper and a sharply truthful tongue as well as a bark that belied the toothlessness of his bite; for this reason the archduke had not been especially beloved. But if he had not been a figure for popular times, he was nevertheless recognized as possessing energy, goodwill, and good sense. Some said, and many hoped, that he would have had some political magic up his sleeve that would have proved to be the means to put an end to the quarreling among Austria's nations.[34] After all, the nationalist perspective was the real interest of only a few; indeed, for the many, nationality in Austria was viewed as a fatal malaise that in the last analysis was not to be taken seriously because it was not seriously meant. The deed of Gavrilo Princip, of course, had demonstrated otherwise.

The journalist and gadfly Karl Kraus, by no means uncritical of the dynasty, perhaps best put into words what the loss of Franz Ferdinand signified for Austria-Hungary. Making use of his elegant, double-edged style while writing for his somewhat cranky *Die Fackel,* Kraus noted:

> Franz Ferdinand was the hope of this state, the hope for all those who believed that an orderly civil life could be grafted over the chaos of the half-formed

realm. He, who was the focus of so many high-flown hopes, was no Hamlet; he was Fortinbras. But if he were Fortinbras, then there is something very rotten beyond the borders of this state. . . . All in all . . . Franz Ferdinand's ways were the motive force within Austria's constitution . . . but still he will not be posthumously praised fifty times over in Waltz dreams. . . . He was no hail-fellow-well-met.[35]

If there was a public flare-up that caught the attention of the Austrian public during those summer months before Europe went to war, it was not fear over the approach of Armageddon; rather, it was consternation over what appeared to be a high-handed and disrespectful burial of the archducal couple by the Hofburg. The emperor's master of ceremonies, Prince Alfred von Montenuovo, seemed to have decreed that the duchess's lack of royal blood mandated a ceremonial outside of the baroque embrace of the vaunted Spanish court etiquette.[36] Many Austrians, and especially those of liberal outlook among the high aristocracy and haute bourgeoisie, were incensed by what they took as a mean-spirited and ungrateful handling that fell far short of fitting. Hindsight shows, however, that this public outburst was nothing more than a tempest in a teapot and that it was neither an intended slight nor an oversight. It was rather that the timeworn strictures of court ceremony indeed did bar the archducal couple from a customary imperial and royal burial. The emotions of the moment were not sufficient to cause either the old emperor or his major domo to unbend. Karl Kraus especially was outraged by what he viewed as an all too lackadaisical handling of a solemn event and held that his view reflected broad opinion when he wrote

> We will overlook the embarrassment that took place during the consecration at the railway station, where the casual activities of the public were allowed to be carried on as usual. Veterans and volunteer firemen forgot the seriousness of the moment and amused themselves in the vestibule of the station with beer and wursts; gentlemen with cigarettes on their lips walked about in the vicinity of the coffins, which had lain for more than an hour, stripped and bare, on the stone floor of the entranceway.[37]

Beyond the contretemps, however, councils of state were meeting, and they decided on war. So it was that during the sun-flecked days of July, Austria-Hungary, if with little outward show, slid irrevocably toward unsheathing the sword. While the public groused about the mismanaged fanfare surrounding the burial of the murdered archducal pair, the old emperor, perhaps a bit senile, certainly alone and isolated within his antediluvian nimbus, misread the international political landscape and daydreamed of reasserting the political influence of his dynasty. Worse, Franz Joseph's ministers also misread these same portents, while others among his courtiers used them to intrigue for their own advantage. Nothing appeared clear as the first week of August approached.

> Grief and indignation quarreled with one another. The heir is dead, a fact which this foul, self-seeking and irresponsible society that today governs over

us finds useful. And because he is dead, these flunkies triumph unashamedly. The old gentleman is entirely locked up within his senile egotism and thinks only of himself while the sole reaction one senses at court today is malicious joy.[38]

Despite the fact that it was action by Austria that triggered the process by which Europe marched to do battle, Vienna was the last of the capitals to formally involve itself in world war when, on the sixth of August, a declaration of war was issued against the Triple Entente. Franz Joseph, who had continued his holiday at Bad Ischl, immediately returned to Vienna so as to oversee Austria-Hungary's mobilization. Security dictated that the emperor occupy his apartments in suburban Schönbrunn rather than the usual ones in the Hofburg. In the company of Archduke Karl Franz Joseph, now the newly designated heir to the throne, the emperor left the imperial train at the Pensinger Bahnhof, where, under the watchful eyes of tense, silent onlookers, he settled into his waiting carriage and set off toward his golden-hued castle. There, after receiving the customary greeting from Mayor Joseph Weiskirchner, Franz Joseph disappeared into his private apartments. The Viennese, from that moment on, rarely caught sight of their old emperor until more than two years later, when his lifeless body was taken to the Hofburg by way of the Mariahilferstrasse to lie in state upon a flag-bedecked bier.[39]

It cannot be denied that Franz Joseph's magisterial isolation, perhaps only natural in the existence of a mid-nineteenth-century European monarch, had disastrous impact in the lives of Europe's states as the nineteenth century gave way to the twentieth. The nature of government by 1900, no doubt concomitant with the changes induced by the spread of capital and industry, had undergone, if silently, nevertheless the completest of transformations. Government now was less cohesive, less easily confined in the hands of a few, to say nothing of a single individual, no matter how invested with mystical authority. Indeed, by the twentieth century even the most authoritarian ruler could not have the reins of decision-making solely in his grasp. But what made matters unusually fluid for Austria-Hungary was that the old monarch not only thought he had a firm grasp, but at the same time was motivated by a perspective completely at odds with the unfolding complexities of the real political world. For example, his view of the assassination of a prince belonging to his house as first of all an insult to his blood and a blow to its pretensions prevented the old man from properly focusing on the wider, significant issues threatening to drive the realm into a war it could not win.[40]

At one level it is hard to fault the old emperor, for Franz Joseph himself was a victim of the hoary tradition of his house. The perception that the House of Habsburg ruled by the grace of God was officially reinforced every day, in many different ways; his likeness was on coinage and postage stamps; the emperor and his house were apostrophized in history textbooks and on monuments as well as on the facades of grandiose public buildings. Indeed, the hydra-headed apparatus of state evoked his presence. No wonder that Franz Joseph accepted the idea of a God-ordained mission for his house. Looking back from the late twentieth century as well as from the view of an outsider, it is all too easy to critique this perspective. But perhaps it is entirely different if one has never been on the outside. The emperor did not enjoy much personal comfort, and his vast wealth was in reality no more than an abstraction for him; indeed, he had a miserable existence in the center of splendor, for his life was full of worry, full of work and care. As he once summed up his position to the journalist Emmanuel Singer, "You are lucky, you can go to a coffeehouse!" And his letters to his wife repeatedly contain the phrase "I want out" *(aussi möchte i)*.

What must be stressed also is the idiosyncratic position in Austrian political culture occupied by the Habsburg dynasty at the moment of decision. Friedrich Austerlitz, editor of the Social Democratic *Arbeiter Zeitung,* insightfully assessed the significance of this fact when he observed that "it is remarkable how little absolutism has to do with the crown [in Austria], and therefore the emperor doesn't understand how power, absolute power, pushes in and positions itself so as to drive a wedge between the crown and the people.[41] What Austerlitz meant was that politicians in Vienna promoted their own agendas. But they did so always in the name of the emperor and so could carry their programs very far, even to the point of spilling over into the abyss.

What gave the emperor especially decisive authority at the fatal moment during the summer of 1914 was that democracy in Austria had taken a startling twist into parliamentary breakdown, with the result that the entire democratic process was enmeshed in hapless inaction. The government found it necessary to resort to Article 14 in order to function even at a minimum level. This recourse made the monarch the chief executive, if only in a de facto sense. Hence it was the peculiarities of the way the crown was operating within the political culture at the point of crisis that permitted the octogenarian emperor, once persuaded, to sanction Austria's embrace of war. In other words, there existed at that point of political confluence in the summer of 1914 little or no antidote to the danger resting in the senile egoism residing at the center of the state.

At the foreign office, Count Berchtold was rightly concerned to maintain the credibility of Austria-Hungary in the face of the subversive activities of its enemies. To ignore this problem was to weaken the future viability of the state. Hence, Vienna did have to react in some way to Serbia. However, if Serbia was dealt with faint-heartedly, Austria would lose Germany's backing and Berchtold would lose his personal credibility. Thus the foreign minister's posture all too easily made him a pawn of Berlin's policy.

In 1918 Friedrich Adler, after having been released from jail through the emperor's pardon for his murder of Count Stürgkh, claimed to have ironclad evidence supplied to him, albeit indirectly, by the Bavarian minister of war that the Austrian government had decided on war with Serbia by July 17 and informed Berlin of this decision.[42] If Adler was correct, then Vienna had taken the decision for war before it was so decided upon by Franz Joseph. Hence there may be some truth in the report of Field Marshal Alois Klepsch-Kloth, Austria's representative to German headquarters during the war, that in 1915, while discussing his role in the declaration of the war, the emperor stated: "What do you think! I am a constitutional monarch and not an absolute ruler, and I could do nothing else. I had all the official advisors to the crown lined up against me. I defended vigorously my position [for peace] against every position that would result in war. I did not easily allow myself to be convinced. But after my vain endeavors for fully three weeks, I had to give in."[43]

This view is reinforced by a statement made by then Minister of Finance Alexander Bilinski that on July 20 the emperor had before him, unsigned, what Franz Joseph considered to be an unacceptable ultimatum to Serbia because "it would be impossible for Russia to ignore this note."[44]

In any event, following the outbreak of war, knowing how frail the emperor was but fully aware that his office was the keystone in the apparatus holding together the disparate parts of the Habsburg realm, the emperor's entourage did all that was possible to shield Franz Joseph from the bad news that daily flowed from Austria's battlefronts. How successful this isolation was is moot, but certainly the emperor was spared some torment. However, the price was high: almost total withdrawal of the emperor from what already had been a minimum of normal human contact. So, for example, the gardens of Schönbrunn were closed to the public and the monarch was persuaded to eschew his daily trips into the city. There was no more theater, and the visits of his dear and close friend, Frau Schratt, were short and infrequent. The pleasures at Bad Ischl were forsaken, and thereby he deprived himself of his most usual opportunity for the company of his daughters and grandchildren. More than ever, the emperor chained himself at his desk, reading in his gloomy, drafty apartment those reports that his advisors had permitted to filter through from the outside.

The Viennese, perhaps because they were giving vent to their own apprehensions concerning the future, took to conjuring up an image of their emperor as a sorrowing as well as lonely figure:

> Out in Schönbrunn Park
> Sits an old man
> Full of care and concern . . .
> Beloved, good old man,
> Do not be heavy of heart;
> That you are our emperor,
> Vienna rejoices.
> Beloved, good old man,
> Do not be heavy of heart.
> Beloved, good old man,
> In Schönbrunn.[45]

The old monarch's subjects had gone to war readily enough. Indeed, foreign observers, given to predicting Austria's quick demise, were surprised by the number of Franz Joseph's boisterous subjects who had gathered on the squares throughout the Dual Monarchy to rejoice that at last their old sovereign had unsheathed his sword against the unholy demons that for so long had been menacing his realm. Smiling back at pretty girls, young men, like those throughout Europe, marched off in a shower of flowers, buoyed by the cheering and singing populace, to commit murder. At the same time Franz Joseph Hayden's "Gott erhalte" was heard as Austrians everywhere reaffirmed their loyalty to their emperor. Patently, many Austrians did not immediately share that anguish so pervasive in Franz Joseph's war manifesto.

Austrians hardly were to be blamed for their optimism. The man in the street knew no more than he read, and this he did very little of. He had been told, and he believed it passionately, that this war was a just one. He also had been assured that it would be short; moreover, human instinct caused him to believe that the sacrifices chiefly would be borne by the enemy. The Austrian soldier would return home to a hero's welcome, garlanded and at the same time unburdened of the anxiety spawned out of nearly a half century of unresolved conflict among Europe's great powers. So, for example, even Vienna's socialist daily, assuredly no rubber stamp either for the House of Habsburg or for the idea of war, threw its support behind the Austrian government. The *Arbeiter Zeitung* told its readership that "events threaten the soil of the Fatherland. Not only the state but the nations within it are threatened. The state must defend itself if the nations are to remain free. . . . In time of danger everyone must support his country."[46]

If, however, the masses responded to the cue given by their leaders, who were brimming over with enthusiasm for the idea of war, the initial confidence of those same leaders evaporated as soon as they saw that it was one matter to act with rifles cocked and quite another after the trigger had been released; that is, as soon as the full damage stood revealed as unexpectedly great, all saw that a fatal step had been taken that now was irreversible. The first weeks of war witnessed resolve replaced by vacillation; then vacillation turned into consternation. At that point, those councils that initially had favored war now stood haplessly backtracking. For example, the Hungarian minister-president, Count Stephan Tisza, perhaps always fearful of this war in his heart, now proclaimed that he felt Serbia could not be forced to feel repentance, and further announced he wanted no more unruly Serbs annexed and added to the lands of St. Stephen.[47] Conrad von Hötzendorf, faced with a collapsing Austrian front in Galicia under the pressure of Russian troops especially in and around the fortress at Przemysl, no longer displayed his usual overweening confidence in the Dual Monarchy's war machine but rather watched the growing threat to the realm in an agony of apprehension.[48] Indeed, because Conrad feared that advancing Russian troops were on the threshold of spilling over onto the Carpathian basin, thereby bringing the war into the very heart of Hungary, Conrad demanded immediate peace with Russia.

If St. Petersburg was not deflected, argued the chief of staff, Italy, joined by Rumania, would seize the moment to side with the Entente so as to rob the Dual Monarchy of those coastal territories vital to its continued existence.[49]

Franz Joseph seems belatedly to have recalled that he had always been unlucky in war. In this respect, when Archduchess Zita congratulated the emperor in June of 1915 because of some initial success by his troops in holding back the Russians, Franz Joseph, to Zita's consternation, responded by

> laugh[ing] benignly and say[ing] to me:
> " Yes, so it had begun. And now it will go worse and worse. . . . This time the outcome of the war will be completely disastrous."
> "But Your Majesty! That is not possible," I answered. "Is it not for a righteous cause for which we stand ?"
> But he laughed a little and said in his peculiar, rueful way:
> "You still are very young that you believe in the victory of right. . . . This time it is the end."[50]

There could, however, be no retreat from the complexities that had led to mobilization. Perhaps even if it had been otherwise, the existing atmosphere of political carnivorousness only would have made stepping back be taken as a sign of weakness and thereby a signal to the other powers that they might fall on Austria's carcass. There was nothing other than for the Dual Monarchy to carry on with the war and hope against hope that its iron-fisted ally, the German Empire, would pull the fat out of the fire. It was too late to heed the warning words of the murdered heir to the throne, written in 1913 in his hyperbolic style, that

> it would be our misfortune should we become embroiled in a great war with Russia. Should we engage in a preventive war against Serbia, we would overrun the rabble in a short time; but what then? What should we have achieved? All of Europe would view us as the destroyers of peace. And God preserve us if we should annex Serbia, a totally criminal land of king-murderers and rogues.[51]

Ironic as it was that it was his corpse that proved to be the casus belli of the very war he warned against, events proved Franz Ferdinand percipient; by the close of 1914, the full horror of world war stood exposed and, as a result, chauvinism had lost its refulgence. And even after her auspicious start, by the autumn of 1914 the Dual Monarchy had lost out in a murderous contest with the Russian army in Galicia. More embarrassing, the *K.u.K.* army had failed in its initial efforts to take Belgrade, the little Serbian capital just south of her border with Austria-Hungary.[52]

Reluctantly, but nonetheless according to time-honored precedent when viewed from within the parameters of her history, Austria-Hungary turned to diplomacy in an effort to quiet the political storms raging at her borders. Wags shook their heads and noted that whereas for Prussia war might be viewed as an extension of diplomacy, for Austria diplomacy seemed the extension of war.

Nevertheless, the men on the Ballhausplatz moved quickly in the hopes that, as so often before during the long, unlucky reign of Franz Joseph, territory might be ceded on Austria's perimeters so that the core might be preserved. Finesse was to end what war had begun.

That Austria-Hungary desired a shift from fetid battlefields to green baize tables of conciliation was signaled by the resignation of its foreign minister, Count Leopold Berchtold—as accident would have it, on the sixty-sixth anniversary of Emperor Franz Joseph's accession to the throne in what by then must have seemed as a distant and far simpler past.

Berchtold was replaced by Baron Stephen Burian, an experienced diplomat cast in the traditional mode of guileful caution long associated with the men working in the Metternichian Ballhaus.[53] Burian faced two immediate tasks: he was to keep the Kingdom of Italy a partner, albeit an inactive one, in the Triple Alliance, and he was to bring about an end to the war by means of wide-ranging negotiations.[54] His tasks were large, and the obstacles to these monumental. By promising, for example, even small chunks of territory to ambitious Italy, Vienna put the Entente in the position, should it be victorious, of being able to outbid her so as to offer Rome even more territory at the expense of Austria-Hungary. Italy, consequently, met Vienna's proposals with more demands until a point was reached where even the emperor bridled at Italy's desire to tear from the Austrian crown lands great slices of the Tyrol, the city of Trent, and the district of Trentino, and all of this in return for Rome's adhesion to a pledge already made in the first instance as a partner in the Triple Alliance.[55] On being rebuffed by the old emperor, Italy then turned to a willing Entente and concluded clandestinely in March of 1915 the Treaty of London, whereby in exchange for the most sanguine expectations with regard to Austrian territory, Italy would declare war against the Central Powers the following May. Italy's joining the Entente came in the wake of, and to some extent because of, Austria's military reverses, suffered at the hands of the Russians in Austro-Galicia. Most fatefully, however, by joining in with and thereby bolstering the perception in the Entente of an increased chance of victory, Italy also greatly weakened Burian's chance of achieving a negotiated general settlement.[56]

Burian's task was made more difficult in that he sought a negotiated and rational settlement, meaning one that as nearly as possible would be based on the status quo ante bellum. But this task had to be carried out in an era of popular government, when the emotions of the masses had been stirred violently by unforeseen, unparalleled, and escalating human and material losses. Burian confronted a situation not faced by diplomacy previously, where polite private bargains always were possible when the efforts of mercenaries failed on the field of battle. Burian had the nearly impossible task of delivering a rational and reasonable settlement in the face of the belligerent governments' need to produce a peace that would both justify and sanctify the outpouring of young blood since August of 1914. Burian tried, but—perhaps because his motivation was framed by his having operated for far too long within rarefied circles of the aristocracy's last preserve—hardly was aware that diplomacy now required popular support. Defeated on the field of battle, her people demoralized, Austria was bereft of that leverage necessary to extricate herself by means of negotiation at the peace table. Nevertheless an appeal did go out from the Ballhausplatz urging that the belligerents publicly state their war aims in preparation for coming together at the peace table. At the same time, the Dual Monarchy assured world opinion that it had no territorial ambitions. That Serbia be chastened so that in the future Austria-Hungary might rest in peace was sufficient. It was at this point that Berlin presented Burian with a rude awakening. Unlike Austria, German arms had experienced overwhelming tactical success on the battlefield; moreover, the German high command had taken these for strategic victories with permanent increased power advantages for the *Reich*. Berlin's response to the Ballhaus was both aggressive and bullying. The German *Reich* demanded British and French colonies as well as territory in Europe belonging to Belgium, France, and Russia. German megalomania stood exposed; but worse, Vienna unwittingly had demonstrated her inability to curb the appetite of her ally.[57]

More wisely (but perhaps it was more of a display of diplomatic cunning than a reflection of sincere statesmanship), the Entente chose the high road; the hapless Burian therefore had only presented Austria's enemies a forum in which to recount apologues. Dragging a reluctant St. Petersburg along, London and Paris came forth with self-indulgent but inspiring aphorisms brimming over with words expressing democracy, justice, and the right of nations to self-determination. If in fact, when compared with those deeds that created the British and French empires, the Entente response really was not credible, nevertheless it did seem so at the time and went far in tilting neutral opinion in the Entente's favor. Burian's peace initiative had fallen far short of its goal; he had succeeded, albeit abetted by the arrogance of his ally on the Wilhelmstrasse, only in handing a propaganda victory to Austria-Hungary's enemies. Their own clumsy performance notwithstanding, the Germans were furious; Vienna was depressed; and the fighting went on.[58]

The Austrian position worsened as the spring of 1915 faded into the heat of summer. The Austrian high command was faced with not only shoring up the Russian front but also dealing with the Italians on the southern front along the Piave. In the apportioning of her military resources so as to meet these expanding threats, it became obvious that the war had reached proportions far beyond Austria-Hungary's strength. There was nothing else, however, but to fall in with Berlin's demands that the *Reich* augment both the *K.u.K.* forces as well as its command so as to render the Dual Monarchy's military resources subservient to the German war machine. And so the monarchy submitted to this humiliation.[59] But more than humiliation was involved, for the loss of her independence of military action—and in time of war, the loss of military independence signified a concomitant loss of political independence—rendered proud Austria no more than a cog in a potential German central European empire. This change in the relationship between Berlin and Vienna also seemed to signify that the Habsburgs no longer might act as defenders of Austro-Slavdom from pan-German impulses. And finally, submission to the German *Reich* meant that the realm of the Habsburgs was tied to German megalomania, for only Berlin could play the role of Vienna's savior, and that only providing Berlin wrested victory from its opponents.[60]

Unlike members of the emperor's entourage, and perhaps the emperor himself, the Austrian high command, dominated by German Austrians drawn from the traditional officers' corps, was not unhappy in its subservient role to Germany. This attitude was not because the command was predisposed toward disloyalty to the Habsburgs or because of pan-German sentiments, but because it saw in this subservience the only means of preserving the traditional position of the dynasty in south-central Europe.[61] Moreover, German military rule was soft-pedaled in Hungary as well because the Magyar-dominated government in Budapest quite rightly saw the preservation of its domination in the lands of St. Stephen as grounded on German support. Thereby, Magyar support of Germany's role in the Dual Monarchy ensured continued Magyar hegemony within its own lands, an aim already achieved even before the war but certainly enhanced because of hard-pressed Vienna's dependence on Hungarian foodstuffs; in any event, this was an aim that was always at the root of Magyar policy.[62]

Gradually it dawned on Austria's Slavs that because the House of Austria was second to that of the Hohenzollerns within the Dual Alliance, the Habsburgs no longer could play the arbitrator between German and Slav and hence the ancient house no longer exercised what had been viewed as its historic function within south-central Europe. Many Slavic Austrians, frightened that their ruling house had submitted to an aggressive and brutal German regime, began to move away from Vienna and toward whatever might preserve for them their cultural sense of self. At first the Slavs' slide away from Austria was imperceptible. But it gained momentum with the escalation of privation and war-weariness.[63] Nevertheless, the desertions of her Slavs took many of those German Austrians faithful to old Austria by surprise:

> The aristocrats all were German-speaking Austrians attending the imperial court in Vienna. A few, like the Lobkowitz and Chotek and so on, regarded themselves as being Bohemian ... [but only] used Czech as a colloquial speech. The industrialists almost always were German; bank directors and lawyers mostly of Jewish stock [also] stood on the side of the Germans. Small business people, mostly Jews, made no distinction.[64]

It was against this massively darkening background that the old emperor was heard to mutter half out loud that if by the end of the year success could not be wrested on the battlefield then he, Franz Joseph, would bring the war to an end.[65] Brave words, but irrelevant ones; once begun, the course of the struggle lay well beyond the reach of the will of the senile old emperor, who, after all, perhaps was only confusing his past sovereign pretensions with the powerlessness of his present. For in point of fact, the mundane and daily operation of government had, by 1915, passed into other hands. The usual apparatus within which Franz Joseph worked had been modified so as to take into account not only his great age but also military exigencies. So representatives from army headquarters were placed alongside the state-appointed governors. The military appointees in turn developed an administrative apparatus parallel to the civilian ones and, as a consequence of the demands of war, tended to supersede them. Under the circumstances, it was only natural that primacy would redound to the military command at the expense of the constitutional, civil arm of government. It was only natural too that de facto constitutional modifications took place by which the crown came to coordinate all political policy through the army's general staff. The unavoidable result was that the civil administration lost leverage in the overall decision-making processes of government. A reflection of the escalating military influence within Austria's war government was the abridgement of popular civil rights—as provided within the framework of the emergency powers granted the crown by Austria's constitution, to be sure, but thereby too strengthening antidemocratic, antinational, pan-German impulses that could be only obnoxious to citizens identifying with Austria's subject nations.[66]

A normal check to military rule in Austria-Hungary might have been expected to come from the two parliaments belonging to the two halves of the state. But in addition to the disinclination of the Magyar-dominated Hungarian parliament at Budapest to overcome rule through military fiat, the parliament in Vienna remained prorogued. Although unruly, the latter was popularly based and reflective of the nationality makeup of the Austrian crown lands. As such it was under the thumb of no political party or person. But even prior to the outbreak of war, the lower parliamentary house, the Austrian Abgeordnetenhaus, had been mired in political obstructionism emanating out of Austria's apparently never-ending nationality strife; moreover, Franz Joseph had been forced to adjourn that body in 1913 by making use of his emergency powers for executive government in time of legislative breakdown. While not necessarily answering the dispute as to whether it was wise policy or not, the chaotic precedent set by the Abgeordnetenhaus in the course of Austria's prewar nationality strife does provide an argument as to why that body was convened neither during the summer of 1914 nor during the first two years of war. Neither the emperor nor his minister-president, Count Karl Stürgkh, wanted to chance a demonstration of those infamous centrifugal nationality forces at the very moment that the monarchy was beset by war. It must be admitted, however, that the failure of the political leadership to convoke the parliament (especially during the crisis days in 1914), although in strict conformity with the terms of Austria's constitution, gave ammunition to those who would claim that the Dual Monarchy was both decrepit and unworthy of salvation.[67] More damaging in the longer run was that without a viable parliament sitting in Vienna to guard over the state's constitutional life, the executive branch, at the head of which was the by now enervated crown, lacked the potential support of a strong and legitimate political force that might have been set against the waxing Austrian, and German, military authority, which was threatening to destroy those delicate and interlocking forces that made the Dual Monarchy viable in the first place. Indeed, in the eyes of the majority of Austrians who desired both political and cultural democracy, there seemed to have returned to the fore those elements that would turn back the clock to the era of the flood tide of antidemocratic German-Magyar ascendancy.[68]

The most vivid protest against the Austrian war government—and indeed, against the reality of the war itself—came from within the political establishment and took place in a most unlikely forum: a proper dining room in Vienna's fashionable Hotel Meissl und Schadn. For it was in that dining room on the Neuermarkt that Minister-President Stürgkh, on October 18, 1916, violently met his end at the hands of an assassin. The murderer turned out to be a well-known Social Democrat and Marxist idealist, Dr. Friedrich Adler. Adler, who also was the son of Dr. Viktor Adler, the doyen of the Austrian Social Democratic Workers' Party, cut down Count Stürgkh by shooting him at close range while the minister-president was taking lunch. The young man afterward proclaimed that he had committed his crime self-consciously in protest against the government's refusal to convoke the parliament. But the public perceived, and to some extent applauded, more substance to the deed. They saw in it a protest against the conditions of the war itself, and instead of damnation, Adler won outpourings of support, albeit much muted in the press because of war censorship, from usually legitimate political quarters. Indeed, the young assassin became a kind of heroic antihero and gave substance to some of the twists and turns in Karl Kraus's notorious book, *The Last Days of Humanity*.[69] In time, almost as if they were in some sort of theater rather than dealing with political reality, the Viennese came to be divided between those who would condemn the murder and those who would praise it.[70] The contradiction and pathos surrounding young Adler's act of defiance is observed not only in official memoranda but also in the agony of sundered loyalties that surface in the letters of those closest to the event. So, for example, the heartbroken father, Viktor Adler, wrote sorrowingly to the Social Democratic publisher Karl Kautsky that "one can no longer question which side is right, but only on which side is there the greatest frequency of unright. . . . It [is a question] that has to do with our hearts as much as with our heads."[71]

So great was the public stridency surrounding young Adler that the government could only remain on the sidelines in hapless embarrassment, for patently the murderer's champions extended far beyond the political confines of Austro-Marxism; indeed, his act, wrapped in its own genre of political liturgy, appeared to symbolize the growing frustration and anger that was the concomitant to the spread of war-induced deprivation and death. Moreover, it seemed to some observers that the murder of Count Stürgkh opened the wellsprings of malaise that went beyond issues of war and government to the very heart of well-nigh organic but intractable questions having to do with the very fundamentals of Europe's evolving military-industrial civilization. By now a new terror had supplemented older ones: the horror of youth being sacrificed with cold-blooded calculation. There was abhorrence too in the accompanying destruction of traditional values that was certainly one consequence of the human destruction taking place on the battlefields, all cloaked in catchwords that appeared to serve hoary traditions now irrelevant to the well-being of those young men forcibly marched to igno-minious slaughter. The resulting spread of apathy in politically responsible quar-ters, and the gathering hostility among the generality, later was aptly put into words by Friedrich Adler during his trial, when he chastised those who would "praise the Fatherland . . . no matter what the cost and without regard to what is uncovered that is reprehensible about its policies."[72]

The circumstances of Count Stürgkh's murder might be viewed as a harbinger of Austria-Hungary's political disintegration. But the death of the old emperor and king, Franz Joseph I, on the evening of November 21, 1916, can be viewed as the great psychological divide between old Austria and the unfolding agonies of modern Danubia. Moreover, Franz Joseph's death came at a moment before a final resolution had been reached on the grim fields of battle and hence perhaps when the presence of an Austrian King Candaules was more than ever required by the state. The deceased monarch, his reign extending back to 1848, had ruled for more than two generations, and indeed had outlived many of his subjects within those generations. In this sense, the old emperor had transcended ordinary human mortals to become a remote but nevertheless fixed pole in an otherwise rapidly shifting sociopolitical universe.

Despite the opposition of his perspective to the unfolding political reality, Franz Joseph's death was a loss deeply felt by his subjects. They had long been accustomed to drawing a sense of stability from his remote but all-pervasive presence. Many were convinced that his ubiquity ensured that, behind the vast and impersonal facade of his government, Franz Joseph exerted a benign influ-ence working to set right small matters and thereby preserving his subjects' tight little world from the uncertain political tides that threatened to overwhelm from without. In a word, he had been their leader. Now the grim, conservative old monarch was dead, and his departure had been a shock for, despite his eighty-six years, the visit from the grim reaper had been both sudden and unexpected.[73] Long inclined toward bronchitis, Franz Joseph had suffered a severe attack in the early autumn of 1916. However, drawn to his desk by his unyielding sense of duty, the old gentleman had spurned the rest that he required. On the twentieth of November, the bronchitis turned to pneumonia; early the following evening his aides found that the emperor was unable to rise from a short nap. Several hours later, Franz Joseph quietly slipped into unconsciousness, and then into death.

Timeworn protocol was maintained to the very end. The emperor's death watch was kept by his children and grandchildren and, because custom also demanded it, by the heir to the throne, more distant members of the dynasty, his entourage, and his personal servants. It was the ascendant emperor, Karl I, who broke protocol by personally escorting the deceased's closest personal friend, Frau Katharina Schratt—who was widely known as "Die Freudin"—to the emperor's bedside. Karl had found the actress shut out and grieving at the entrance to Franz Joseph's apartments. He wanted her to have the right to bid adieu to her old friend. And the actress did so gracefully, giving Franz Joseph a silent kiss while placing symbols of their enduring friendship, two red roses, in his hands. The tormented emperor thereby departed from life at the instant of the most grievous troubles for his realm; yet, at the same time, he left it having been enfolded, albeit in the very last seconds of life, in that human warmth and sympathy that he rarely had experienced as the reigning patriarch of the House of Habsburg.[74]

It was with resignation born out of a premonition of overriding fate that the Viennese observed the prescribed seven days of obsequies that followed the emperor's death. Not a few understood that in bidding farewell to the monarch, they were casting off not only from the state that for so long had both exasperated and shielded them, but from a tradition and culture as well. What had been ebbing away during two years of bloodletting finally seemed to have departed with the soul of Franz Joseph.

No court in Europe better knew how to evoke the phantasmic mood of imperial last rites than Austria's *Hofstaat*. Supervision belonged to the court's major domo, Prince Montenuovo, and he minutely saw to it that these last rites were carried out with traditional and somber Habsburg pomp. The prince appeared to command even the weather for the sharp, gray November days gave added solemnity to the ceremonies. The sun was banished most of an entire week. A frosty mist clung to the surface of things, creating a baleful lens that transformed the elegant forms lining the Ringstrasse into vaporous funeral props. The dark greatcoats worn by the imperial entourage complemented and enhanced the macabre ambience called forth by the Catholic funeral mass.

Stubbornly clinging to the Spanish court etiquette, Montenuovo had the emperor's body placed in state at Schönbrunn for forty-eight hours. Then, always strictly as prescribed, the imperial bier was hoisted aboard a huge and majestic ebony catafalque, which possessed its own brooding aura from having borne past Habsburgs to their last resting place, and carried to the hallowed Hofburg in the heart of the residence and capital city. A second period of lying in state followed, culminating in a private burial service in the old castle's ancient Gothic chapel.

The public rituals were resumed on the Switzerhof. Once again the great catafalque, drawn by eight carefully matched black steeds, funeral bunting muffling the sound of hooves striking on cobblestones, bore the imperial and royal remains. Entering the mourning-draped Heldenplatz by way of the Switzertor, the procession was joined by a flock of black-clothed courtiers. Slowly, exuding majestic resignation, the dark spectacle made its way through the Heldentor and on into the midst of the crowd massed on the Burgring and all along the Ringstrasse. The procession wound its way over the Rotenturmstrasse by way of the Schwarzenburgplatz and the Franz Joseph Kai, toward the great, Gothic Stephensdom.

After a second public mass within the cavernous cathedral, the body of Franz Joseph a third time was hauled onto the catafalque and brought by way of the Kartnerstrasse on to the Neuermarkt and before the faded magenta facade of the Church of the Capuchins. There the bier was stripped of its splendid trappings and laid bare while, in stylized cant, Prince Montenuovo begged admittance so that the body of his poor cousin might be placed alongside those of his wife and son, resting deep in the building's vault. The bier was admitted, not carrying the remains of the emperor and king but carrying those of a humble man and sinner. And so the door closed on the Kaiser's burial vault.[75]

The baroque rite was at an end. With it passed the last fragile link between the old Austria and the violent, bleeding Austria of 1916. At the moment of this flood tide of grief there was no hand capable of steadying the helm of the Austrian ship of state. Not a few Viennese understood that an era irrevocably had come to an end. A young member of the bourgeoisie, Alice Herdan-Zuckmayer, recalled that

> My mother and I were invited by a friend, who had a great apartment over-looking the Kartnerring, to come and watch the funeral procession. For the last time we saw archdukes, princes, and counts parading before us on horses or in wagons in their splendid uniforms and representing the monarchy from Hungary, Poland, Bohemia, Croatia, Slovenia, and many other lands. The new Emperor Karl and the Empress Zita walked together with the little heir to the throne in this long parade, this beautiful procession of outworn significance and beauty. My mother and I stood alone at the window. Suddenly I took her left hand with my right one as if we ought to hold fast to one another. . . . On returning home, Luise took our coats and followed us into the salon. Luise sobbed, wrung her hands, and asked: "Is it all gone, is it all over?" "Yes," answered my mother, "it is all over, not right now, Luise, but soon!"[76]

Notes

1. Field Marshal Conrad von Hötzendorf, chief of the (Austrian-Hungarian) general staff, quotes the emperor as saying, on July 28, 1914, "If the monarchy must go to the ground at least it should go to the ground honorably." See Franz Count Conrad von Hötzendorf, *Aus Meiner Dienstzeit: 1906–1918*, 5 volumes (Vienna: Rikola Verlag, 1923), vol. IV, p. 162.

2. See Albert Freiherr von Margutti, *Vom alten Kaiser: Personliche Erinnerungen an Franz Joseph I* (Vienna: Leonhardt Verlag, 1921). The historian Hugo Hantsch maintains that the chief reason why Austria-Hungary went to war was to underscore its great-power status, thereby maintaining the viability of the Triple Alliance. See Hugo Hanstch, "Kaiser Franz Joseph und Probleme der Franzisko-Josephineschen: die Aus-

senpolitik," *Probleme der Franzisko-Josephineschen Zeit 1848–1916* (Vienna: Schriftenreihe des österreichischen Ost-Sudosteuropa Institut, 1967), vol. I, p. 31. Another historian, F.R. Bridge, agrees with Hantsch with the added admonition that if the Dual Monarchy had failed to react forcefully to the murders in Sarajevo, the result would have been the creation of another anti-Habsburg Balkan league dominated by Russia, which would have been the severest threat yet to Austria's great power position. See F.R. Bridge, *From Sadowa to Sarajevo: The Foreign Policy of Austria-Hungary, 1866–1914* (London: Routledge and Kegan Paul, 1972), pp. 371–375ff. For a view that takes into consideration the above points but that nevertheless still comes down hard on the Austrian decision, see Samuel R. Williamson, "Influence, Power and the Policy Process: The Case of Franz Ferdinand, 1906–1914," *The Historical Journal* 17, no. 2 (1974).

By 1912, the Eastern Question, an elastic euphemism for the eternal quagmire of Balkan politics, had heated up to a bellicose and dangerous level for Austria-Hungary. While fully appreciating that wars among the Balkan powers, especially given that the sinister foreign policy of the Russian Empire often stood behind these outbreaks, might spill over and flood Austria-Hungary with its virulence, Vienna had stopped short of military intervention either because Franz Joseph did not view them as directly challenging his sovereign power or because Archduke Franz Ferdinand refused to countenance a war policy. Premeditated murder directed against his house was another matter for the old emperor. Beyond removing a chief opponent of war from the scene, the treacherous assassination, in the eyes of the old dynast whose perspective had been forged in an era reaching back to Napoleon Bonaparte, hit at the very core of dynastic credibility necessary for the House of Habsburg if it was to carry on its duty, given through divine inspiration, to uphold God's Catholic and Christian order. Modern tenets of popular government notwithstanding, the old emperor personally had clung to his view that the source of political authority was divine, not popular, and that the divisions seen in the worldly political order of states lay not in those envisioned by the emerging nationalities but in the existing dynastic ones apotheosized by history. See Josef Schnieder, ed., *Kaiser Franz Joseph I und sein Hof: erinnerungen und Schilderungen aus dem Nachgelassenen Papieren eines persönlichen Ratgebers* (Vienna: Paul Zsolnay Verlag, 1984), pp. 155–165. See also Roberta Kann, "Erzherzog Franz Ferdinand und Graf Berchtold als Aussenminister, 1912–1914," in *Erzherzog Franz Ferdinand Studien* (Munich: R. Oldenbourg, 1976), pp. 206–240, and Heinrich Graf von Lützow, *Im Diplomatischen Dienst der K.u.K. Monarchie* (Munich: R. Oldenbourg, 1971), pp. 202–217. Lützow writes of a general depression that took hold in Austria's governing circles because of the Russian-inspired Balkan wars of 1911–1912 and the consequent pressure exerted on the Dual Monarchy to intervene into these matters.

3. Franz Joseph's parting words to Field Marshal Conrad Hötzendorf, on August 15, 1914, as the latter left the Hofburg to take up his position on the Russian front were indicative of the emperor's mood: "God grant that all goes well; however, if it should go wrong, that I will hold up *[durchhalten]*." Hötzendorf, *Aus Meiner Dienstzeit,* vol. IV, p. 399.

4. See, for example, Nora Furstin Fugger, *Im Glanz der Kaiser-Zeit* (Vienna: Amalthea, 1980), p. 437.

5. See Ferdinand Fauland, *Vorwiegend heiter: Von einem, der auszog General zu werden* (Vienna: Styria, 1980) and Erich Alban Berg, *Als der Adler noch zwei Köpfe hatte: Ein Florilegium: 1885–1918* (Vienna: Styria, 1980), especially pp. 184–187.

6. Quoted in Berg, *Als der Adler noch zwei Köpfe hatte,* p. 186.

7. Erich Feigl, ed., *Kaiserin Zita: Legende und Wahrheit: Nach Gesprachen und Dokumenten herausgeben von Erich Feigl* (Vienna: Amalthea, 1977), pp. 165–167.

8. Fauland, *Vorwiegend heiter.* The above, from Fauland, is quoted in Berg, *Als der Adler noch zwei Köpfe hatte,* pp. 181–187. This description is verified by the military

governor of Bosnia-Herzegovina, Count Potiorek, in his report to the Austrian minister-president on June 29, 1918. See Ludwig Bittner and Hans Uebersberger, ed., *Österreich-Ungarns Aussenpolitik von der Bosnischen Krise 1908 bis zum Kriegsausbruch 1914,* 26 volumes (Nendeln/Liechtenstein: Kraus Reprint, 1972), vol. 26, pp. 215–218.

9. For another, if quite similar, summary of these same tragic events, see Friedrich Weissensteiner, *Franz Ferdinand, Der verhinderte Herrscher: Zum 70. Jahrstag von Sarajewo* (Vienna: Österreichischer Bundesverlag, 1983), pp. 10–51.

10. See Egon César Conte Corti and Hans Sokol, *Kaiser Franz Joseph* (Vienna: Verlag Styria, 1965), pp. 357–367.

11. Ibid., p. 367.

12. Erich Graf Kilemansegg, *Kaiserhaus, Staatsmäner und Politiker* (Vienna: Verlag für Geschichte und Politik, 1966), pp. 97–98.

13. It would seem that the emperor's personal dislike of the marriage and/or all or some of the actors in the dispute determined to some extent the decision that the archduke's marriage be morganatic. For a thorough discussion surrounding Franz Ferdinand's morganatic union, see Johann Christoph Allmayer-Beck, *Ministerpräsident Baron Beck: Ein Staatsmann des alten Österreich* (Munich: R. Oldenbourg, 1956), pp. 34–55.

14. The historian R.A. Kann pointed out that the "essence [of dynasticism] was neither in personal contacts nor in so-called monarchical solidarity so as to maintain and achieve common objectives . . . much more, [it was] a matter of common allegiance to self-preservation within each system of Machtpolitik. Humanitarianism steps into the background." See Robert A. Kann, *Erzherzog Franz Ferdinand Studien* (Munich: R. Oldenbourg, 1976), p. 11. See also Kann's "The Aristocracy of the Habsburg Empire in the Eighteenth Century," *Encyclopedia Britannica,* 15th edition, 1974.

15. See Josef Schneider, *Kaiser Franz Josef I und sein Hof,* pp. 8–10, 13–15, 73.

16. See F.R. Bridge, *The Habsburg Monarchy Among the Great Powers, 1815–1918* (Oxford: Berg, 1990), pp. 245ff.

17. Ibid. Francis Roy Bridge also gives substance to this view when he states that Austria-Hungary went to war in 1914 because failure to react firmly would have brought about another Balkan League centered on Serbia and Rumania, but dominated by Russia, which would have put the Dual Monarchy's great-power position in question, presumably to Germany's intense dissatisfaction. See Bridge, *From Sadowa to Sarajevo,* pp. 371–372.

18. The minister of finance, Leon, Ritter Leon von Bilinski, stated that in October 1911, Franz Joseph told him regarding Serbia's occupation of Montenegro that "if they [the Serbs] don't give in within a week, we will let it [war] come about." See Robert A. Kann, *Kaiser Franz Joseph und der Ausbruch des Weltkreiges: Eine Betrachung ueber den Quellenwert der Aufzeichung von Dr. Heinrich Kanner* (Vienna: Akademie der Wissenschaft, 1971), p. 22, and in general pp. 20–23. More than the guilt of one, the obscure Gavrilo Princip, was involved in what Franz Joseph saw as an inexorable process compelling him to punish. Whether by omission or commission, the government of the Serbian king, Alexander Karageorgevič, himself descended from murderous brigands, was culpable as well. The Karageorgevič dynasty therefore must meet its fate before the force of Austrian arms. And so it was that an order of priorities long outworn in the workaday world of the European twentieth century welled up to engulf not only the realm of the octogenarian ruler but the entire continent (and eventually the United States of America) in violence of unheard-of proportions. It was the hoary view of a fading world that became the ideological linchpin that altered the course of world history. In one perspective, but of course the narrowest of ones, the First World War was Franz Joseph's war in that it was a by-product, at least insofar as Austria's role was concerned, of political myopia rendered more acute because of the emperor's age. That same myopia,

moreover, had engulfed the *Hofstaat* as a result of the interaction between the Dual monarchy's internal political problems and Franz Joseph's view toward the position and prestige of its emperor and king. Room thereby was allowed for the machinations of members of the imperial entourage, which, in turn, obfuscated other issues belonging to the wider, international political sphere. This obfuscation abetted those considerations that led to the conclusion of war. There were too many who were responsible for Austria-Hungary's power position who thought they foresaw a little war with Serbia that would win Vienna cheap political victories; they imagined too that such a war would be a useful instrument for the advancement of one's career.

The perspective, and priorities, of the old emperor and his councils also must be understood within the larger context of the aspirations and conduct of the other European great powers. Here it is clear that the position taken by Austria-Hungary against Serbia, and made manifest by the dubious ultimatum dispatched to Belgrade on July 21, 1914, had little to do directly with the general factors that escalated the Austro-Serb fracas to the level of world war. The complex, often eccentric, motives yielding those decisions that triggered the First World War, complex in that a plethora of individuals scattered throughout Europe were involved and eccentric because motive always is interlaced with the subjective judgment of individuals, could not be overcome or otherwise dominated by a single will. World War I therefore has to be understood as being the end product of the interplay of perspectives and interests of a myriad of individuals belonging to a sociopolitical aggregate, and as such, the whole defies a rational and orderly rendition.

But an understanding of history is computed on different levels, and on one of these levels of history, causation can be seen as emanating out of the perspective of individual actors. There can be little doubt as to Franz Joseph's perspective, and that it sadly was out of focus with the realities of the opening of the twentieth century. His perspective had little experience in common with an era that centered around the machine, mass literacy, and the spread of political egalitarianism and, along with the enfranchisement of the masses, the growth and spread of nationalism. Born during the era of Metternich and in the afterglow of the great Napoleon, it was beyond the ken of Franz Joseph to fit into a era conducive to the political perspective of the likes of Woodrow Wilson, Georges Clemenceau, Lenin, or Leon Trotsky. Hence, one source of Austria's tragedy is prosaic enough: Her emperor had outlived his age.

At another level, however, Austria-Hungary's decision for war was the result of political posturing and hyperbole because the foreign office insisted that Vienna punish Serbia for reasons of credibility and prestige. Reinforcing the views formulated on the Ballhausplatz was the opinion in Berlin that Austria must stand firm for the sake of the Dual Alliance, if not for her own sake. The German *Reich,* in seeking a diplomatic coup against her perceived enemies by supporting Vienna in 1914, perhaps was envisioning a scenario that essentially was reminiscent of the 1908 annexation crisis. Six years previously, the German Empire had demonstrated its determination by taking advantage of Russia's discomfort in the wake of its imbroglio with Japan to force St. Petersburg to back away from mobilization in defense of Serbia because of the Dual Monarchy's annexation of Bosnia and Herzegovina in the face of Belgrade's claim for those same territories. For its part, the German government had continually made it clear that the Dual Monarchy must stand up to her enemies if Vienna expected continuation of the Berlin-Vienna alliance. It was in this vein, for example, that Kaiser Wilhelm II, in November of 1913, told the chief of the Austrian-Hungarian foreign service, Baron Ludwig Freiherr von Flotow, that "I will always stand by you if the German core of Austria became endangered." (See Erwin Matsch, ed., *November 1918 auf dem Ballhausplatz: Erinnerungen Ludwig Freiherrn von Lützow des Letzten Chefs des österreichischen Auswartigen Dienst, 1895–1920* (Munich: Hermann Böhlau Nachf., 1982), p. 316.)

In 1914, however, while on the surface diplomatic currents had appeared to change very little since 1908, these currents, in fact, had been moving swiftly in favor of the Entente, and with deadly force. Hence, while once again in 1914, Berlin and Vienna danced in tandem vis-à-vis Serbia, a variety of internal and external pressures pushed the Russian Empire over into mobilization. And it was the czar's order that Russia mobilize that caused the Austro-Serb crisis to trigger a European war. See Kann, *Kaiser Franz Joseph,* pp. 3–23. See also Ernst Trost, *Kaiser Franz Joseph I, von Gottes Gnaden Kaiser von Österreich apostolischer König von Ungarn* (Vienna: Fritz Molden, 1980). p. 74.

19. Kann, *Kaiser Franz Joseph,* p. 11.

20. See Williamson, "Franz Ferdinand," *The Historical Journal,* XVII/2, 1974. See also, Kann, *Erzherzog Franz Ferdinand Studien,* pp. 206ff.

21. Ernst Rutkowski, ed., *Briefe und Dokumente zur Geschichte der österreichisch-ungarisch Monarchie: unter besonderer Berücksichtigung des böhmisch-mährischen Raumes,* Teil I: "Der Vafassungstreue Grossgrundbesitz, 1880–1899" (Vienna: R. Oldenbourg, 1983), p. 662.

22. Vienna, Neues Politische Archiv, 01/1a, Karton 143, I/II. This telegram is reproduced in Bittner and Uebersberger, *Österreich-Ungarns Aussenpolitik,* vol. 26, p. 942.

23. Vienna, Neues Politische Archiv, 01/1a, Karton 143, I/II. Also reprinted in Bittner and Uebersberger, *Österreich-Ungarns Aussenpolitik,* vol. 26, p. 944. Whether the Austro-Serb crisis meant world war or not brings the computation of history to its broadest level: that of describing relations among the world's greatest powers. The crux of whether there would be war or not at the broadest level of international relations lay quite beyond the power relationships directly involving Austria-Hungary; rather, this decision centered on long-festering rivalry, at all manner of levels, that had arisen out of the protracted economic competition between Europe's two preponderant powers: Great Britain and the second German Empire.

The link bringing Anglo-German rivalry into the boiling political cauldron in central Europe has been well delineated: While Germany was allied to Austria-Hungary through the Dual Alliance, England, along with France, was tied to the Russian Empire by means of the Entente. Thereby, concerted action by Vienna and Berlin inspired like but opposing concert among the British, French, and Russians on the other. So it was that the deepening rivalry that had existed between the German and British empires pushed London and Berlin to opposing one another with regard to the Austro-Serb conflict; moreover, this division worked itself out in such fashion so as to increase enmity between France and Germany while the latter's ally, Austria-Hungary, found itself pitted against the Russian Empire. And so the sides were drawn: Austria and Germany against Russia, France, and Great Britain.

24. Kann, *Ausbruch Weltkriegs,* pp. 14–15. See also Kann, *Erzherzog Franz Ferdinand Studien,* p. 157ff.

25. Kann, *Erzherzog Franz Ferdinand Studien,* especially pp. 100ff. The archduke perhaps always was inclined toward authoritative solutions; for example, as early as 1896, Franz Ferdinand wrote, concerning the *K.u.K.* army: "In these difficult times which the monarchy is experiencing, I question who and what upholds the throne [and] the dynasty? And there is only one answer to this question: The army: the army is not only for the defense of the fatherland from its external enemies; its chief task is for protecting and maintaining throne [and] for battling every one of its internal enemies." Quoted in Weissensteiner, *Franz Ferdinand,* p. 102.

26. See for example, Rutkowski, *Briefe und Dokumente,* pp. 321–322.

27. Kann, *Ausbruch Weltkreiges,* pp. 22–23.

28. Heinrich Graf von Lützow, *Im diplomatischen Deinst der K.u.K. Monarchie* (Munich: R. Oldenbourg, 1971). p. 219. The German ambassador to Vienna, Count Heinrich

von Tscherchky, wrote at this time to the German foreign secretary in Berlin, Gottlieb von Jagow, that the "Austrians remain Austrians, a combination of courage and thoughtlessness" (ibid., p. 229). Yet Conrad von Hötzendorf insists that initially, that is, on July 5, neither he nor Franz Joseph was by any means sure of Germany's position. Further, the emperor told Hötzendorf on that date that, when asked by Franz Ferdinand in the spring of 1914 about Germany's position in case of a war between Austria and Serbia that would also involve Russia on the side of Belgrade, Kaiser Wilhelm II sidestepped the question. Neither did the German emperor return to it during the remainder of his visit at the archduke's Bohemian estate, Konopist (Konopiště). The answer to Germany's position, according to Hötzendorf, seems first to have come only on July 7; and moreover, not from the German emperor but from the German chancellor. Even so, Bethmann-Hollweg's answer, given to Vienna's special emissary, Count Alexander Hoyos, was guarded, allowing only that "the monarchy can count on Germany as a friend and an ally . . . [that] he viewed that a quick step on [Austria's] part against Serbia was the most radical and best solution to [her] difficulties in the Balkans, and [further] from an international perspective, now was better than later." See Hötzendorf, *Aus Meiner Dienstzeit: 1906–1918,* IV, 36, 5–56.

29. Kann, *Ausbruch Weltkriegs,* p. 7.

30. Quoted in Hugo Hantsch, "Kaiser Franz Joseph und die Aussenpolitik," *Probleme der Franzisko-Josephenischen Zeit: 1848–1916,* vol. I., p. 31. See also Corti and Sokol, *Kaiser Franz Joseph,* p. 399, and Max Polatschek, *Franz Ferdinand: Europas verlorene Hoffnung* (Vienna: Amalthea, 1989), pp. 157ff.

31. Quoted (and reproduced) in Georg Markus, ed., *Der Kaiser Franz Joseph I, Bilder und Dokumente* (Vienna: Amaltha, 1985), p. 150.

32. See Fauland, *Vorwiegend heiter.* The above quote from Fauland is quoted in Berg, *Als der Adler nach Zwei Köpfe hutte,* pp. 184–187.

33. Edward Crankshaw, *The Fall of the House of Habsburg* (New York: Viking Press, 1965), pp. 244–288.

34. See Polatschek, *Franz Ferdinand,* pp. 213ff.

35. Quoted in Berg, *Als der Adler noch Zwei Köpfe hatte,* pp.187–188.

36. Also Franz Joseph's cousin, being the grandson of the Archduchess Marie Louise, in turn wife of Napoleon I, by the lady's second husband, Count Neippieg.

37. *Die Fackel.*10, no. 400 (July 1914).

38. Quoted in Feigl, *Kaiserin Zita,* p. 171. "Danzer" evidently refers to C.M. Danzer, editor of the *Armee Zeitung.*

39. See Hilde Spiel, "Der liebe gute alte Herr," in *Wien: Spketrum einer Stadt* (Vienna: Biederstein, 1971), pp. 80–95.

40. The historian Fritz Fischer speaks of the possibility that Franz Joseph's age and isolation served as the basis whereby Austria's German allies, wanting war, obtained the cooperation of the men around the Austro-Hungarian chief of staff, Conrad von Hötzendorf, to encourage Franz Ferdinand to be in Sarajevo on June 28, a national feast day for the Serbs, in hopes that something would happen that would produce a casus belli. Then, this having been accomplished, Franz Joseph was kept in the dark and was misled to believe by this same cabal that the Serbs would accept Austria's ultimatum as delivered. Fischer goes on to conjecture that, given the old emperor's focus on the insult dealt to his house, it was easy enough to convince him of Serbia's weakness. It is difficult, however, to find any documentary evidence supporting this line of conjecture even if, at the same time, it might seem plausible.

41. Transcript of the trial of Friedrich Adler, May 1917, p. 227, in Archives, Institute for Social History, Amsterdam, "F. Adler 1917."

42. See undated letter of Friedrich Adler to (Fritz Lang?) in Archives, Institute for Social History, Amsterdam, "F. Adler vor 1923," box 7.

43. See Trost, *Kaiser Franz Joseph I,* pp. 74–75.

44. Quoted in ibid., p. 74.

45. Quoted in Spiel, *Wien: Spektrum einer Stadt,* p. 80.

46. *Arbeiter Zeitung,* August 5, 1914.

47. Conrad von Hötzendorf to Emperor Franz Joseph, December 4, 1915. Haus, Hof-und Staats Archiv, PAI, 597, Liasse xlvii/la, c: "Krieg, 1914–1918."

48. See Hötzendorf, *Aus Meiner Dienstzeit: 1906–1918,* vol. IV, especially pp. 594ff.

49. See Hötzendorf, *Aus Meiner Dienstzeit: 1906–1918,* vol. IV, especially pp. 399ff.

50. Feigl, *Kaiserin Zita,* p. 191. See also confirmation by Alois Klepsch-Kloth, quoted in Trost, *Kaiser Franz Joseph I,* pp. 74–75.

51. Feigl, *Kaiserin Zita,* p. 173.

52. See Arthur J. May, *The Passing of the Habsburg Monarchy* (Philadelphia: University of Pennsylvania Press, 1966), vol. I, pp. 84–116.

53. May, *The Passing of the Habsburg Monarchy,* vol. I, pp. 152ff.

54. Vienna, Haus Hof-und Staats Archiv, PA xl/Interna, "Tagesberichten des K.u.K. Ministerium des Aussen."

55. Vienna, Haus Hof-und Staats Archiv, Liasse xlvii/3 (17–22), "Krieg 1914–1918," ff. 162–167.

56. Vienna, Haus Hof-und Staats Archiv, Liasse xlvii/3 (17–22).

57. See Ottokar Czernin und zu Chudenitz, *Im Weltkrieg* (Berlin: Ullstein, 1919), especially pp. 289–347.

58. Czernin, *Im Weltkrieg,* pp. 183–193.

59. May, *The Passing of the Habsburg Monarchy,* vol. I, pp. 97–123.

60. See Ingebord Meckling, *Die Aussenpolitik des Grafen Czernin* (Vienna: Verlag für Geschichte und Politik, 1969), pp. 128–132, 338ff. See also Czernin, *Im Weltkrieg,* especially pp. 28–35, and May, *The Passing of the Hapsburg Monarchy,* pp. 582ff. On German views toward Mitteleuropa, see Friedrich Naumann, *Mitteleuropa* (Berlin: Ulstein, 1915).

61. See, for example, Hötzendorf's memo to (the German) Generaloberst von Prittwitz (in Marienburg), in Hötzendorf, *Aus Meiner Dienstzeit,* vol. IV, pp. 391–393.

62. See, for example, a letter from Hungarian Minister President Werkerle to Czernin in which the Magyar leader argues against any Berlin-Vienna tariff arrangement as strengthening the Germans in the monarchy and hence threatening to Hungarian autonomy (Vienna, Haus Hof-und Staats Archiv, PAI, Liasse xlvii/la, c: "Krieg 1914–1918." This same box contains a twenty-eight-page missive written to the foreign minister by Count Tisza stating what is in effect Werkerle's position far more emphatically: "The 1867 Compromise . . . the minimum necessary for a great-power position and the maximum, from the point of view of the Hungarian state and its [right of] an independent existence, cannot freely be sacrificed for the common goal." Ibid.). Austria's deepening debility because of food shortages is starkly outlined by Czernin in a record of his discussions with German officials in Berlin in March and April of 1917. See Vienna, Haus Hof-und Staats Archiv, PAI, 504, Liasse xlvii/3 (17–22), c. "Krieg, 1914–1918," ff. 7/5–7/10.)

63. This attitude perhaps best summed up in a famous letter to Emperor Karl by Count Czernin on April, 12, 1917, in which he tells the monarch

> [that Austria has] completely run out of raw materials and manpower resources and there is widespread suffering among the people as a result. . . . The statesman, who is not blind or stupid, and who daily sees what is going on among the population, must hear the rumbling within the broad masses. . . . Your Majesty has the reports of the governors. Two things are clear: our Slavs are

strongly affected by the Russian Revolution . . . but the consequences are greater for . . . this land held together by the bond of dynasty and where the people battle for their national autonomy *[Selbständigkeit]*. Your Majesty knows that it is a simple fact that the press of the people for this has grown extraordinarily. . . . Your Majesty has the duty to God and to your people to do all that you can to defend them from the catastrophe that would go with the collapse of the monarchy.

Karl responded by writing, "I completely identify with what you say and you have summarized the situation exactly as I see it" (Vienna: Haus Hof-und Staats Archiv, PAI-504, Liasse xlvii/3 (1722), c.: "Krieg 1914–18," ff. 981–986).

64. This already well-documented phenomena is again underscored by this quote drawn from the unpublished memoirs of Frau Gabriele Deuticke (née V. Werther) entitled "1895–1975: Mein Leben Eine Zeit-und Familiengeschichte," pp. 27–29. See also Arthur Count Polzer-Hoditz, *The Emperor Karl* (Boston: Houghton Mifflin, 1922), pp. 211–280.

65. Margutti, *Vom Alten Kaiser: Persönliche Erinnerungen an Kaiser Franz Joseph I,* p. 421.

66. See Czernin, *Im Weltkrieg,* especially pp. 253–263, and Meckling, *Die Aussenpolitik des Grafen Czernin,* especially pp. 221–249.

67. See, for example, Friedrich Adler, *Gegen Krieg und Absolutismus* (Jena: Thüringer Verlaganstalt, 1925). Adler's book constitutes his justification, based on the transcript of his trial for his assassination, in November 1915 of the Austrian minister-president, Count Karl Stürgkh, on whom, somewhat unfairly, he placed the entire blame for the suspension of democracy in Austria. Adler's annotated copy of the transcript is in the Archives, Institute for Social History, Amsterdam, box labeled "F. Adler voor 1917."

68. Adler, trial transcript, especially pp. 30ff.

69. See Karl Kraus, *Die Letzten Tage der Menscheit: Tragodie in Funf Akten* (Munich: Kösel Verlag. 1957).

70. Adler, trial transcript.

71. Archives, Institute For Social History, Amsterdam, Kautsky Archiv, KD1/268.

72. Adler, trial transcript, p. 37.

73. See, for example, Trost, *Kaiser Franz Joseph I,* pp. 256–260.

74. Corti and Sokol, *Kaiser Franz Joseph,* p. 443.

75. Margutti, *Vom Alten Kaiser,* pp. 455–458.

76. Alice Herdan-Zuckmayer, quoted in Trost, *Kaiser Franz Joseph I,* p. 260.

✧ 8 ✧

Socialism: Between the Shoals of Nationalism and Internationalism

Pressures generated by the First World War focused the Austrian Social Democratic Workers' Party on preserving the fatherland, which, at least in a de facto sense, came to mean not a transformed state, but Austria-Hungary as she actually was, warts and all. The state was to be preserved if for no other reason than so that it might be around to be reformed once the war was brought to an end. The Brünner Program thereby was put on the sidelines as the party's leadership concentrated its energies on convincing its following of the necessity of maintaining the state. To this end, Friedrich Austerlitz, editor of the party's highly respected *Arbeiter Zeitung,* gave his front page over to calling upon Austria's proletariat to celebrate "Der Tag des deutschen Nation."[1] He framed the spreading conflagration with urgent tones tinted in moralistic hues, but, in something of an abrupt about-face, Austerlitz ended his appeal by noting that events now made it necessary to defend civilization from assault by a barbarous Slavdom. Austerlitz went on to conclude: "events threaten the soil of the fatherland. Not only the state but the nations within the state . . . must be defended if the nations are to remain free. . . . In times of danger everyone must support his country."[2] Austerlitz thereby succeeded only too well in giving tangibility to the suspicion of non-German Austrians (and not only the working class among them) that when push came to shove, German Austrian social democracy's high-sounding words regarding a supranational proletarian international based on working-class solidarity was nothing more than highfalutin rhetoric. And in fact not a few close to the center of the party's leadership were aghast that Austrian socialism apparently could forget so easily its fundamental canons. Not the least among these dissidents was Viktor Adler's own son, Dr. Friedrich Adler. But young Adler was not alone. On July 25, 1914, the south German Karl Kautsky, whose land of birth was Austria, had written to Viktor Adler expressing his shock over the terms in Austria's ultimatum to Serbia of July 1914, and he urged the Austrian leader to organize demonstrations against this war policy on the part of Vienna. "The ultimatum came so unexpectedly as I had assumed that the old Franz Joseph and the *Junge* [Karl] wished for their peace and quiet. And now suddenly a declaration of war."[3] Kautsky further noted that now war was "a foregone conclusion" and the moment had arrived in "Austria when there should be a mass strike on the part of the proletariat to protest against war. But," lamented Kautsky, "one notices not the slightest stir of protest action on the part of the party."[4]

Particularly frustrating to more insurrectionist spirits like young Adler was the fact that when war had begun the Austrian parliament, having been prorogued in 1913 because of its perennial tendency to obstructionism, had not been called to discuss either Emperor Franz Joseph's declaration of war against Serbia on July 25 or the state's participation in world war as of August 6.[5] Hence, from Adler's standpoint, Austria sent her young blood to war by imperial fiat. No less galling was that the party's leadership seemingly not only went along with this state of affairs, but also was content to permit the government of Minister-President Karl Stürgkh to carry on the business of war in the name of all of Austria. Hence, to the likes of young Adler, social democracy had abandoned not only its time-honored positions of class struggle, working-class solidarity, and internationalism, but also its insistence on democratic government. On October 21, 1915, young Adler gave sensational vent to his unhappiness and frustration by shooting dead Minister-President Karl Stürgkh while the count was taking lunch in Vienna's Hotel Meissl und Schadn on the Neuermarkt. With this, Friedrich Adler took what came to be the first step in a process that soon would split his party and give over its majority to a more radically inclined leadership.[6] In the process, the Brünner Program passed into history unfulfilled and unmourned.[7]

The actual shooting is best described by Friedrich Adler himself. He was interrogated immediately after the deed, and the resultant transcript, which was read out during his trial, portrays a coolly collected Adler who, once determining that he would kill the minister-president as a way of protesting both the war and the Austrian war government, sought out Count Stürgkh at his well-known luncheon haunt. Adler slipped a revolver into the right-hand pocket of his coat, went over to the Hotel Meissl und Schadn, situated on the Neuermarkt in the capital's first district, and took a table in its second-floor dining room, a few seats from Count Stürgkh and his party. Adler noted that he was lucky to obtain a table because at the time the room was crowded with diners. Adler described how he was so nervous that he was not sure that he would be able to follow through with his plans. Further, he was having difficulty keeping an eye on the minister-president because a column blocked his view and because ladies passing by his table interrupted his surveillance. But nevertheless Adler kept in sight the minister-president, who was talking with animation to his companions. Finally, gathering up his courage and convictions, young Adler walked over to Stürgkh's table, stood by his head, took out the revolver, and shot the minister-president in the head "three or four times." As he did the deed, Adler cried out, "Down with absolutism, we want peace!" As the minister-president slumped forward, spurting blood, the soldiers around him drew their swords and rushed toward Adler, who, having decided in those split few seconds that he did not want to be cut down and so be remembered as having met his end as a "seedy assassin," cried out, "I am Dr. Adler!" Thereby Adler sought to establish his identity through his nominal membership in that establishment that habitually lunched at the Meissl und Schadn. Quickly two detectives seized young Adler by the arms and led him, in the midst of shouts for an ambulance, into the next room.[8]

The mainstream of the German Austrian party, including young Adler's father, nevertheless stuck to the course as articulated in July and August of 1914. Indeed, this view was given fuller expression even after almost three years of war when, during the spring of 1917 and in the face of deepening tumult, socialists from some of the neutral European states thought they saw a means in this same tumult not only to salvage but also to elevate the fading second international. To this end, socialist leaders from Denmark, Sweden, and the Netherlands suggested that revolution in Russia presented an opportunity that must be seized, as the outbreak in St. Petersburg clearly indicated that Europe's masses had enough of war. The governments of the belligerent powers, they reasoned, now were ready to save themselves from what surely would be the spread of revolution by latching on to a peace agenda if a credible one could be found. Given that social democracy in Russia had been one of the engines for revolution, the neutral socialists called for an all-socialist peace conference to be convened in Stockholm.[9] The task of the conference was to make use of what some socialists perceived to be the international's newly minted credit, due to the rise of the Mensheviks in Russia, to produce such an agenda for peace.[10] The fall of the Romanovs, then, would serve as a warning. The rising tide of revolutionary public opinion would fuse with socialism's prewar reputation as the party of peace to render the international an apt vehicle for both the fabrication and the imposition of a peace program. That peace program, in turn, would reflect the priorities of an emergent populist, democratic, and triumphantly socialist world order. The neutral socialist leadership was confident that under the pressures that would be generated in Stockholm once the international met, the increasingly frightened war-making governments would have no choice but to adopt the results of socialist deliberation. Certainly the neutral socialist leadership was not alone in this view. For example, Kaiser Karl's foreign minister, Count Ottokar Czernin von und zu Chudenitz, informed his sovereign on April 12, 1917, that

> it is completely clear that [Austria] has come to the end of [her] military power. We have . . . run out of raw material and manpower. . . . It is of the greatest urgency that we begin negotiating peace before the enemy is conscious of our utterly exhausted condition. . . . Five monarchies are threatened by this [war], even the strongest monarchy in the world, England. . . . This war has begun a new era in world history, it has no predecessor or example. The world is no longer the same as three years ago, and consequently, no analogy out of the past will do to explain the current course of world history.[11]

As a first step toward an all-socialist get-together, the neutral leaders proposed that a steering committee, headed by socialist organizers from the neutral states, be created to hold a preliminary conference at which socialist representatives from states all over the world, one by one, would lay out their agendas for peace.[12] The resultant testimony would then form the material from which a definitive proposal would be drawn up to be placed before the main conference, which was to be held, also at Stockholm, during the late spring or early summer of 1917. Among the delegations that attended and testified before the Dutch-Scandinavian steering committee was one representing the Vienna-based Austrian Social Democratic Workers' Party and headed by Viktor Adler.

Adler and his colleagues worked closely with the Austrian foreign office for, like the German Austrian socialists, the men on the Ballhausplatz apparently were in agreement with the neutral socialists that the outbreak of revolution in Russia indeed had transformed Europe's political landscape. The political atmosphere now was fraught with both hope and catastrophe. Socialists and monarchists alike believed that the time had arrived when the war both must and might be ended, but as far as the Ballhaus was concerned, it had to be done in such a way as to preserve the Habsburg state, and yet permit restructuring and reform. Adler and his colleagues would go to Stockholm and insist on recognition for the nationalities in Austria. But the Vienna socialist leadership sought this recognition strictly within the political-cultural framework of autonomy rather than one defined by political independence; that is, rather than one based on the nation-state principle founded on ethno-cultural self-determination. Beyond provision for autonomy, central Europe's nations still were to exist within the parameters of the traditional states, and above all those historically associated with the Dual Monarchy within Austria-Hungary. It was quite natural, therefore, that the Ballhaus, desperate for a peace that would ensure survival of the Habsburgs, saw in the socialist agenda possibilities for Austria's salvation. Accordingly, the Vienna government did all that it could to expedite the presence of Adler and his colleagues at Stockholm. Further, the men on the Ballhausplatz worked fervently behind the scenes to promote the conference among both allies and enemies.[13]

Not a few of Czernin's cohorts, and especially Hungarian Minister-President Count Stephan Tisza, took a dubious view of the foreign office's apparent flirtation with socialism. In defending his policies against Tisza's attacks, Czernin admonished the hard-nosed Magyar leader:

> I hear that you do not approve of the delegation of socialists for Stockholm. To begin with, it is not a delegation. The men came to me of their own accord and applied for permission to travel, which I granted. . . . The first two [Wilhelm Ellenbogen and Viktor Adler] are capable men, and I value them in spite of the differences that exist between [me and] them. . . . All are genuinely desirous of peace. . . . If they secure peace, it will be a socialistic one, and the emperor will have to pay out of his own pocket; I am sure too, dear friend, that if it is not possible to end the war, the emperor will have to pay still more.[14]

A few days later, in a similar vein, the foreign minister responded to Tisza's criticism by insisting that "all [the Viennese socialist leadership] genuinely is desirous of peace and [Viktor] Adler in particular does not wish for the downfall of the realm.... After the war, we shall be forced to have a socialist policy whether it is welcome or not, and I consider it extremely important to prepare the Social Democrats for [this task]."[15] Czernin, however, was more frank about his feelings toward the socialists when, while corresponding with his close friend, the Austrian ambassador to the Ottoman Porte, Margarve Johann Pallavicini, he allowed:

> The reason why we wish none of our socialists to make peace lies on the hand [it is obvious].... We must ... do all that we can to forward the convening [of the Stockholm Conference] ... through our choice of delegates.... Requests at the right moment will set off the doctrinaire elements and the existing gulfs within the international will not be bridged.... [This circumstance will present] us with the opportunity to take over demands [of the Austrian delegation and present them] as our [own] proposals.[16]

The Vienna delegation arrived in Stockholm in April of 1917 and while there maintained close communication with the Austrian-Hungarian foreign office. For its part, the Ballhaus assigned Prince Emil zu Fürstenberg, first legation counselor at Stockholm, the responsibility of keeping an eye on the delegates and generally to monitor and report back to Count Czernin on anything that appeared pertinent to the foreign minister's agenda. Count Maximilian Futak von Hadik and Baron Gomirje Alexander von Musulin were assigned to assist the delegation.[17] As a result of these arrangements, a steady stream of reports flowed to Vienna, eliciting, in turn, Czernin's observations, admonitions, and orders. The paper trail thereby created between Vienna and Stockholm demonstrates that a viable working relationship had developed between the German Austrian socialist leadership and the Ballhaus.[18] The same paper trail also conclusively demonstrates that Viktor Adler and his colleagues were working strenuously to preserve the outlines of the old monarchy. But to render their argument for Austria persuasive, they chose Metternichian principles on which to ground their logic. Like the chancellor of yore, the German Austrian socialist delegation invoked history in order to legitimate the state and focused on arguments granting national recognition by means of autonomy within Austria as a whole according to the existing historic states. To obtain the international's support for resolving the nationality struggle within the framework of Austria's historical *Länder,* the party apparently deserted the Brünner Program. Perhaps this desertion vindicated earlier accusations by Czech socialist separatists that the real socialist loyalties of the Vienna leadership were on deposit in the camp of the Habsburgs. Further, this change in approach demonstrated that the German Austrian leadership, above all the senior Adler and Ellenbogen, no longer adhered to nation-state principle in the potential national and socialist sense once touted by them prior to the outbreak of the war. Rather, they now exposed themselves to be

Austrians and socialists in an older sense; that is, in the sense of mid-nineteenth-century liberalism combined with the utopian socialism of Ferdinand Lasalle. One suspects too that when push came to shove, Adler's brush with liberalism during his student days had rendered him still an indefatigable promoter of German culture as the best vehicle for the spread of higher civilization in central Europe. The idealism of youth sometimes does survive even the most searing experiences of the adult.[19]

At Stockholm, the Adler delegation made its appearance before the Dutch-Scandinavian committee and pressed its conviction that cessation of war should be immediate and should involve neither indemnities nor annexations. Moreover, the delegation called for peace within a framework of a twelve-point program upholding the territorial integrity, albeit a restructured one, of the Dual Monarchy.[20] For example, the Austrians insisted that the south Slav territories of Bosnia and Herzegovina remain with the Austrian state. Further, and most explicitly, the delegation insisted that all of Galicia be given autonomy only within Austria. With regard to the remainder of nationality questions as it concerned the Dual Monarchy, Adler, in the name of the party's Vienna leadership, rather stridently declared that

> only an Austrian could speak with authority on [the Austrian nationality question]. The idea of the suppression of nationalities [in Austria] is a fable. The authority of the [Austria-Hungary] state generally protects, and with success, minorities, as the existence [within Austria] of even the smallest fragment of a people demonstrates. Only the nationalities [themselves] make life difficult for one another.[21]

The German Austrian delegation's testimony, as might be imagined, caused a bit of an uproar among Entente supporters. As also might be imagined, the Vienna delegation's approach hardly pleased a number of socialists representing Austria-Hungary's subject nations. For example, Czech socialist separatists (the Czech delegation was now divided into supporters of Adler's view, called separatists, and those who wanted to entirely cut loose from Vienna, called deserters) were in sharp disagreement with the German Austrians.[22] The separatists demanded the reorganization of Austria-Hungary into a confederation that would permit an autonomous Czech-Slovak state, while the national-socialist-inclined deserters demanded an independent Czech-Slovak state.[23] For its part, the Dutch-Scandinavian committee tried to maintain impartiality as it steered a course between the treacherous shoals of state and nation. And perhaps it did so with no more success than its capitalistic and dynastic counterparts, for the great influence of Viktor Adler, and with it the nuances of change of socialist tactic toward Austria's nationality question, shaped the deliberations of that same committee. Indeed, the Dutch-Scandinavian committee not only affirmed that peace should exact no annexations or indemnities but further decided to draw on Adler's convictions when it placed its final proposals for Austria's future before the upcoming socialist conference. Its preliminary resolution proposed that

> the solution to the Bohemian question should be resolved in the sense that the districts within which the majority are Czechs should be pulled together so that these would constitute a confederation within Austria-Hungary. The south Slav peoples of Austria-Hungary should possess cultural freedom and the completest equality in their internal economic relations and should be constituted so as to possess their own administrative territories. Austria's Italian districts that do not join Italy should enjoy cultural autonomy.[24]

It requires no repetition here that the conclusions of the Stockholm Socialist Peace Conference came to nothing.[25] For one thing, it had become clear by August 1917 that, given America's entry into the war the previous April, the western powers were now in possession of the necessary edge in manpower and raw materials to overcome Austria-Hungary and Germany. Further, by the opening of 1918, and as Czernin was only too well aware, because the Central Powers had completely exhausted their manpower and material reserves while unsuccessfully trying to break through Allied lines on the western front, their superior tactical position on Europe's battlefronts meant little in practical terms. Also important was that the Allied leadership, and the Americans in particular, did not view either the 1917 revolution or the apparent socialist triumph in Russia as an opening for peace. Rather—and especially with the surfacing of the Bolshevists as the coming power in Russia by November of that fateful year—the Allies viewed these changing circumstances as all the more reason why the Central Powers must be defeated; it was essential to impose a new democratic and capitalist world order on Europe before the red tide swept westward out of Russia. And to the extent that too many in the governments in the west could see little distinction between Bolshevist and socialist, the conclusions at Stockholm were viewed not as a basis for peace but, more alarmingly, as an opening for the spread of Bolshevist communism.[26]

Woodrow Wilson in particular would undercut Bolshevism and thereby make the world safe for democracy. The American president was convinced that the pursuit of this dream required a new Europe existing in a world without war, which in turn demanded her stately reordering on the basis of democratic national self-determination.[27] The American president hinted what he had in store for Austria when he told Congress that

> Austria-Hungary for the time being is not her own mistress but simply a vassal of the German government. . . . [Regarding the peoples of the Dual Monarchy,] I am thinking of Austria herself . . . as well as of Serbia and Poland. Justice and equality can be had only at a great price. We are seeking permanent, not temporary foundations for peace in the world and we must seek them candidly and fearlessly. As always the right will prove to be the expedient.[28]

Wilson's view not only had primacy within the Allied camp because of America's possession of the material means by which the balance of power had shifted to the Allies, but his strong ideological adherence to a simple application of the nation-state principle rendered, to his mind, the preservation of multinational states in central Europe inadmissible for any reason and in any shape or form. It was a foregone conclusion, then, that an Allied victory signified the dissolution of the Dual Monarchy. And of course such dissolution meant that the Brünner Program also was dispatched to history, its potential untested.[29]

To celebrate, as it were, the changing order of the socialist perspective, Heinrich Tuma, a Social Democratic political writer hailing from Austria's south Slav lands, informed his colleagues within the party that

> only by building a homogeneous Europe held together in a federation of [nation-states] between the Baltic and Adriatic, [and between] the Aegean and Black Seas is there a solution to the ongoing development of Europe . . . [for] the battle of nationalities . . . has brought [Europe] to the brink of ruin. . . . The surest way in which Austrian-Hungarian Social Democrats can join European social democracy is by constructing an Austrian international on the principle of self-determination of nations.[30]

Tuma's language, because of the prevailing military censorship, had to be carefully couched. But Karl Mann, a German Austrian politician, took the point, declaring that all Germans in central Europe ought to belong to a common German nation-state. After all, Mann reminded his readers, if the fallout from the Russian revolution permitted the resurrection of the Polish state, so did the probable defeat of the Central Powers presage an end to that division of the German nation dictated in 1866 by the Peace of Prague.[31] Sensing the coming breakup of his old Austria, Karl Renner bitterly remarked that "the inability of the Austrian-Hungarian government to grant a halfway acceptable constitution is permitting the imperialist Entente to turn the war into one for national freedom. But at the same time these [powers] are laying the foundation for their imperial expansion in the Middle East . . . and [in] the . . . Balkans."[32]

Through default, given that the traditional political parties had been wrecked on the shoals of defeat and collapse, the leadership of the provisional German Austrian republic that emerged out of the breakup of the Dual Monarchy during October of 1918 fell to Vienna's Social Democratic leadership. However, the party, due to the sudden death of Viktor Adler in November of 1918, was bereft of a strong leader and was run by an informal and uneasy collective leadership dominated by Karl Renner, Otto Bauer, and Karl Seitz.[33] Even before Viktor Adler's death, the German deputies to the old Austrian Reichsrath had reconstituted themselves as a National Assembly to form a democratic republic and, on the twenty-ninth of October, sent a note to President Wilson stating its intentions to form a German Austrian state consisting of Lower Austria and the traditional German-Austrian Alpine regions. The new leadership, socialist all, also announced its intention, while appealing to Woodrow Wilson's articulation of the principle of democratic national self-determination, to include those thirty-six districts in Bohemia where there was a German majority. In addition, this social-ist-dominated National Assembly intended that the new republic would include those districts in Austrian Silesia, southern Moravia, and the south Tyrol where it held that there was a clear German majority. Further, Wilson was informed that the new government in Vienna would undertake to negotiate these matters with the Czech and south Slav successor states and, where necessary, submit to plebi-scites conducted under neutral auspices in those areas where the negotiating parties could not reach agreement.[34]

Otto Bauer had become convinced in the course of the First World War (perhaps not least while witnessing events in Russia, where he had been a prisoner of war during the outbreak of the Russian revolution) that class struggle was not a viable tactic for revolutionary socialism as long as the powerful sirens of nationalism were present to draw away the worker from his primary task of doing battle against capitalism. Bauer had become convinced that Europe required political reorganiza-tion on the basis of the nation-state principle, but only as the first necessary and preliminary step toward the creation of a potent pan-European workers' movement *(Gesamteuropäischerarbeiterbewegung)*. In other words, Bauer was following, or thought he was following, the tactic demonstrated by the socialist left at the 1915 Zimmerwald Conference of advocating national self-determination as a first step in creating the proper preconditions deemed necessary before commencing the final march toward the socialist millennium. Thereby too, Bauer abdicated his former insistence, proposed in 1907, in his renowned work *Die Nationalitätenfrage und die Sozialdemokratie* that the nations must be reconciled to one another within the framework of Europe's historic multinational states.[35]

Indeed, upon his return from revolutionary Russia to Vienna in 1918, Bauer had organized a conference made up of the Austrian socialist left, which, meeting in the spring of 1918, chastised Marxism in Austria "for all too long failing to pursue the right of [national] self-determination of the Slavic nations against the German bour-geoisie."[36] Further, the Czech socialists were taken to task for demanding "the right of self-determination of the Czech nation without recognizing [the demands] of the Germans in the Sudetenland."[37] The conference concluded with a program that was to belong to the German Austrian republic during Bauer's tenure at the Ballhausplatz between 1918 and 1920. Old Austria was to be

> (1) divided into seven speech territories: German, Czech, Polish, Ukrainian, south Slav, Italian and Rumanian. . . . (2) Each speech territory is to be deline-ated through equal and direct elections by all men and women [within the context of] a national convention [that would] decide the constitution and administrative organization of these independent speech territories. (3) Each [resultant] nation . . . will achieve a nation-state with their *Volksgenossen* (na-tionals) outside of [old] Austria. (4) Each nation[-state] will regulate its rela-tions with the other former Austrian nations through its national convention. (5) National minorities will be protected by treaties between these nation[-states].[38]

It is clear that by the end of October 1918, forced, so to speak, by the press of events, the German Austrian socialist leadership had abandoned the reconstruction of the old Habsburg state along the lines of its national communities as they had existed in the crown lands as a whole; that is, as outlined in the now discarded Brünner Program. Neither was the party any longer interested in pursuing nationality equality within the historic *Länder* as implied before the steering committee in Stockholm in the spring of 1917. Now, for example, Bohemia would be pulled apart according to ethno-cultural demographics, and the ancient kingdom would disappear into the evolving German Austrian and Czech-Slovak republics.

The matter that was not presented to Wilson in the initial note of October 29 was the intention of the government of the new Austrian republic to join Vienna's new German political creation with the then-evolving German republican *Reich*. Such a creation, bringing all Germans under a single stately umbrella, would render the German nation, now no longer divided by the existence of the old Habsburg and Hohenzollern states, dominant, if not in Europe as a whole, at least in central Europe. Such a political state was considered by many non-Germans in central Europe to be a severe threat to their emergent independence. In addition, neither the French nor the English were inclined, having won the war, and at great cost, to lose the peace.[39]

The American president received word of Vienna's intention to achieve what might be called an extended version of *Anschluss* only when, on November 13, 1918, the socialist leader Otto Bauer, now in charge of the Foreign Office, requested affirmation of such a union

> on the basis of the right of national self-determination. . . . German Austria was divided from Germany 52 years ago by the sword. . . . [We hope that the American president] will support this striving of the German Austrian people. . . . [that] the German Austrians will possess the same right that is being granted to the Poles, Italians and south Slavs who formerly belonged to the old Austrian state.[40]

Otto Bauer thereby heralded still another shift in nationality policy, this time away from a *Vielvölkergesamtdönauischstaat* (centralized multinational Danubian state) concept, as the Vienna socialist leadership now maneuvered between the shoals of war, defeat, and revolution.[41]

It is self-evident that foreign policy of the first German Austria republic emanated directly out of Otto Bauer's 1918 manifesto. Old Austria, and indeed Europe as a whole, now would be reordered on the basis of the nation-state principle. Then, when the reordering was accomplished and nationality struggle had died out as a consequence, not only in Danubia but in all of Europe, it would be time enough to build a new socialist international that would rest on this new foundation of European nation-states. Not all socialists agreed with the party's new Weltanschauung. For example, in the spring of 1919, one elderly veteran fighter for socialism wrote Friedrich Adler, who had been pardoned in 1918 by Emperor Karl for his role in the assassination of the Austrian minister-president and then a member of the German Austrian National Assembly:

> I see that you are on the left and thereby in the principal stream of the Social Democratic Party whereas I am on the other and have been for 29 years! I wish to remark on my astonishment over the call next Sunday for a demonstration favoring *Anschluss* between German Austria and the German *Reich.* I see a fundamental contradiction between this goal and socialist principles. Previously, for a quarter of a century, we have taken a position ... that the proletariat and its representatives should have nothing to do with [the nation-state principle]. In fact, at one time I learned that the proletariat should erect socialism on a given territory and link it to another so as to overcome the state. That hardly interested the bourgeoisie, for whom the state was merely the means to suppress the worker. I am against the idea of using the motto of national self-determination to erect a state founded on the cultural community because it divides the worker and robs him of the means by which he might found a state based on socialism.... The end result [of the nation-state] is that it enhances capitalism.[42]

He might have added that the program now being pursued by Otto Bauer and his socialist colleagues was one that perhaps was driven by nationalism. But one thing was for certain: The implications for the distribution of power in central Europe contained in the nationality program of the left would be hard to sell to the peacemakers when they gathered in Paris. There the focus would be on limiting the power of the old German *Reich,* and Bauer's assumptions could only add to the Allied determination to accomplish this task. Fully aware of the danger of what they viewed as misunderstandings over the application of the principle of national self-determination in German-speaking Europe, the socialist guardians of the new Austrian Republic undertook a campaign to educate the victors on its perspective of the changed circumstances now defining central Europe. This task prompted Friedrich Adler, newly appointed in November 1918 as editor of Vienna's socialist daily, to write:

> What should happen [to Austria]? Should we remain in the tragic-comic situation where we would be a free state along with an emperor of Austria ... or should German Austria be reconstructed as a republic and have done with the Habsburgs once and for all? ... But we German Austrian Social Democrats wish to make no secret that we generally do not desire such a [republic] even if it were possible. This German Austria does not produce enough food and cannot produce enough. Without sugar, without coal, it cannot be saved from economic disaster. What then, as socialists, should we do? ... We want life. We wish to struggle rather than to rot. The great German republic is also of the same mind—and our place, our future is there. The republic of German Austria is a constituent and indivisible part of the great German republic. The Entente will not, cannot, forbid it because it knows that, if not today, we will carry out

[Anschluss] after the peace so as to ensure our security. In any case, recognition of the free decisions of a free people, who have decided to both build and join a republic, is an honorable and fundamental right belonging to all humanity.[43]

One could argue that such an energetic drive for *Anschluss* coming from the mouths of socialists was certain to dampen acceptance for it among the capitalists in the west. But even more off-putting, perhaps, was that Austria's socialist leadership used the likes of Friedrich Adler, a convicted assassin, to promote what in the eyes of many in Paris was the most dubious of propositions. Nor did it help matters that Vienna's socialist activists were sprouting forth at the same time that their apparent colleagues in Russia (for who in London or Paris knew the difference between a socialist and a Bolshevist?) were sliding toward a tactic of violent repression. But neither were all within the Austrian socialist rank and file happy with Adler's rationale, which, as was his wont, he pronounced in high-handed and dogmatic tones. One of the party's followers, for example, reacted strongly against

> these . . . political policies of German Austria. . . . The Social Democratic party should not be immune from free speech. The time has come to knock the leaders of the party on the head. . . . We find German nationalist ecstasy manifest in the print of the *Arbeiter Zeitung*. First there was an article by Otto Bauer threatening the Czechs with *Anschluss* with the German *Reich* and then it followed that the *Arbeiter Zeitung* was transformed into a German nationalist organ, propagating and proclaiming union with the German *Reich*. . . . Where does the [socialist] state council get the right to make such fundamental and far-reaching decisions without first determining the position and the mood of the people? What is left of the democracy once associated with the *A[beiter] Z[eitung]* and the Party leadership?[44]

Also confusing the issue of *Anschluss* in the autumn of 1918 was the fact that it was still uncertain which of the German-speaking lands belonging to the old monarchy would constitute a part of the new German Austrian republic, that same republic that the provisional socialist government in Vienna intended to unite with the newly emergent provisional socialist German republican *Reich*. In addition to the South Tyrol, claimed by Italy, as well as thirty-six districts situated in Austro-Silesia, Bohemia, and Moravia, claimed by the emerging Czecho-Slovak republic,[45] Vienna also laid claim to some districts on the Austria-Hungary border then occupied by Budapest as well as lands further south claimed by the Slovenes and Croats.[46] Hence, Otto Bauer, Karl Renner, and indeed the whole of the Vienna socialist leadership, which by now was nearly the same thing as German Austria's provisional government, were in hot pursuit not of a restructured Danubian state as outlined in the Brünner Program or in their works on the subject published in a plethora of books and articles before the First World War, but in tearing out as many of the German-speaking regions as possible from the corpse of the old state and joining them with the German

Social Democratic and republican *Reich.*[47] One could argue, of course, that Vienna now had no other choice, for not only was the old Dual Monarchy irrevocably lost in the wreckage of the three central and east European states, but inasmuch as both Berlin and Vienna apparently were now socialist, not only were the conditions ripe for *Anschluss* but it was, as Friedrich Adler had pointed out, the only logical solution for the weak German Austrian remnant of Habsburg *Hausmacht.*

German Austria's nationalist agenda opposed at least two other obvious solutions to the political vacuum that had emerged in the heart of Europe: the recasting of south-central Europe into a federation of Danubian nation-states and the acceptance of the emergent successor states (formed on the basis of the nation-state principle) as the new order for the region.[48] That Bauer and Renner accepted the successor states as the basis of a new stately order was implicit in their seeking an *Anschluss* solution for German Austria. However, at least on the surface, a Danubian federation that included German Austria certainly more closely reflected the old Brünner Program than did *Anschluss*. Why, then, did Vienna pursue *Anschluss?*

Bauer perhaps gave a preview of his changing rationale toward the German nation when, in 1917, he wrote: "the proletariat will overthrow German Prussian imperialism by means of revolution and then will reconstruct the . . . national community, embracing the entire German nation, on its ruins."[49] The catastrophe of world war had demonstrated, at least by 1917, that the Austrian, German, and Russian states were not immutable. Further, a entirely new stately order now might be constructed in central and east Europe. At any rate, Austria had, for Bauer at least, lost her utility by 1917. Culpable for the Great War, and now sinking in the same morass overtaking the old monarchical states governed from Berlin and St. Petersburg, the Habsburg state no longer served human material needs. Compromise between the concepts of state and nation, painfully wrested in the political atmosphere of prewar times whereby Marxist socialism's ideas for restructuring of the state were forced to fit within the framework of Austria-Hungary, no longer was necessary. The party's leadership now was free to indulge both their nationalist and socialist instincts, to fuse them together within a new, if still de facto, state, a socialist one driven by nationalism. Further, both the Habsburg dynasty and its *Hausmacht* had lost their authority among many Austrians because of the spreading perception, especially among Austrian Slavs but also among not a few of its German citizens, that the traditional Habsburg state no longer could protect her subjects from German expansionist lust.

> Germany went to war as a "loyal ally" of Austria-Hungary; but today Germany is not an ally, she is the military leader, the political and economic sovereign of "independent" Austria-Hungary. . . . Austria-Hungary opens up the road to Constantinople; it is the "Alliance" with Austria-Hungary which has enabled

Germany to invade the Balkans. . . . The Allies must meet the German plan of Central Europe . . . by the plan of Central Europe freed from German control.[50]

To the north, again in 1917, Poland was a primary recipient of national aspirations unloosed by the Russian Revolution. But the Polish question then became the central one for Austria. Polish Austrians now saw the possibility of living out one of their most exigent political desires: rejoining Galicia to a newly emergent Polish state that had commenced to reappear out of the wreckage of czarist Russia.[51] Henceforth, relations between the House of Habsburg and its subjects, both Pole and Ruthene, living in Galicia was problematic. The possibility of the reconstruction of an independent Poland signified the detachment of Galicia from the Dual Monarchy. This detachment, in turn, added force and tangibility to the idea of national self-determination for all of Austria's nations. Unforeseen changes had altered those circumstances that had defined the Habsburg Austrian state. Naturally, the German Austrians must look to their future. One possible conclusion was only too obvious: German Austria's future belonged with that of Germany. So too did these events presage an end to that division of the German nation dictated by the circumstances that in 1866 produced the Peace of Prague.[52]

Of course, even in 1917 not all of Otto Bauer's colleagues had entirely given up on the Austrian idea. One of the more notable holdouts for an old Austria was he who turned out to be the first and provisional Chancellor of the First Austrian republic, Karl Renner. But even Renner's defense against the flow of circumstances had become a weak one. He could only retort to Bauer that "in reality . . . self-determination . . . can be effected in many different forms."[53] But the currents against Renner's views proved too strong. And so as chancellor, Renner found himself sponsoring, through Otto Bauer, *Anschluss* as the best solution for the future of the first German Austrian republic.

But why not create an independent German Austria as a part of a Danubian federation? One answer is only too obvious: the fear that such a federation, especially if it included Budapest and Vienna, might serve as a vehicle for the restoration of the Habsburg, if not the Hohenzollern, rulership.[54] But others held a federative state solution no more workable than old Austria. French sources let it be known that a Czech state, to say nothing of a Danubian federation, was unworkable for the same reason:

A Czech state of six and one half million Czechs, three and one half million Germans, two million Slovaks and some 100,000 Poles and a few Magyars won't work as a unitary state. . . . A Swiss Confederation maybe. . . . [And while] the loss of German Bohemian industry and coal is catastrophic for Austrian life . . . a Danubian federation offers no solution [for German Austria]. The Germans would be too weak as against the Slavs and would therefore be laboring under a foreign regime repeating thereby the history of the Czechs in old Austria.[55]

The question of a Danubian federation continued to be bandied among the capitals of western Europe. But little interest could be generated for the idea within central Europe. The leaders in the various successor states, having finally gained power, feared that they would lose their hard-won gains to the restoration of the old regime. And so those in the Vienna government who would bring all Germans residing in central Europe into a single state continued to work toward *Anschluss*. These same elements used talk of Austria joining a Danubian federation of states merely as a ploy to divert hostile speculation away from the flirting between Berlin and Vienna. For example, when the Americans were upset because the German National Assembly greeted Ludo Hartmann with festivities out of all proportion to his position in Berlin as German Austria's ambassador, Otto Bauer suggested that the Ballhaus encourage Great Britain to chair a committee seeking ways and means for creating the federation. "Let the Czechs and south Slavs," it was suggested, "take the odium for the undoubted failure of such negotiations."[56]

To preempt the unveiling of the peace treaties in Paris, Berlin, and Vienna completed a comprehensive protocol for the implementation of *Anschluss*.[57] The protocol consisted of seven articles dealing with questions ranging from the legal basis for the union to special problems involving the teaching of Catholicism in Austria's schools and the protection of selected Austrian industries from German competition. And neither was Austrian pride overlooked in the process. Vienna, for example, was to be recognized as the second capital, and hence the president of the German republic was to have a residence in the city on the Danube; the parliament was to gather there at least once a year, and an undetermined number of the *Reich* ministries were to have Vienna as their permanent home.[58] The protocol was signed in the friendliest of ceremonies in Berlin on March 2, 1919, by the socialist Dr. Otto Bauer and the aristocratic pan-Germanist Count Ulrich Brockdorff-Rantzau. In addition, there is also the fact that to a great extent the agreement was in part brokered by Social Democrats of the likes of Germany's Karl Kautsky and Austria's Friedrich Adler and Ludo Hartmann as well as the executive director of the former second international, Belgium's Camille Huysmann.[59]

Certainly before the First World War, the prevailing state system appeared to be immutable in that the Romanov, Habsburg, and Hohenzollern states were taken as more or less permanent and that to the extent that there might be change, it would have to be within the framework of these existing states. Existence for the Ottoman state was more problematic, but certainly by 1914, those changes within it that might spill over to influence the fundamental European state order were perceived as already having taken place. Hence, given these assumptions, it is understandable why Austro-Marxism would seek reconciliation between state and nation within the existing political framework. It would appear that many of the Vienna socialists of Viktor Adler's generation, while strongly viewing themselves as belonging to the German cultural nation, nevertheless also strongly held that Vienna was their home and Austria was their fatherland. For example, Viktor Adler's personal background, while perhaps suffused with more material prosperity than many, was not fundamentally untypical of many of the capital's bourgeois socialist leaders: born in the non-German hinterland (Moravia, in the case of Adler) of economically upwardly mobile parents with Jewish roots. Moreover, this upward mobility was pursued within the framework of the emerging modern society governed socioeconomically by industry *(Grossindustrie)* and capital *(Grosskapital)*. Adler grew up in Vienna's Ringstrasse quarter during the period of the Austrian Grunderzeit that created the social ambience within which the family converted to Protestantism. He was educated at the Schöttengymnasium and then went on to the University of Vienna, where the young Viktor pursued both medicine and psychiatry.[60] To be truly Viennese and Austrian, however, meant a certain developed and self-conscious obeisance to the Habsburg monarchy in the abstract; hence the source of the drive of the likes of Viktor Adler to pursue reform within the framework of Habsburg Danubia. Men from a somewhat younger generation who also were bourgeois, if not haut bourgeois—men like Otto Bauer—might have entertained somewhat more ambivalent attitudes toward the dynasty and might therefore have been more inclined to lean away from political tradition, especially when energized by the impact of war, revolution, and disintegration.[61] It was men such as Bauer, like so many of the well-educated of his generation, be it a Thomas G. Masaryk or a Marshal Josef Pilsudski, who proved open to the sirens of nationalism.[62] Hence, the leap embodied in the left's nationality-based program was an easier one for Otto Bauer than it would have been for Viktor Adler. And for this reason, one might conclude that even among Marxist socialists, a brew combining elements of nationalism and socialism within the nation-state principle was buried, and always had been, in the political rhetoric of socialist internationalism well before the First World War. It took the unforeseen collapse of central and east Europe's multinational states to make explicit what was implicit in the political rhetoric of the turn of the century.[63] And hence by 1918, many varieties of a nationalist and socialist amalgam were unloosed in what had been Austrian Danubia. Unfortunately, these varieties extended from gutter national socialism to that well-intentioned variety pursued by Otto Bauer as minister of foreign affairs. Nevertheless it must be conceded that the operative word in all these varieties was *nationalism*.[64]

Notes

1. *Arbeiter Zeitung,* August 5, 1914.
2. Ibid.
3. Karl Kautsky to Victor Adler, July 25, 1914. "Viktor Adler, II, Kopien, 1889–1918," Archives, Institute for Social History, Amsterdam.
4. Ibid.
5. See the telegrams between Franz Joseph and Wilhelm II in the Austrian State Archives, N.P.A., 01/la, Karton 143 I/II.

6. See the trial transcript, p. 270, in the Friedrich Adler papers, "Voor 1921," on deposit in the Archives, International Institute for Social History, Amsterdam.

7. Adler was pardoned and freed by Emperor Karl in the course of a general amnesty declared for political prisoners in November of 1918.

8. Adler, trial transcript, pp. 260 ff.

9. The neutral socialists at the time were thinking more of the Mensheviks than of the Bolshevists, whom they considered too radical and less likely to succeed.

10. Especially active in the socialist-inspired Stockholm peace movement were the secretary for the second international, Camille Huysmanns, a Belgian national; Branting of Sweden, Stauning of Denmark, and Trolestra of the Netherlands. See Olga Hess Gankin and H.H. Fisher, *The Bolshevists and the World War* (Stanford: Stanford University Press, 1960). Attending the preliminary Stockholm conference under the patronage of the Ballhaus and under the umbrella of the Viennese German Austrian Party, besides Viktor Adler, were Wilhelm Ellenbogen, Karl Renner, Ludo M. Hartmann, Karl Seitz, A. Hubner, E. Burian, G. Habermann, V. Stein, (Burian, Habermann, and Stein were actually Czechs loyal to Austria), H. Diamant, Daszynski (Austrian Pole speaking for Galicia); Herren D. Glumač and F. Martic (representing Bosnia-Herzegovina). In addition, Anton Němec and Dr. Bokumir Šmeral came as spokesmen for Czech social democracy; Herren Bokayni, Buchinger, Garami, Jaszai, Kunfi, and Welther for Hungarian social democracy; Herren V. Pittoni for Austrian-Italians; G. Grigorovici and H. Tuma for Yugoslavia (south Slavs); Herren H. Temmyzski and Hankievitsch for Austro-Ruthene social democracy. See Fürstenberg to Czernin, Haus Hof-und Staat Archiv, 959, PAl, Liasse Krieg 25z (Friedensverhandl), ff. 276, May 24, 1917. See also ff. 276–274, containing similar reports to the Ballhaus from various worthies. With the exception of Dr. Kunfi (actually a Hungarian) and representatives speaking for Czech social democracy, most of these men usually were designated socialist patriots by the Vienna party's left wing, which included members of the so-called Karl Marx Club such as Friedrich Adler, Therese Schlesinger, Franz Koritschöner, and Frau Luzzato. He who was to be the most notorious among these latter, Otto Bauer, was incommunicado at this time because he was a prisoner of war in Russia. See Merle Fainsod, *International Socialism and the World War* (Cambridge: Harvard University Press, 1935), pp. 136–137. See also Ludwig Brügel, *Geschichte der österreichischen Sozialdemokratie* (Vienna: Volksbuchhandlung, 1925), vol. V.

11. Czernin to Kaiser Karl, April 12, 1917. Vienna, Haus Hof-und Staats Archiv, 504 PAl, Liasse XLVII/3 (17–22), c. "Krieg 1914–1918," ff. 981–986.

12. This steering committee a short time later became known as the Holland (or Dutch)-Scandinavian committee. After July 11, 1917, when Russia's Mensheviks supported the Stockholm idea, it became known as the Dutch-Scandinavia-Russia committee.

13. Documents on the Stockholm conference from the point of view of the Austrian foreign office are found in Vienna, Haus Hof-und Staats Archiv, 960–PAI, Liasse Krieg 25z, Friedensverhandlung 25/21.

14. Ottokar Czernin, *Im Weltkrieg* (Berlin: Ullstein, 1919), pp. 187–188. Ottokar Czernin went out of his way to lure to Stockholm socialists from foreign states within which Austria had influence, in the hopes of adding to the weight of the likes of Viktor Adler. Sometimes these efforts of Czernin went sour. At the same time, however, they betray an element of urgency, if not desperation, in the foreign minister's maneuvering. For example, at Viktor Adler's request, the Ballhaus promoted the presence of two Serbs at the preliminary conference only to find out at the last moment that the men in question were in fact hostile to the integrity of the Austrian state. (958–PA1, Liasse Krieg 25z, Friedensverhandlung, ff. 2–40.) Another instance when expectations soured had to do with Czernin's facilitation of passage to Stockholm of two Turkish socialist delegates at

the behest of the Austrian ambassador to the Porte, Count Pallavicini. However, as it turned out, the Turks in question (Mukim Eddin, Akil Bey, and Ali Abbas) not only proved to be Russian citizens, but the delegates evidently were only interested in escaping out of Turkey, for once in Stockholm these Turks disappeared. Vienna, Haus Hof-und Staats Archive, 958–PAl, 25z, I 204, ff. 2–50.

15. See Czernin, *Im Weltkreig,* p. 188.

16. Vienna, Haus Hof-und Staats Archiv, PAl, 958, 25z, ff. 6–11. For an overview on Czernin's foreign policy, see Ingebord Meckling, *Die Aussenpolitik des Grafen Czernin* (Vienna: Verlag für Geschichte und Politik, 1969). The Ballhaus, viewing them as the coming power in Russia, also thought that socialist activity in Stockholm would bring Menshevik leaders to the Swedish capital, where contact then could be made that might lead to a separate peace between the Central Powers and the Russian state. The Swiss (left) socialist leader Karl Moor in fact did function as a go-between for the Austrian Embassy in Stockholm and Menshevik leaders such as Rozanoff and Martov. See Fürstenberg and Hadik to Count Czernin, Vienna, Haus Hof-und Staats Archiv, PAl, Liasse 959, ff. 405–409, 426–432.

17. Musulin was at this time the Dual Monarchy's legation in Bern. Switzerland, of course, being a neutral land easily accessible to members of the Central Powers and the Entente alike, was a hothouse of extracurricular intrigue; hence Musulin's usefulness to Czernin in this matter. For his part, Count Hadik was ambassador plenipotentiary to the Swedish crown. (See Vienna, Haus Hof-und Staats Archiv, 959, PAl, Liasse Kreig 25z, Friedenverhandlung., Kr. 25z, ff. 101.)

18. See Vienna, Haus Hof-und Staats Archiv, especially 959, PAl, Liasse 25z. The socialist cooperation with the Ballhaus, as might be expected, was not always appreciated by the party's rank and file. Indicative perhaps was Friedrich Adler's statement, made by him during his trial in May of 1917, in which he roundly condemned his father (and those associated with him) for cooperating with the Austrian government in defending not Austrian interests, but German interests in Austria. See the trial transcript of Friedrich Adler in the Friedrich Adler papers, "Voor 1923," on deposit in the Institute for Social History in Amsterdam.

19. See William J. McGrath, *Dionysian Art and Populist Politics in Austria* (New Haven: Yale University Press, 1974), especially pp. 17–86.

20. Vienna, Haus Hof-und Staats Archiv, PA1, 959, 25z, ff.180. See also Brügel, *Geschichte,* vol. V, pp. 290 ff. The twelve points in addition to no annexations or indemnities and the demand that Austria's Slav lands, including Bosnia, remain within the state were as follows: Italian demands for Austrian territory must vigorously be denied; autonomy for Poland and Finland (but the Poles in Galicia and Prussia also must be granted autonomy within Austria and Germany respectively); Alsace-Lorraine should be a *Bundesstaat* within Germany with guaranteed protection for its national minorities; Belgium must be reconstructed so as to give equality between the Flemish and Walloons; Bulgaria's demands regarding the Dobrudja must be fulfilled; Serbia must be reconstructed and united with Montenegro so as to possess access to the Adriatic; freedom of the seas is not to be disturbed in the future by economic warfare; setting aside the question of war guilt; the conclusion of armament limitation treaties; the abolition of secret diplomacy.

21. Vienna, Haus Hof-und Staats Archiv, 958K PAl, ff. 18. See Karl Renner's bitter comments against Britain and France (partly cited in this chapter) in his "In Stockholm und Daheim," *Der Kampf* X (1917), p. 237.

22. Vienna, Haus Hof-und Staats Archiv, 958–1, 25z, 1–109.

23. Ibid.

24. Ibid.

25. For a fuller discussion of the Stockholm Peace Conference and its counters, the Zimmerwald Conference (held in Switzerland) and the so-called Socialist and Workers Conference in London, see Olga Hess Gankin and H. H. Fisher, *The Bolsheviks and the World War* (Stanford: Stanford University Press, 1960) and Merle Fainsod, *International Socialism and the World War* (Cambridge: Harvard University Press, 1935). The Zimmerwald Conference was driven by the socialist left, and especially by the Bolsheviks, who thought that they were on the brink of seizing power in Russia. As a first step toward the goal of world revolution, they desired the breakup of the existing state system in central and east Europe. It was logical, therefore, that the Zimmerwald Conference came out for the reordering of Europe on the basis of national self-determination. The conclusions arrived at by the conference participants establish the difference in the objectives sought by the socialist left as against the socialist right. This becomes clear when the former's call for the breakup of Europe's states is compared to the caution of the Stockholm steering committee that "it is in the interest of advancing society to put a stop to the splintering of economic territory. It follows, therefore, that social democracy should handle nationality questions in line with the right of self-determination of peoples but within the framework of the advancement of the [general] good of society. Where a people cannot constitute an independent state, the freedom of their development should be secured by means of their political autonomy *[Selbstbehältung]* as a member of a democratic federal state." See "Kündigung des (Neutraler) Parteien des Internationalen," October 10, 1917. A copy of this is to be found in Vienna, Haus Hof-und Staats Archive, PA 1, K958, k25z, ff 76 ff. In addition, a socialist conference at London was held under the auspices of the British government so as to deflect criticism of its not allowing socialists visas to take part in the Stockholm peace conference. The Americans and French also denied socialists visas.

26. An ongoing debate over the Stockholm conference and the intention of some British socialists to attend took place in the British Parliament during May of 1917. Reports of parts of these debates appeared in the *London Times.* Philip Snowden, for example, pursuing the implications of the agenda being set through the Dutch-Scandinavian committee in Stockholm, proposed in Commons "that this House welcomes the declaration of the new democratic government in Russia repudiating all imperialistic aggrandizement and conquests." See *London Times,* May 17, 1917.

27. Woodrow Wilson's Fourteen Points articulated national self-determination of nations in the sense of independence rather than in the sense of autonomy for the first time only on January 7, 1918. See George V. Strong, "Woodrow Wilson, Thomas G. Masaryk and the Regeneration of Europe," paper presented at the Virginia Humanities Conference, "The Treaty of Versailles: The Shaping of the Modern World" (Staunton, Virginia, 1989). Wilson's change of nuance from autonomy to independence undoubtedly was due to British pressure, which in the late summer of 1917 not only saw that the Allied war effort was lackluster but feared a German militarist empire was in the making, with the end result of seriously transforming the European balance of power. So, in September of 1917, Prime Minister David Lloyd-George wrote to President Woodrow Wilson that "the allies had confidently expected to have produced very serious results for German military power. . . . Their failure is, of course, mainly attributable to the military collapse of Russia. . . . At a very early stage of the war Germany established a practically despotic dominion over her allies . . . so that the central empires and Turkey are to all intents and purposes a military empire with one command. For some time past it has seemed to me that we ought to consider very carefully whether we cannot achieve decisive results by concentrating first against Germany's allies. They are weak not only militarily but politically. They are also very anxious for peace, so that comparatively small success might produce far reaching results." See Arthur J. Link, ed., *The Woodrow Wilson Papers* (Princeton: Princeton University Press, 1983), 44, pp. 125–129.

28. Link, *The Woodrow Wilson Papers*, vol. 43, p. 127.

29. These matters can best be traced in Link, *The Woodrow Wilson Papers*, especially volumes 42 and 43, dealing with the First World War. The American view was heavily influenced by that of the British, the result of the most intense lobbying (not without the help of its Propaganda Office) by the latter. See especially "General Correspondence for 1917, British Foreign Office: British Mission to the United States," FO 800/214, filed in the British Public Record Office at Kew (London). That British propaganda had its helpers in America is attested to by George Creel in *How We Advertised America: The First Telling of the Amazing Story of the Committee of Public Information that Carried the Gospel of America to Every Corner of the Globe* (New York: Harper Brothers, 1920). See also Victor S. Mamatey, *The United States and Central Europe, 1914–1918: A Study of Wilsonian Diplomacy and Propaganda* (Princeton: Princeton University Press, 1957). Also useful in understanding the relationship between the American and British perspective is Hugh and Christopher Seton-Watson, *The Making of a New Europe: R.W. Seton-Watson and the Last Years of Austria-Hungary* (Seattle: University of Washington Press, 1981). The matter as viewed from Vienna is well summarized in Richard Georg, ed., *Die Auflösung des Habsburgerreiches, Zusammenbruch und Neuorientierung in Donauraum* (Munich: Oldenbourg, 1970). See also Adam Wandruszka and Peter Urbanitsch, eds., *Die Habsburgermonarchie: 1848–1918*, 4 volumes (Vienna: Verlag der österreichischen Akademie der Wissenschafter, 1980), and Winfried Baumgart, *Deutscher Ostpolitik 1918: Von Brest-Litovsk bis zum Ende des Ersten Weltkriegs* (Vienna: R. Oldenbourg, 1966). Variations on a theme came from many quarters. See, for example, Thomas G. Masaryk, later first president of the Czechoslovakian Republic, who had a rather fluid view of the future of central Europe. In 1915, Masaryk wrote seeking an independent Slav state out of "industrial Bohemia and agricultural Serbo-Croatia . . . [possessing a] corridor lead[ing] from Bohemia to the Serbo-Croatian ports. The corridor would, of course have great military significance . . . prevent[ing] the Germans from colonizing the Balkans and Asia Minor, and . . . would prevent the Magyars from being the advance guard of Berlin. . . . The Bohemian politicians think that Constantinople and the Straits can only belong to Russia . . . Bohemia is projected as a monarchical state, a Bohemian republic is advocated only by a few radical politicians. The dynasty could be established in either one of two ways. Either the allies could give one of their princes, or there could be a personal union between Serbia and Bohemia. . . . The Bohemian people are thoroughly Russophile. A Russian dynasty, in whatever form, would be most popular." Quoted in Robert W. Seton-Watson, *Masaryk in England* (Cambridge: Cambridge University Press, 1943), pp. 125–133.

30. Heinrich Tuma, "Zur Sudstawischen Frage," *Der Kampf* II (1918), pp. 92, 94.

31. Karl Mann, "Das Selbstimmungsrecht der österreichischen Nationen," *Der Kampf* IV (1918), pp. 214–215.

32. Karl Renner, "In Stockholm und Daheim," *Der Kampf* IX (1917), pp. 233–240.

33. Initially, on November 12, 1918, there was confusion in Vienna as to who was who in the emerging provisional government of German Austria. Originally, Karl Renner was thought to be director of the Office of Foreign Affairs *(Leiter des Staatsamt fur ausseres)*, in addition to being chancellor *(Staatskanzler)* and secretary of foreign affairs. This de facto dictatorship was ended a few days later when Dr. Viktor Adler assumed the office of secretary of foreign affairs *(Staatssecretär für Ausseres)* where Otto Bauer was undersecretary of the same. Karl Seitz became head of defense *(Heerwesen)*. Adler's unexpected death further clarified things when Bauer became secretary of foreign affairs, an office he held until October 17, 1919, when Renner, retaining his position as chancellor, assumed Bauer's position as well. By the beginning of 1920 the term Staatssecrētar was dropped in favor of *Bundesminister*. So, for example, on November 20, 1920, Seitz

was replaced by Egon Glanz as *Bundesminister fur Heerwesen.* (See Vienna, Austrian State Archives, N/P.A./209, Liasse Österreich 2/1. Prinzipielle innere Fragen, ff. 37–39.)

34. Austrian State Archiv, N.E.P. 304, Liasse Österreich 12/2, 1918–19, vol. 1–183, ff. 4–6. The note, while reflecting the views of the German Austrian leadership, was signed by the *Abgeordneten* Dindhofer, Fink, and Seitz for the National Assembly.

35. For a shorter summary of Bauer's ideas, which he held before to the First World War, whereby nationality recognition must be given only within existing state structures, see Otto Bauer, *Deutschtum und Sozialdemokratie* (Vienna: Volksbuchhandlung, 1907).

36. See Otto Bauer, "Notizen: Ein Nationalitätenprogram der Linken," *Der Kampf,* April 1918, pp. 269–274. Bauer's conclusions here contrast diametrically with his older ideas, expressed in his *Deutschtum und Sozialdemokratie.*

37. Ibid.

38. Ibid.

39. As one would suspect, there is no lack of evidence either in the press or in archival materials in general denouncing the *Anschluss.* Typical is a report that appeared in Madrid in November of 1918, in which Monsieur Paul Deschanel reported a conversation with Prince Bülow, which supposedly took place in Rome during September of 1914, and in which the former German chancellor stated, "We will win the war. But if we should not win it, we will win it anyway because in the latter case of the nine million German Austrians which would be annexed [by Germany]." At the same time, press releases planted by French opponents of *Anschluss* insisted that German Austria, due to her history, is much too diverse "nationally speaking" to be attached to Germany under the principle of "national self-determination." Vienna, one article claimed, did not have merely 100,000 Czech-speaking citizens, as stated by the Austrian Republic, but 500,000. See Vienna, Austrian State Archive, NPA-106, ff. 16–31.

40. Austrian State Archive, N.P.A. 106, "Anschluss Fragen mit Deutschland, 1918," ff. 8–11.

41. See Otto Bauer, *Die Österreich Revolution* (Vienna: Wienervolksbuchhandlung, 1923).

42. F. Horn to Friedrich Adler, May 9, 1919, found in the F. Adler papers at the Institute for Social History, Amsterdam, Box II, "Friedrich Adler voor 1921."

43. Friedrich Adler, "Deutsch Österreichs Zukunft," *Arbeiter Zeitung,* November 10, 1918.

44. Heinrich Fleischer to Friedrich Adler, November 19, 1918, in Archives, Institute for Social History, Amsterdam, "F. Adler voor 1923," Box 7.

45. Vienna, Austrian State Archive, NPA 209, ff. 26–27, dated March 2, 1919. For a general litany of German Austria's border difficulties with her new neighbors, see Vienna, Austrian State Archive., NPA 209 2/II, "Selbstandigers Vorgehen," ff. 26–27, dated February 3, 1919.

46. For explicit border problems with the south Slavs, see Vienna, Austrian State Archive, NPA, 167, ff. 11–12 and 60–61.

47. Germany seemed apparently under Social Democratic control between November 1918 and February 1919 in the guise of its provisional republic.

48. On the viability of a Danubian federation, see C.A. McCartney, *National States and National Minorities* (London: Royal Institute of International Affairs, 1934). Useful as background is a thesis (University of Basel) by Otto Sammuel Freiherr von Beck, *Die Wirtschafts-Gebiete an der Mittel-Donau vor dem Weltkreig* (Vienna: Manzsch, 1922).

49. Otto Bauer, "Wurzburg und Wien," *Der Kampf* November/December 1917, p. 330.

50. Thomas G. Masaryk, quoted in Seton-Watson, *Masaryk in England,* pp. 190–193. That at that time the Austrian government was fully conscious of this drift on the part of her Slavs away from Vienna, see Vienna, Haus Hof-und Staats Archiv, PAI

(Weltkrieg), especially XL/Interna, Karton 261, "Korrespondenz des K.u.K. Minister des Aussen."

51. See Vienna, Haus Hof-und Staats Archiv, letter from Count Czernin to Kaiser Karl of 12 April 1917, in PA I, Liasse xlvii/3 (17–22), 11Krieg 1914–18." See also the report, dated December 7, 1918, to Czernin, and the reasons for it, detailing why the "Polish Club" stood against the military budget in the Austrian Abgeordetenhaus, in PA I, XL/Iterna: "Korrespondenz des K.u.K. Ministers des Hauses des Aussen mit der Ministerium, 1911–1912," Karton 26. See also Ingebord Meckling, *Die Aussenpolitik des Grafen Czernin* (Vienna: Verlag für Geschichte und Politik, 1969).

52. For more on this point of view, see Ludo M. Hartmann, "Deutschland und Wir," *Der Kampf*, April 1918, and Karl Mann, "Das Selbstbestimmungsrecht der österreichischen Nationen," in the same issue. In 1918, Hartmann became Vienna's ambassador to Berlin and worked hand in glove with Bauer (and with the foreign office in Berlin) to achieve *Anschluss*. For an exchange of letters between Hartmann and Otto Bauer during the winter of 1918–1919, see Vienna, Austrian State Archive, NPA K428, ff. 226 passim; also NPA 107, ff 60–89 and NPA 167, f. 72, where Hartmann reports his telling the new president of the German Republic, Friedrich Ebert, that reconstruction in Austria would be very difficult if not impossible without union with Germany.

53. Renner's writings on the nationality question were extensive during the war period. His views however, increasingly were defensive. See, for example, Karl Renner, "Stockholm und Daheim," *Der Kampf*, October 1917, and his "Wirlichkeit oder Wahnidee," *Der Kampf*, January 1916. For a summary of Renner's ideas on nationalism through time, see Robert A. Kann, *Renners Beitrag zur Lösung Nationaler Konflikte im Lichte Nationaler Probleme der Gegenwart* (Vienna: Verlag der österreichischen Akademie der Wissenschaft, 1973). A letter written to the *Arbeiter Zeitung* on March 19, 1919, by a Herr Heinrich Fleischer against *Anschluss* typifies the arguments against it. Fliescher, responding to strong pro-*Anschluss* editorials written by Friedrich Adler, who became editor of the socialist daily upon his pardon and release from prison in November 1918, points out that he opposed "*Anschluss*, because it threatens to make Austria subservient to *Reichdeutsch* culture, finance and industry. . . . [Further,] it precludes all chances of some sort of relinkage with the states of the former empire." Fliescher went on to recall *(Reich)* German anti-Slavism as at least one reason why Austria should not be pulled away from her Danubian heritage, and he decried the likes of Otto Bauer and the socialist Karl Leuthner along with "politicians, journalists, professors of political science" along with their "indolent students" who favor *Anschluss*, maintaining that, other than the above, no one else favors it. See the Friedrich Adler papers deposited in the Archive, Institute for Social History, Amsterdam, Corr. 1918–1919. II, L-Z, varia for a number of similar dissents.

54. The atmosphere was replete with scare stories, seriously taken, over plots to restore both the Habsburgs and the monarchy. One example relates that Archduke Josef, son of the former Hungarian Palatine, Archduke Joseph, was to marry the Italian Princess Jolanta. This Italian connection, in turn, was to be used as a springboard for Josef to become king of Hungary and to bring into being a Danubian federation consisting of Hungary, Austria, and Rumania, under Italian auspices. The terrain for all of this was to be prepared by Constantine of Greece. Following this report is a series of reactions as diverse parties sought to squelch the romance in case it was more than mere rumor. See Vienna, Austrian State Archive, NPA, "Praesidium," K233 ff. 1–9 (dated August 25, 1921) and passim.

55. See letter by Bertha Zuckerkandl to Otto Bauer on her talks with the French consular official Chateauneuf at Bern on November 21, 1918. Vienna, State Archive, NPA-Praesidium, 233. f. 787. Interestingly from the standpoint of current history,

Chateauneuf also thought that "the Slovaks are too different in culture, history and somewhat in speech" to form a workable unitary state with the Czechs (ibid.). On similar doubts concerning the viability of a Danubian federation, see ibid., ff. 919–957.

56. Vienna, Austrian State Archives, Counselor Haupt in Bern to Otto Bauer, February 6, 1919. Vienna, Austrian State Archive, NPA-Praesidium-233, ff. 821–822.

57. Since the instrument was never ratified due to the forbidding of *Anschluss* written into both the Treaties of St. Germain and Versailles, it cannot be called a treaty. See *"Protokoll: Verhandlungen Zwischen Deutsch Österreich und Deutschland am 27 Feb. bis zu 2 Marz, 1919."* Vienna, Austrian State Archive, NPA 108, ff. 2–7.

58. Ibid.

59. Huysmann told the Ballhaus, through the Austrian Consul at Bern, where the socialists were holding a conference to forward a just peace, that he, like an overwhelming number of French socialists, supported national self-determination in Woodrow Wilson's sense. However, Huysmann interpreted such national self-determination to mean, for German Austria, *Anschluss*. Huysmann also thought that the new Germany would have the right to the cities of Danzig and Trieste. See Vienna, State Archiv, NEP Prasidium, 233, f. 795 (dated January 21, 1919).

60. See Julius Braunthal, Viktor Adler, and Friedrich Adler, *Zwei Generationen Arbeiterbewegung* (Vienna: Wiener Volksbuchhandlung, 1965). A proper setting for understanding the likes of the Adlers is given in Steven Beller, *Vienna and the Jews, 1867–1938: A Cultural History* (Cambridge: Cambridge University Press, 1989). Also useful is William O. McCagg, Jr., *A History of the Habsburg Jews: 1670–1918* (Bloomington: Indiana University Press, 1989) and Arthur Schnitzler, *My Youth in Vienna,* trans. Catherine Hutter (New York: Holt, Rinehart & Winston, 1970) Schnitzler paints a very interesting portrait of life among the Jewish haute bourgeoisie in Vienna ca. 1900 in his *The Road to the Open,* trans. Horace Samuel (New York: Knopf, 1923).

61. See Friedrich Austerlitz, "Der Kaiser," *Der Kampf* IV (1911), pp. 143–143.

62. Whether Masaryk was nationalist in a Czech sense or in a greater Czech sense or merely anti-Habsburg, anti-Austrian, or anti-German remains an open question. See note 44 above. In any event, his final evolution is frozen in his *Thomas Garrigue Masaryk, The Making of a State: Memoirs and Observations, 1914–1918,* trans. Henry Wickham-Steed (New York: Frederick A. Stoakes, 1928).

63. Emperor Franz Joseph, quite naturally, was one of the last articulators of an older view wherein old Austria had more than a mere historical mission, for "more than the historical events of the past have brought our peoples together. [They have been brought together] by the absolute necessity of their present and future well-being. The monarchy therefore, is not merely and artificial creation, it is an organic one and as such even doubly necessary, for it is a refuge, an asylum for all the national splinter groups in central Europe which, if they stood alone, must lead a doubtful and troubled existence, as they would become a football for their more powerful neighbors." Quoted in A. Freiherrn von Margutti, *Vom Alten Kaiser: Persönliche Erinnerungen Franz Joseph I* (Leipzig: Leonhardt Verlag, 1922), pp. 261–262.

64. See Bruce Pauley, *Hitler and the Forgotten Nazis: A History of Austrian National Socialism* (Chapel Hill: University of North Carolina Press, 1981).

✧ 9 ✧

Interment

F rau Herdan's premonition, given vent as she and her daughter clutched one
another in the face of some felt but unseen terror, turned out to be something more; indeed, it turned out to be a recognition of fact. The triumph of
nationalism for the old monarchy indeed was interred symbolically with the
actual burial of Emperor Franz Joseph I. And not a few observers, like the
Herdans, understood that they were witnessing for the last time old Austria's
ceremony of the whole as the imperial funeral procession made its way, in
somber, hushed splendor, from the Hofburg out across the Heldenplatz and along
the Ringstrasse toward its final destination, the ancient Church of the Capuchins
on Vienna's Neuermarkt. And so too did Luise's tears express what was to be the
lot of Danubia's peoples as the remnants of the old state searched for a new order
during the tumultuous decades following the First World War. And while inherently such a search is always ongoing, it must be observed that to this day,
despite a glimmer of promise from time to time, a stable order like that which
was lost to central Europe in 1916 has yet to be found. Stately order is more
easily destroyed than created.

Franz Joseph's death came at a moment when not only he but many of his
ministers responsible for state policy had recognized that the war was beyond
Austria's strength and that, in the emperor's words, "[it would] have to be
brought to an end."[1] It is doubtful, however, whether even the strength of the old
man's hoary authority would have been sufficient to overcome the hydra-headed
thrust for war. Not only was Great Britain, on the Entente side, resolved to
continue the struggle against Germany, but the war party had also come into
control of policy within the *Reich* as well.[2] Hence, the opinion makers within the
Central Powers were no less resolved to continue to do battle than were those
within the Entente. And while it was true that there was a considerable
groundswell within official circles in Austria to find a way out of belligerency,
these sentiments were not shared by the power brokers in Berlin and London,
and feelings in Vienna counted for little in the German and British capitals.

Austria's apparent initial success against the Russians on the Russia-Galicia
border had collapsed in September of 1914, as was made patently clear with
Austria's loss of the pivotal stronghold of Przemysl. Matters became worse for
the monarchy when, in May of 1915, Italy deserted the alliance for the Entente,
resulting in the opening of a second front for Austria. And while until the very

last weeks of the war Italy's forces were held down by Austrian troops, the Dual Monarchy remained dangerously exposed to Russian troops north and east of the Carpathians.[3] Given Berlin's overwhelming successes against the Russians in Poland, and given the need for stable battle lines in the east while the Germans concentrated on breaking through French and British positions on the western front, Berlin decided to shore up Vienna's efforts against the Russians, with the result that the German General Erich von Falkenhayn had become de facto generalissimo of the Austrian war effort. Falkenhayn had accomplished this feat by interspersing Austrian units with German troops so that the Austrian army, and hence the government of the Danubian realm itself, was hostage to the German army.[4] And since the German army command came to control the decision-making process in Berlin, Austria-Hungary fell into the hands of the German general staff *(Oberstkriegsheerleitung)* and hence had little real independence from Berlin of its own. The Austrians might recommend, but the Germans commanded. Gradually central Europe was thereby transformed into a German empire. Given the historic tensions between the Germans and the Slavs, and given the Dual Monarchy's supposed mission to adjudicate these differences, Vienna's subservience to Berlin won no friends for the Habsburg dynasty among disaffected Austrian Slavs.[5] Moreover, perceptions as to circumstances were not improved by the widespread feeling that the new Habsburg chief, unable to fill the imperial nimbus left vacant by the departed Emperor Franz Joseph, was helpless in the face of the monarchy's aggressive German ally.

After his death in November of 1916, the new standard-bearer for the House of Habsburg was Franz Joseph's grandnephew, the twenty-eight-year-old Karl I. If the times had been more ordinary, Karl might have been just what the dynasty required to bridge the absolutist perspective of his great-uncle with the requirements of a modern, popular, and constitutional monarchy. The new emperor had the advantage of comely youth; he was well educated and, moreover, had had his education within a more democratic framework than had ever been possible in the era when the old emperor had been young. In addition, standing by the side of the amiable, darkly handsome, and diffident monarch was his attractive consort, Zita of Bourbon-Parma. But unlike her husband, the young empress carried the strongest of wills behind her smiling visage and personable demeanor. Indeed, perhaps the ignominious fate that awaited the dynasty might have been otherwise if their roles could have been reversed, for where her husband lacked discipline and stamina, Zita displayed purposeful resolve. More significant, she was endowed with considerable natural political savvy, and if somewhat uneducated formally in the ways of modern politics, she was nevertheless in possession of a mind and character that complemented her determined ambition that she and her husband succeed in the task assigned to them by Providence.[6]

The picture-book-handsome couple would have made popular monarchs if 1917 had been more ordinary times, for Karl and Zita in every way deported themselves as popular and constitutional sovereigns. But of course 1917 was hardly ordinary, and so the couple paid a heavy personal price for the conditions fate had handed them. [7]

The young couple had been married only a scant four years when Franz Ferdinand and his consort were assassinated. They heard the news as they were sitting in their garden, savoring a rare quiet moment and enjoying together the clear blue summer afternoon—a rare moment because even then Karl and Zita were only too conscious that they were not an ordinary couple, for they were at the same time both indulged with every luxury and inordinately burdened by the oppressive ceremonial of their high-born life. If ostensibly they were fairy-tale prince and princess, they also were Habsburg and Bourbon, scions of Europe's august dynasties and all too conscious that not only they themselves but their children as well were destined to play their part in the fortunes of the House of Habsburg-Lorraine. From earliest childhood the couple were accustomed to yielding up their private moments to the demands of their greater fate, and so too it was no different on that sunny, summer afternoon—with one exception: The clarion call that summoned them from their summer's idyll was one that would turn their life, and the course of the entire world, upside down. So it was that the news of the death of Franz Ferdinand and Sophie reached Karl and Zita in the garden of Villa Wartholz (as irony would have it, the parental home of both Karl and the murdered heir to the throne). In later years, Zita recalled:

> It was one of the most emotional moments of my life. In this park belonging to Villa Wartholz, Franz Ferdinand's father (he who was also my husband's grandfather), Archduke Karl Ludwig who, like all Habsburgs, was a passionate and skilled craftsman, had created a summer house out of logs with the help of only one old carpenter. They had given it a lovely sitting room and a small veranda. Later [Karl Ludwig] had surrounded it with a hedge within which he had created a little garden of flowers and vegetables . . . [and] it was in this little garden, on June 28, 1914, that Karl and Zita sat waiting for the main meal which was unbelievably long in coming. . . . What's the matter? Something must have happened since no one had come. In the end, it was the bearer of a telegram and not a waiter who finally made an appearance. . . . Archduchess Zita sat up with fright as Karl suddenly turned white as a sheet. Silence. And then [Karl] took a deep breath.[8]

Karl's first thought was that the assassination of his uncle made him the presiding heir to the throne. His second thought seems to have been that he must speak with his great-uncle, the eighty-three-year-old Franz Joseph, who already must have been informed of the tragedy at his summer quarters in Bad Ischl. And so it was that a few days later the new Habsburg heir awaited the old, physically frail emperor at the Penzing train station, located on the western fringes of Vienna near the imperial castle of Schönbrunn. Moving through a crowd of humanity who had come to wish kaiser and nephew well, the sovereign and the archducal heir went off to the palace, where the mayor of Vienna, Joseph

Weiskirchner, waited armed with the customary welcome the local worthies were expected to provide when their emperor returned to his capital and residence city.[9]

As kaiser and king, Karl had to deal with a political system not only in crisis but shot through and through with men and women of an older generation and a different experience, men and women therefore perhaps incapable of understanding that time and events had rendered their perspective unsuited to the task before them. If Karl and his empress (Zita was far more than merely his consort) had been an integral and visible part of the political scene over a long period of time—like, for example, the dead heir to the throne, Franz Ferdinand—then the imperial and royal couple might have possessed the kind of authority that would have surmounted these encrustations of time. But until that fateful day, June 28, 1914, the young couple had not been widely visible in the public eye. Instead, it was Archduke Franz Ferdinand, in any event a very strong personality, who was presumed to have a long life before him as Austria-Hungary's kaiser and king. Naturally all eyes had focused on the Belvedere and not on one of the minor castles occupied by Karl and Zita. In addition, although humane, friendly, and well-intentioned, Karl's character was not aggressive. And certainly it was not domineering. In addition, Karl lacked the capacity for long hours of sustained and disciplined work that had transformed his great-uncle into that proverbial manikin whose existence apparently was limited to long hours behind his desk when he was not otherwise occupied with reviewing his troops, opening new buildings, and the like. And of course Karl could not possess the authority derived from being a living legend, the mystique that had devolved on Franz Joseph simply because of his longevity and his associations with a hoary past in which few of his living subjects had participated.[10]

The imperial couple carried an added burden in that Zita was a Bourbon and hence, as it was often said, a member of a dynasty that was the "wormwood of royalty."[11] More salient to the times was that her family, because it belonged to the Franco-Italian House of Bourbon-Parma, was identified in the public mind with two of the monarchy's continental western enemies, France and Italy, despite the fact that the family had lived in exile within Austria for decades. Moreover, one of the empress's brothers, Sixtus, was an officer in the French army, while another fought under the Belgian banner.[12] In an another era, where loyalty to one's chief was on the basis of a personal oath, these supranational, pan-European relationships natural within the aristocratic circles of the ruling elites would not have disturbed opinion. But in a chauvinistic era concomitant with the age of public and popular government, people expected their political leaders to be defined in every way possible as belonging in their camp. And indeed, in the spring of 1917, when it came to light that the emperor had been dealing secretly with France for peace, that he was ready to return Alsace-Lorraine to France, that his German ally had not been consulted, and that the intermediary had been none other than Zita's brother, Prince Sixtus, the public's outcry against Zita was comprehensible if nevertheless misplaced.[13]

Karl first displayed his disconcerting, perhaps even fatal, inability to stand against the weight of time when, on succeeding Franz Joseph, he immediately succumbed to the demands of the Hungarian minister-president, Count Stephan Tisza, that Karl be publicly crowned king of Hungary. This coronation took place with unseemly haste in Budapest in February of 1917 amid a degree of pomp patently insensitive in the face of Austrian deaths on the battlefronts and hardship on the home front. But more significant was that Karl took an oath, ceremoniously before all the world, to uphold the Hungarian constitution and hence the current dualistic state structure. In so playing to the Magyars, Karl thereby preempted most of the options open to him for restructuring the state so as to accommodate the demands of cultural nationalism. Whether Karl fully realized his commitment to the Magyars, or if he would have honored these commitments under other circumstances, can only be guessed at. But it is certain that Count Tisza knew what he was about; that is, he set out not only to carve the *Ausgleich* in stone but to tie Karl's hands regarding future reform. Austria's Slavs, already observing Vienna's subservience to Berlin, could not be faulted if they concluded that, given this further bowing before the politics of power, the likelihood of cultural-national fulfillment for the Slavs under Karl and Zita, though the royal couple might be well-intentioned, was dim indeed. Hence, beyond giving an incongruous if interesting display of a splendid but anachronistic exercise, the coronation in Budapest only increased the centrifugal swirl of nationalism.[14]

Until the spring of 1917, it still could be argued that the despotic forces of oriental barbarism said to be inherent in czarist Russia's lust for expansion continued to be a factor threatening international life. Hence arguments for Austria's continuation in the war, like, for example, that given by Friedrich Austerlitz in his famous essay "Der Tag des deutschen Nation" on August 5, 1914, still had considerable force within broad elements of Austrian public opinion. However, the beginning of the Russian Revolution in February of 1917, followed by the overthrow of the Romanov autocracy and the apparent disintegration of its empire only weeks after the outbreak of rioting in St. Petersburg, deprived Vienna of the last shreds of a rationale for continued participation in the war. By May of 1917 the moment had arrived for Vienna to cut bait, so to speak. However, Austrian authorities were only able to demonstrate Vienna's inability to take the helm and maneuver the Habsburg ship of state free of Berlin's demands that Austria fight on until the Alliance had achieved peace with victory. In short, Karl's government proved that it was German intransigence that governed in Vienna.

Perhaps nowhere was Austria's role as the tail of the German dog more manifest than in the controversy that broke out between the two allies over the future of Poland. Although the issue of whether Poland would be autonomous, and if so, whether under German or Austrian auspices, had been simmering even before the death of the old emperor, it broke out in full force during the spring and summer of 1917. Vienna, to preserve Galicia for the crown lands, wished to reconstruct Poland so that the resurrected state would possess autonomy within the framework of the monarchy and its king would be the Habsburg archduke Karl Stephen. The German general staff made it clear, however, that it preferred its own solution whereby the Poles would be tied to the *Reich* under the rule of the duke of Hesse. Although the dispute never reached settlement, it had become clear in the course of the debate that the price exacted by the Germans for acquiescence to the Austrians' solution would be so high as to contradict its basic advantage for Vienna. The *Reich* government gave Austria to understand that even if Vienna were permitted to reign, the concessions extracted by Germany would ensure that Berlin would command.[15]

Vienna's helplessness in the grip of her German ally dovetailed with Great Britain's decision, independently arrived at, to work for the breakup of the Dual Monarchy. To be sure, London was not especially focused on bringing about the collapse of Austria-Hungary per se, but Whitehall had concluded that victory over the German *Reich* would be facilitated if Berlin were forced to fight alone.[16] This British policy, while implemented from London, was heralded not from the British capital but by the American president in Washington. Destiny, it seems, had presented London with an agent for the fulfillment of its intentions in the form of America going to war against the Central Powers.[17] For his part, Woodrow Wilson, by character inclined toward a certain self-righteousness, seemed not at all unwilling to pit the power of the American colossus against what he deemed to be the autocratic and unwanted political anachronism seated in Vienna. This view perhaps demonstrated that Wilson had only a simple grasp of Europe's ethno-political complexity. That Wilson tended toward reducing complexity to simplicity is attested to by his close confidant, Colonel House, who wrote that once while talking about education, the president

> expressed himself as not being in agreement with the general modern trend against the classics. He thought the world had gained as much by untruths of history as by the truth. He did not believe that the human mind should be held down to facts and material matters. . . . German thought expressed itself in terms of machinery and gasses. The reading of Romance languages and the higher flights of fancy in literature led one to spiritual realms which, to say the least, was as advantageous to the world as its material progress. [The British foreign secretary, Lord] Balfour said that he had never heard this view expressed but agreed with it, whether from politeness or not I do not know.[18]

In any event, the American president grandly announced that America had entered the war to fight to end all wars, and she would use victory to create a world safe for democracy. A democratic world would be a world at peace. But it required that Austria's nations be given the right of democratic national self-determination.[19] Pronounced in this vein in December of 1918, Wilson's fiat not only launched what was to be America's nearly century-long ideological war from across the

Atlantic, but her proclamation coincided with the demonstration that Austria was no longer necessary to Europe, as had once been proclaimed by Frantisek Palacky, because Vienna possessed no independence of action from Berlin and, at the same time, the perceived threat from czarist Russia had evaporated. Hence, a constellation of circumstances, unimaginable even the year before, now conspired to bring down not only the Austrian state but that political order that extended from the Rhine eastward across Asia to the Pacific. Certainly neither Karl nor his weakening government could any longer channel these gargantuan centrifugal forces. It was quite clear in Vienna by the end of March 1918, and especially after the monarchy had been compelled to march in lock step with Germany as a consequence of the debacle surrounding the Prince Sixtus affair as well as her forced acquiescence to the Peace of Brest-Litovsk in March of 1918, that if Germany were victorious, Austria would survive, but her survival would be both unhappy and seriously flawed, for she would be merely a political creation within a Hohenzollern, pan-German Mitteleuropa. On the other hand, if Germany went down in defeat, it was just as clear that Austria-Hungary would disintegrate in some fashion along some of the lines defining her component parts. But what was most clear and disheartening was that whatever the outcome, Vienna could have little input in its determination.[20] Great Britain, by the same token, would have her way, if only because of London's hold over the imaginations of America's politically articulate.[21] And so world war had destroyed that European framework within which old Austria had defined her mission. Time and events had outstripped the *raison d'être* of the realm of the Habsburgs. But, of course, the outcome of the Great War had destroyed much else as well.

In the years immediately following the end of the First World War, south-central Europe was a political vacuum. The Dual Monarchy had been replaced by a series of successor states of which none but rump Austria and rump Hungary could be called nation-states. The trauma emanating out of this sudden, certainly unexpected, transformation rendered these successor states badly disarrayed to varying degrees; the disarray was magnified by the general debility that was the inevitable outcome of the immoral squandering of human and material resources in the course of more than four years of war. Catastrophe too is a hydra-headed behemoth.

The German and Russian nations to the northeast and east respectively had suffered hugely as well. But even though the German and Russian states had been destroyed, the two nations still were whole, and were in a vengeful mood. And in fact the German Austrian republic stood as a potential addition to the territorial power of the German nation-state. In south-central Europe, however, there were no other nations, states, or nation-states that might counterbalance the vengeful dynamic implicit in the existence of the German and Russian nations. Should the vindictive mood of the Germans and Russians find the leadership that could tame and harness this lust for vengeance, then vengeance stood poised to fill the political void that defined south-central Europe after 1918. And indeed, there was even the possibility that Danubia might become the battleground on which the two nations, historically at one another's throats, might continue their struggle for hegemony over one another. But now there existed no mitigating power like that once exercised by Austria-Hungary. There was in Danubia only a gaggle of defenseless and feuding peoples living within states convulsed by irredentist sentiment. In short, the region was open to whichever won hegemony over the other: Germany or Russia. The advent of modernism had unleashed forces too powerful to be contained by the old political state systems. In Austria-Hungary, modernism took the form of cultural nationalism and so too provided the perfect weapon her enemies might use to destroy the political synthesis of the old monarchy.

The old state systems in central Europe had, up until the twentieth century, successfully subsumed, harmonized, and synthesized the ethnic diversity contained within them so as to give space wherein human creativity was unfettered to produce a civilization; that is, a high culture characterized by a dynamic intelligence. However, this collapsed in the crucible of cultural nationalism.

Two additional powerful forces were unleashed during this process: nationalism and socialism. The vacuum left by the collapse of the old political culture permitted these two ideologies to combine with one another to bring about national socialism. This bizarre amalgam, while a precondition for both Stalinist Russia and Hitlerian Germany, did not necessarily have to lead to the fascist juggernaut that arose in Europe between the two world wars. It was a combination that might have remained in the hands of the likes of an Otto Bauer or a Rudolf Hilferding. But the historical fact is that the Hitlers and Stalins triumphed over the latter.

At bottom, nationalism (a sort of tribalism) and socialism (a sort of communal approach to the holding of material property) are, of course, instinctive to human nature. Human beings do generally run with the herd, and that herd, so to speak, seeks free and unfettered rights to the common pasture. But these group impulses, perhaps locked in biology and surmounted by the fire of reason only when society permits the individual to exercise it, obtain political leverage only when the herd instincts are institutionalized in popular political culture. Of course, it requires no telling here that the variety of national socialism that ultimately was institutionalized proved to be a vastly destructive centrifugal force especially because this same variety emanated from a national self-consciousness that had deep ethno-cultural roots.

Nationalism, if the experience of central Europe is a trustworthy measure, appears to be a kind of cultural "scent"—expressed through language, but sometimes concurrently through other factors such as religion—by which human beings identify with one another. If in addition there is a perception of national turf, coming from the occupation of territory by a now self-conscious national group, these self-perceived ethno-cultural national groups then lay exclusive claim to that turf. Marxist socialists learned that nationalism transcends class distinctions, while the elite of old Austria learned that it overrides high culture. Nationalism, then, is a powerful instinct but most so when it is linked to a sense of national turf.

It is perhaps too facile to state that socialism simply is a natural expression of the human desire for a free ride, but to some extent the want of a free ride does explain its emergence. Of course, in modern, complex societies socialism is fueled by much more than a simple desire to be rid of the obligation to labor. Indeed, the instinct has been turned around so that it is an expression of labor's desire to be free of the constraints of capital. Hence, modern socialism is also driven by the search for economic security. In addition, it is driven by the quest for social acceptance. And last, because it is a perspective driven by the need for both security and acceptance, socialism at bottom is an expression of envy. Envy, of course, when it becomes a part of a political culture, is destructive.

Because socialism, in its context in modern Europe, paradoxically is anti-modern—that is, hostile to industry and capital—it is potentially destructive to the political culture of industrial capitalism. And socialism is a natural bedfellow for nationalism because nationalism, which extols the perceived folk community, is antimodern as well. Hence, it is because of its inherent antimodernism that socialism found ready acceptance by national communities such as those extolled by Karl Luegar or Baron Vogelsang. In this fashion, then, socialism and nationalism fused into what became national socialism. By the same token, Marxist social democracy, never seemingly driven by instinct—as demonstrated by the very fact that it had been cloaked in class struggle and internationalism—was rejected by the national community because it was too abstract and modern, and, above all, because it by definition opposed instinct.

The acceleration of the processes of deconstruction of the Austrian idea, the failure of international class socialism to bear fruit, and the very destruction of the old Austrian state itself all attest to the centrifugal power of unfettered national socialism. Many nuances in national socialism were revealed during central Europe's fin de siècle era. In the final analysis, however, the coloration of its different varieties was largely dependent on the character of the leadership that defined and brought it to maturity. Nevertheless, the roots of national socialism appear to be derived from the fundamentals of human nature. Through the experience of popular politics—when, so to speak, leavened by modernism and fermented with industry and capital—it became rooted in political culture. National socialism was then unloosed to generate political storms to which, as with their natural counterparts, human beings must bend. In other words, the collective nature of human existence, like its existence in nature per se, renders human beings potential victims, not only to natural phenomena, but to political phenomena as well.

Because of its ideological dress, social democracy was a potential complement to the Austrian idea. But then the Austrian idea too was ultimately rejected by the national communities in Danubia as too much of an abstraction. What survived was national socialism, a sense of belongingness founded in rooted national communities combined with the need for social security that was promised by the political leadership within those same communities. The likes of the Jewish-dominated leadership of Austro-Marxism, largely known as internationalist, could neither flourish or survive in post–World War I Danubia. And especially they could not successfully compete against the heirs of a Karl Luegar or Georg von Schönerer, with Christian Socialism or Czech and German national socialism. Ultimately, therefore, it was the likes of Engelbert Dollfuss and the lugubrious Adolf Hitler that gave postwar national socialism in Mitteleuropa its final shape. It was Adolf Hitler that led his nationalist socialist community into the Second World War and thereby against counter–national socialist forces much more powerful. And so, too, much of the history of central Europe during the second half of the twentieth century fell into the hands of Joseph Stalin.

The metacenter of a large nation is perhaps sufficient in itself to arrest the centrifugal forces residing in it; that is, to discipline the potential agents of deconstruction in its political culture. But against this same pull, small nations, and especially if these are not dominant within a given territory, lack this necessary gravity. These small nations therefore inherently are vulnerable to disruption from within and occupation from without. A multinational state entity might seem to be a solution to such vulnerability. But the history of modern Europe demonstrates that states of such collective diversity do not prevail when contested by this same diversity. Both the Austrian-Hungarian Dual Monarchy and the Ottoman Empire collapsed early in the twentieth century. More recently, the Soviet Union and its empire evaporated before our very eyes, and the former Yugoslavia has been convulsed by a brutal and bloody civil war. Outside of Europe, in Africa, for example, multiethnic states do not seem to be holding either.

Lastly, how might the Austrian experience encourage historians to examine the state of being within that vast, continental multicultural entity, the United States of America? Is America not a diverse state, a melting pot in the process (one hopes) of transfiguration into a nation-state? Will the force of the American tradition hold while it is in fact being centrifugally reshaped so as to fit the ideal of a truly diverse, egalitarian, and democratic political entity? Historically, most of America's currently self-conscious ethnic groups cannot lay exclusive claim to any of her turf. Historical experience has given over American ground to all of her nations equally (on the other hand, it no longer belongs to the relatively few surviving native Americans who once did claim it exclusively). If, however, a self-identified ethnic group comes to successfully link its sense of its destiny with any part of the American turf, then American history could be pulled in an opposite direction, the state pulled apart by the centrifugal forces of cultural nationalism.

There may be something that can be called psychological turf, a cybernetically approached space issuing out of the psyche that is not tangible. Rather, cybernetic spheres of influence might be delineated from within an otherwise seemingly polyglot culture by self-defined ethnic or professional groups or by more broadly defined groups delineated by class or gender. Will the process of reconstructing, through cybernetics or other approaches, those intangible spaces residing in the human psyche prove deconstructive to America's current state synthesis? Will the gathering perception that America belongs to groups and not to individuals prove fatal to the sense of the wholeness of American political culture? And further, if these new perceptions create powerful centrifugal forces that come to be sufficiently strong to stand on their own, what perceptions might then be even stronger so as to hold the wholeness of America together? Time will tell. In 1900, the deconstruction of the political culture of old Austria seemed impossible. In 1980, the deconstruction of the political culture of the Soviet Union was unimaginable. Clio is ever tending to her spinning.

Notes

1. See Erich Feigl, ed., *Kaiserin Zita: Legende und Wahrheit* (Vienna: Amalthea, 1978), p. 191. See also Ernst Trost, *Franz Joseph I* (Vienna: Fritz Molden, 1980), p. 75.
2. On Germany's war party, see Fritz Fischer, *Griff nach der Weltmacht* (Düsseldorf: Droste Verlag, 1961).
3. For the story of the First World War from the perspective of Austria-Hungary, see Arthur J. May, *The Passing of the Habsburg Monarchy, 1914–1918,* 2 volumes (Philadelphia: University of Pennsylvania Press, 1966).
4. See May, *The Passing of the Habsburg Monarchy,* vol. II, pp. 497–531.
5. See Ottokar Czernin von und zu Chudenitz, *Im Weltkrieg* (Berlin: Ullstein, 1919), pp. 28, 38ff. See also Arthur Count Polzer-Hoditz, *The Emperor Karl* (Boston: Houghton Mifflin, 1922), pp. 94ff.
6. On Zita, see E. Vasari, *Zita, Kaiserin und Königin* (Vienna: Herold, 1976).
7. For a sympathetic and insightful summary of Karl and Zita, see Polzer-Hoditz, *The Emperor Karl* (Vienna: Amalthea, 1928). See also Herbert Vivian, *The Life of Kaiser Karl of Austria* (London: Grayson and Grayson, 1932); Karl Martin Werkmann [von Hohensalzburg], *Der Tote auf Maderia* (Munich: Verlag für Kultur und Politik, 1923); *Kaiser Karls Nachlass* (Berlin: Verlag für Kultur-Politik, 1925). On Zita, see Feigl, *Kaiserin Zita,* and E.H.P. Cordfunke, *Zita, keizerin van Oostenrijk, koningin van Hongarije* (Amsterdam: Bataafsche Leeuw, 1986).
8. Feigl, *Kaiserin Zita,* pp. 167–168 (my translation).
9. Ibid., p. 167.
10. On Karl, see Herbert Vivian, *The Life of Emperor Charles of Austria* (London: Grayson and Grayson, 1932). See also Baron Charles Werkman, *The Tragedy of Charles Habsburg,* trans. L.E. Lockhart (London: P. Allen, 1924).
11. The House of Bourbon was reputedly described in this vein by Franz Joseph himself. See Josef Schneider ed., *Kaiser Franz Joseph I und sein Hof: Erinnerungen und Schilderungen aus des Nachgelassenen Papieren eines Persönlichen Ratgebers* (Vienna: Paul Zsolnay, 1984), p. 139.
12. This seeming crossing of loyalties from the contemporary perspective was explained by the historian Robert A. Kann, who maintained that "the essence of dynasticism was neither in personal contacts nor in so-called monarchical solidarity to maintain and achieve common objectives but much more [it was] a matter of common allegiance to

self-preservation within each system of *Machtpolitik.*" Hence, in the family of Bourbon-Parma, loyalties defined by an older aristocratic state system appeared in conflict with newer ones emanating out of modern state systems. See Robert A. Kann, *Franz Ferdinand Studien* (Cambridge: Cambridge University Press, 1974), p. 11.

13. See Robert A. Kann, *Die Sixtus Affare und die geheimen Friedensverhandlungen ÖsterReich-Ungarn im Ersten Weltkrieg* (Vienna: Verlag fur Geschichte und Politik, 1966).

14. See Polzer-Hoditz, *Kaiser Karl,* pp. 133ff. See also Cordfunke, *Zita,* pp. 59–70.

15. In return for permitting an Austro-Polish solution whereby Poland would have autonomy linked to Vienna by having the Habsburg archduke Karl Stephen as its king, Berlin, its policy in this instance formulated by the OHL, dominated by General Erich Ludendorff, made heavy demands on Vienna. Most significant were: Poland's resources were to be used in ways compatible with Germany's military-economic interests in Poland, future railway development was to be compatible with Germany's industrial and military needs, and Polish migratory workers were to be permitted easy exit to and from Prussia. In addition, Vienna was to agree to a broad series of tariffs favorable to German interests, agree to joint German-Austrian regulation of shipping on the Danube and Elbe rivers and, should Austria obtain territory from Rumania, German goods were to have free access to that territory across Austria-Hungary. Lastly, the German *Reich* would be given naval bases at Valona on the Adriatic, and the Ballhaus would support German efforts to obtain revisions from the Vatican regarding the governance of Roman Catholic dioceses in Lithuania and all of Poland. See Haus Hof-und Staats Archiv, PA-1, Number 504, Liasse XLVII/3 (17–22), "Krieg 1914–1918," folios 757–760: "Summary of talks in Berlin, November 5 and 6, 1917." See also Ingeborg Meckling, *Die Aussenpolitk des Grafen Czernin* (Vienna: Verlag für Geschichte und Politik, 1969), especially pp. 190ff.

16. The nuances of British thinking about Austria-Hungary are revealed in documents found in the British Public Record Office, "General Correspondence for 1917." See especially "British Mission to the United States," FO 800/208, 800/209 and 800/214. See also Link, *The Woodrow Wilson Papers,* especially volumes 43 and 44. For example, Woodrow Wilson's closest advisor, Col. House, told of a talk he had with the British prime minister's confident, Sir William Wiseman. Wiseman, who actually was "Chief of British Intelligence in the U.S.A.," told House that Lloyd-George, in the strictest confidence, had told him "what he had in mind to do. He [Lloyd-George] had not even yet communicated this to the . . . cabinet. The war on the western front . . . bids fair to be a stalemate. . . . [Lloyd-George] believes that another way out must be found, and he has in mind the smashing of Turkey, or the smashing of Austria." (See Link, *The Woodrow Wilson Papers,* vol. 44, p. 202.) On Sir William Wiseman, see W.B. Fowler, *British-American Relations 1917–1918: The Role of Sir William Wiseman* (Princeton: Princeton University Press 1969.

17. The progression in President's Wilson's thinking is clearly evident in documents published in Link, *The Woodrow Wilson Papers.* For example, on April 26, 1917, the British Ambassador reported to David Lloyd-George that Woodrow Wilson "has very clearly grasped the fact [*sic*] that Germany inspired by militarism is [*sic*] the real enemy . . . but both he and Mr. Lansing entertained strong hopes to detach Austria from her domineering partner" (vol. 42, p. 141). "But . . . Wilson appears to be undergoing a change in attitude toward Austria for the . . . President believed that, even if a democratic regime be . . . instituted in the German Empire after the war, the races forming the Austro-Hungarian agglomeration would wish to be emancipated" (vol. 43, p. 468). "On August 7, 1917, the American Ambassador to Paris . . . passed on a message to Jules Martin Cambon . . . that [Wilson believes] the object of the war . . . is the freedom of the peoples and the lasting security of the independent units into which they have formed

themselves. . . . The President believes that if only the Austrian people could be defini-tively satisfied upon these points the present movement in Austria looking toward a peace would become . . . irresistible" (vol. 43, p. 388). The story of successful efforts of the British to influence Wilson are seen in the (British) Public Records Office, "General Correspondence for 1917," especially FO 395/109, 395/134, 395/143. For British efforts from within the British Enemy Propaganda Office to influence American opinion, see Seton-Watson, *The Making of a New Europe,* especially pp. 237ff. See also Victor S. Mamatey, *The United States and East Central Europe 1914–1918: A Study in Wilsonian Diplomacy and Propaganda* (Princeton: Princeton University Press, 1957), and Eduard Beneš, *My War Memoirs,* trans. Paul Selver (London: Allen and Unwin, 1928).

18. Link, *The Woodrow Wilson Papers,* vol. 42, p. 171.

19. Link, *The Woodrow Wilson Papers,* vol. 42, p. 211; vol. 45, pp. 199–200. In a long statement by Thomas G. Masaryk, circulated by the British Enemy Propaganda Office in London in April of 1916, the Czech leader demonstrated how closely he had been attuned to British fears (that the Germans would win the war by maintaining the stalemate on the western front). Masaryk also demonstrated that he knew how to make good use of Wilson's altruistic impulses regarding national self-determination, remarking "that [originally] the allies had no . . . plan, each had a special plan of his own. . . . The allies must meet the German plan of Central Europe . . . by the plan of central Europe freed of German control. . . . I have attempted to show (the allies) that Central Europe contains a peculiar zone of smaller, unfree or half free nations, and that the political organization of this zone is the real task of this present war. . . . Germany's weak spot is in the east, not in the west. By liberating and organizing the smaller nations of Central Europe against German aggression. . . . will weaken [Germany] in the west and that is the only way. . . . The programme of the allies cannot be a mere plan to crush Germany. . . . It must be a plan of defense, a path for promoting the moral and political progress of Europe and of humanity." It should be added that the British Enemy Propaganda Office, under Lord Northcliffe, the publisher of the *London Times,* not only had the aid of the Masaryks, but also had the enthusiastic help of a number of British historians, including Lord Bryce, Arnold Toynbee, and Otto Trevelyn who, and with not with a little boastfulness, placed Clio at the feet of the department's chief. See (British) Public Record Office, "General Correspondence," FO 800/2090.

20. For a thorough discussion of the various political, cultural, and economic ramifi-cations surrounding the collapse of the Dual Monarchy, see Richard Georg Plaschka and Karlheinz Mack, eds., *Die Auflösung des HabsburgerReiches:* Zusammenbruch und Neu-orientierung im Donaurum (Munich: R. Oldenbourg, 1970); see especially the contribu-tion by Fritz Fellner, "Der Zerfall der Donaumonarchie in weltgeschichtlicher Perspektive," pp. 32–42.

21. For example, a Wilson confidant, George Creel, told the American president of a telegram sent to the *London Times* from a Mr. Henry Hall, which stated: "Today, thanks to Balfour [and] Northcliffe [we are] reading [the] American government and people [as] thoroughly convinced of [the] sincerity of British war aims . . . whereas formerly [a] very large [and] influential section [of] American opinion [was] frankly suspicious of Great Britain." Creel goes on to say that the *Times,* whose publisher was Lord Northcliffe, suppressed the telegram, not wanting it published lest it raise a counterpoint. See Link, *The Woodrow Wilson Papers,* vol. 48, p. 447.

Bibliography

Archives Consulted

Amsterdam, The Netherlands. *Archives, Institute for Social History.*
London, United Kingdom. *Public Record Office.*
Vienna, Austria. *Haus Hof-und Staats Archiv.*
Vienna, Austria. *Staats Archiv.*

Periodical Literature Variously Cited

Cambridge, United Kingdom. *The Historical Journal.*
London, United Kingdom. *London Times.*
New York, United States. *New York Review of Books.*
Oxford, United Kingdom, *History of European Ideas.*
Vienna, Austria. *Die Arbeiter Zeitung.*
Vienna, Austria. *Der Kampf: Sozialdemokratische Monatsschrift.*
Washington, United States. *Catholic Historical Review.*

Monographs, Memoirs, and Printed Archival Materials

Adler, Friedrich. *Gegen Krieg und Absolutismus.* Jena: Thüringer Verlaganstalt, 1925.
Allmayer-Beck, Johann Christoph. *Ministerpräsident Baron Beck: Ein Staatsmann des alten Österreich.* Munich: R. Oldenbourg, 1956.
Baernreither, J. M. *Fragments of a Political Diary.* Ed. Joseph Redlich. London: Macmillan, 1930.
Bauer, Otto. *Die österreichischen Sozialdemokratie und die Nationalitätenfrage.* Vienna: Volksbuchhandlung, 1906.
———. *Deutschtum und Sozialdemokratie.* Vienna: Volksbuchhandlung, 1907.
———. *Die österreichische Revolution.* Vienna: Wienervolksbuchhandlung, 1923.
Baumgart, Winfried. *Deutsche Östpolitik 1918: Von Brest-Litowsk bis zun Ende des Ersten Weltkrieges.* Vienna: R. Oldenbourg, 1966.
Beales, Derek. *Joseph II: In the Shadow of Maria Theresa, 1741–1780.* Cambridge: Cambridge University Press, 1987.
Beck, Otto Sammuel. *Die Wirtschafts-Gebiete an der Mittel-Donau vor dem Weltkrieg.* Vienna: Manzsch, 1922.
Beller, Steven. *Francis Joseph.* London: Longmans, 1996.
———. *Vienna and the Jews, 1867–1938: A Cultural History.* Cambridge: Cambridge University Press, 1989.
Benedikt, Heinrich. *Die Monarchie des Hauses Österreich: Ein historisches Essay.* Munich: R. Oldenbourg, 1968.
Berchtold, Klaus. *Österreichische Parteiprogramme: 1868–1966.* Vienna: Verlag für Geschichte und Politik, 1967.
Berg, Erich Alban. *Als der Adler noch Zwei Köpfe hatte.* Vienna: Styria Verlag, 1980.
Bernard, Paul P. *The Limits of Enlightenment: Joseph II and the Law.* Urbana: University of Illinois Press, 1979.

Bittner, Ludwig, and Hans Uebersberger, eds. and comps. *Österreich-Ungarns Aussenpolitik von der bosnischen Krise 1908 bis zum Kriegsausbruch 1914,* 9 volumes. Nendeln/Liechtenstein: Kraus Reprint, 1972.

Blaukopf, Kurt. *Mahler: A Documentary Study.* London: Thames and Hudson, 1976.

Bled, Jean-Paul. *François Joseph.* Paris: Librairie Arthème Fayard, 1987.

———. *Franz Joseph.* Trans. Teresa Bridgeman. Oxford: Blackwell, 1992.

Blum, Mark E. *The Austro-Marxists, 1890–1918: A Psychobiographical Study.* Lexington: University of Kentucky Press, 1986.

Botting, Douglas. *In the Ruins of the Reich.* New York: Meridian, 1986.

Boyer, John. *Political Radicalism in Late Imperial Vienna.* Chicago: University of Chicago Press, 1981.

Brachelle, H.F. *Statistische Skizze der österreichischen-ungarischen Monarchie.* 12th ed. Leipzig: Heinrich, 1889.

Braunbehrens, Volkmar. *Mozart in Vienna, 1781–1791.* Trans. Timothy Bell. New York: Harper, 1986.

Braunthal, Julius. *Viktor und Friedrich Adler: Zwei Generationen Arbeiterbewegung.* Vienna: Wiener Volksbuchhandlung, 1964.

Bridge, F. R. *From Sadowa to Sarajevo:The Foreign Policy of Austria-Hungary: 1866–1914.* London: Routledge and Kegan Paul, 1972.

———. *The Habsburg Monarchy Among the Great Powers, 1815–1918.* Oxford: Berg, 1990.

Brügel, Ludwig. *Geschichte der österreichischen Sozialdemokratie.* 5 volumes. Vienna: Volksbuchhandlung, 1925.

Cachee, Josef. *Die Hofküche des Kaisers: Die K.u.K. Hofküche, Die Hofzuckerbäckeri und der Hofkeller in der Wiener Hofburg.* Vienna: Amalthea, 1985.

Carsten, Francis Ludwig. *Faschismus im Österreich: von Schönerer zu Hitler.* Munich: Wilhelm Fink, 1977.

Cassels, Lavender. *Clash of Generations: A Habsburg Family Drama in the Nineteenth Century.* London: John Murry, 1973.

Clare, George. *Last Waltz in Vienna: The Destruction of A Family, 1842–1942* (London: Macmillan, 1982.

Clary-Aldringen, Alfons. *Geschichten eines alten Österreichers: Mit einem Vorwort von Golo Mann.* Frankurt am Main: Ullstein, 1977.

Cohen, Gary. *The Politics of Ethnic Survival: Germans in Prague, 1861–1914.* Princeton: Princeton University Press, 1981.

Conrad von Hötzendorf, Franz. *Aus Meiner Deinszeit: 1906–1918.* 5 volumes. Vienna: Rikola Verlag, 1921–25.

Cordfunke, E.H.P. *Zita, keizerin van Oostenrijk, koningin van Hongarije.* Amsterdam: Bataafsche Leeuw, 1986.

Corte, Egon César, and Hans Sokol. *Der alte Kaiser, Franz Joseph I.* Vienna: Styria Verlag, 1955.

Crankshaw, Edward. *Vienna: The Image of a Culture in Decline.* New York: Macmillan, 1938.

———. *The Fall of the House of Habsburg.* New York: Viking, 1965.

Creel, George. *How We Advertised America: The First Telling of the Amazing Story of the Committee of Public Information That Carried the Gospel of America to Every Corner of the Globe.* New York: Harper Brothers, 1920.

Czernin, Ottokar von und zu Chudenitz. *Im Weltkriege.* Berlin: Ullstein, 1919.

Deák, Istvan. *Beyond Nationalism: A Social and Political History of the Habsburg Officer Corps.* New York: Oxford University Press, 1990.

de Bourgoing, Jean, ed. *The Incredible Friendship: The Letters of Emperor Franz Joseph to Frau Katharina Schratt.* Trans. and ed. Evabeth Miller Kienast and Robert Rie. Albany: State University of New York Press, 1966.

Deuticke, Gabriele. *1895–1975: Mein Leben: Eine Zeit-und Familiengeschichte.* Vienna: Unpublished manuscript.

DÖSDAP. *Was Will die Sozialdemokratie?* Vienna: Volksbuchhandlung, 1912.

Dreger, Moriz. *Baugeschichte der K.u.K. Hofburg in Wien bis zum XIX Jahrhunderte.* Vienna: Anton Schroll, 1914.

Duffy, Christopher. *The Army of Maria Theresa: The Armed Forces of Imperial Austria, 1740–1780.* New York: Hippocrene Books, 1977.

Eder, Karl. *Der Liberalismus im Altösterreich.* Munich: R. Oldenbourg, 1965.

Edmondson, Clifton Earl. *The Heimwehr and Austrian Politics, 1918–1936.* Athens: University of Georgia Press, 1978.

Ernst, Otto, ed. *Franz Joseph as Revealed By His Letters.* Trans. Agnes Blake. London: Methuen, 1927.

Evans, Robert John Weston. *The Making of the Habsburg Monarchy, 1550–1700: An Interpretation.* Oxford: Oxford University Press, 1979.

Fainsod, Merle. *International Socialism and the World War.* Cambridge: Harvard University Press, 1935.

Fauland, Ferdinand. *Vorwiegend heiter: Von einem, d. auszog, General zu werden.* Vienna: Styria, 1980.

Feigl, Erich. *Kaiserin Zita: Legende und Wahrheit.* Vienna: Amalthea Verlag, 1978.

Fichtenau, Heinrich. *Von der Mark zum Herzogtum: Grundlagen und Sinn des privilegium minus für Österreich.* Munich: R. Oldenbourg, 1970.

Fischer, Fritz. *Griff nach der Weltmacht: die Kriegszielpolitik des kaiserlichen Deutschland, 1914/18.* Düsseldorf: Droste Verlag, 1961.

Fowler, W.B. *British-American Relations 1917–1918: The Role of Sir Wiliam Wiseman.* Princeton: Princeton University Press, 1969.

Francis, Mark E., ed. *The Viennese Enlightenment.* New York: St. Martin's Press, 1985.

Fried, Alfred. *Wien-Berlin: ein Vergleich.* Vienna: Josef Lenobel, 1908.

Fugger, Nora Fürstin. *Im Glanz der Kaiserzeit.* Vienna: Amalthea Verlag, 1980.

Funder, Friedrich. *Vom Gestern ins Heute: Aus dem Kaiserreich in die Republik.* Vienna: Herold, 1963.

Gankin, Olga Hess, and H.H. Fisher. *The Bolsheviks and the World War.* Stanford: Stanford University Press, 1960.

Geehr, Richard S. *Karl Lueger: Mayor of Fin-de-Siècle Vienna.* Detroit: Wayne State University Press, 1990.

Good, David F. *The Economic Rise of the Habsburg Empire, 1750–1914.* Berkeley: University of California Press, 1984.

Graf, Max. *Legend of a Music City.* New York: Philosophical Library, 1945.

Grossegger, Elisabeth. *Der Kaiser Huldigungs Festzug.* Vienna: österreichische Akademie der Wissenschafetn, 1922.

Habsburg, Rudolph, ed. *Die österreichische-ungarische Monarchie in Wort und Bild,* 24 volumes. Vienna: K.K. Hof-und Staats Druckerie, 1886–1902.

Haider, Edgard. *Verlorenes Wien: Adelspaläste Vergangener Tage.* Vienna: Hermann Böhlau, 1984.

Hantsch, Hugo. *Die Nationalitätenfrage im alten Österreich: das Problem der konstrucktiven Reichsgestatung.* Vienna: Herold, 1953.

Hamann, Brigitte. *The Reluctant Empress.* New York: Alfred A. Knopf, 1986.

———. *Meine liebe, gute Freundin !: Die Briefe Kaiser Franz Josephs an Katharina*

Schratt aus dem Besitz der österreichischen Nationalbibliotek. Vienna: Ueberreuter, 1992.

Hayes, Carlton, J.H. *A Generation of Materialism: 1871–1900.* New York: Harper and Row, 1941.

————. *Contemporary Europe Since 1870.* New York: Macmillan, 1958.

Heer, Friedrich. *Der Kampf um die österreichische Identität.* Vienna: Hermann Böhlau, 1981.

Heiszler, V., Szakács, M., Vörös, K. *Ein Photoalbum aus dem Hause Habsburg: Friedrich von Habsburg und seine Familie.* Vienna: Böhlau Verlag, 1989.

Herzog, Max, ed. *Viribus Unitis: Das Buch vom Kaiser.* Vienna: Herzig, 1898.

Hitler, Adolf. *Mein Kampf.* New York: Reynal and Hitchcock, 1940.

Hobsbawm, Eric J. *Nations and Nationalism Since 1780: Programme, Myth, Reality.* Cambridge: Cambridge University Press, 1990.

Hoebelt, Lothar. "Parliamentary Politics in a Multinational Setting: Late Imperial Austria." Center for Austrian Studies Working Paper, University of Minnesota, 1993.

Jaksch, Wenzel. *Europas Weg nach Potsdam.* Stuttgart: Deutscher Verlag, 1959.

Janik, Allan, and Stephen Toulmin. *Wittengenstein's Vienna.* New York: Simon and Schuster, 1973.

Jenks, William Alexander. *The Austrian Electoral Reform of 1907.* New York: Columbia University Press, 1950.

Judtmann, Fritz. *Mayerling ohne Mythos: Ein Tatsachenbericht.* Vienna: Kremayer and Scheriaw, 1968.

Kann, Robert A. *The Multinational Empire: Nationalism and National Reform in the Habsburg Monarchy, 1848–1918.* 2 volumes. New York: Columbia University Press, 1950.

————. *Die Sixtusaffäre und die geheimen Friedensverhandlungen Österreich-Ungarns im Ersten Weltkrieg.* Vienna: Verlag für Geschichte und Politik, 1966.

————. *Kaiser Franz Josephs und der Ausbruch des Weltkrieges: Eine Betrachtung uber den Quellenwert d. Aufzeichungen von Dr. Heinrich Kanner.* Vienna: Akademie der Wissenschaften, 1971.

————. *Renners Beitrag zur Lösung nationaler Konflikte im Lichte nationaler Probleme der Gegenwart.* Vienna: Österreichischen Akademie der Wissenschaft, 1973.

————. *Franz Ferdinand Studien.* Cambridge: Cambridge University Press, 1974.

————. *Dynasty, Politics and Culture: Selected Essays.* Boulder, CO: Social Science Monographs, 1991.

Kann, Robert A., and Zdenek V. David. *The Peoples of the Eastern Habsburg Lands, 1526–1918.* Seattle: University of Washington Press, 1984.

Katz, Jacob ed. *Toward Modernity: The European Jewish Model.* New Brunswick, NJ: Transaction Books, 1986.

Ketterl, Eugen. *The Emperor Franz Joseph I: An Intimate Study by His Valet du Chambre.* London: Skefferington, no date.

Kielmansegg, Erich. *Kaiserhaus, Staatsmänner, und Politiker.* Vienna: R. Oldenbourg, 1966.

Kiszling, Rudolf. *Erzherzog Franz Ferdinand von Österreich-Este: Leben, Pläne und Wirken am Schicksalsweg der Donaumonarchie.* Graz-Cologne: H. Böhlau Nachf., 1953.

Komlos, John, ed. *Economic Development in the Habsburg Monarchy in the Nineteenth Century.* Boulder, CO: East European Monographs, 1983.

Kraus, Karl. *Werke.* Ed. Heinrich Fischer. 14 volumes. Munich: Kösel Verlag, 1952–1966.

————. *Die letzten Tage der Menschheit: Tragodie in funf Akten*. Munich: Kösel Verlag, 1957.

————. *Literatur und Lüge*. Munich: Kösel Verlag, 1974.

Lackey, Scott. *The Rebirth of the Habsburg Army: Friedrich Beck and the Rise of the General Staff*. Westport, CT: Greenwood Press, 1995.

La Grange, Henry-Louis de. *Mahler: The Years of Challenge, 1897–1904*, vol. 2. New York: Oxford University Press, 1924.

Lammasch, Heinrich. *Europas Elfte Stunde*. Munich: Verlag für Kulturpolitik, 1919.

Langseth-Christensen, Lillian. *A Design for Living*. New York: Viking, 1987.

Lechner, Karl. *Die Babenburger: Markgrafen und Herzöge von Österreich 976–1246*. Vienna: Böhlau, 1976.

Leitich, Ann Tizia. *Vienna Gloriosa: Weltstadt des Barock*. Vienna: Wilhelm Andermann, 1947.

Lhotsky, Alphons. *Aufsatze und Vortrage*. 2 volumes. Munich: R. Oldenbourg, 1970.

Link, Arthur S. *The Woodrow Wilson Papers*. 58 volumes. Princeton: Princeton University Press, 1983.

Lobkowicz, Erwein. *Erinnerungen an die Monarchie*. Vienna: Amalthea Verlag, 1989.

Luft, David S. *Robert Musil and the Crisis of European Culture, 1880–1942*. Berkeley: University of California Press, 1980.

Lützow, Heinrich. *Im Diplomatischen Dienst der K.u.K. Monarchie*. Munich: R. Oldenbourg, 1971.

McCartney, C. A. *National States and National Minorities*. London: Oxford University Press, 1934.

Mamatey, Victor S. *The United States and East Central Europe, 1914–1918: A Study in Wilsonian Diplomacy and Propaganda*. Princeton: Princeton University Press, 1957.

————. *The Rise of the Habsburg Empire, 1526–1815*. New York: Holt, Rinehart and Winston, 1971.

Margutti, Albert Alexander Vinzenz. *Vom Alten Kaiser persönlich errinerungen an Franz Joseph I, Kaiser von Österreich König von Ungarn*. Leipzig: Leonhardt, 1921.

Markus, Georg, ed. *Der Kaiser: Franz Joseph I, Bilder und Dokumente*. Vienna: Amaltha Verlag, 1985.

Martin, Gunther. *Als Victorianer in Wien: Errinnerungen des britischen Diplomaten*. Vienna: österreichischer Bundesverlag, 1984.

Masaryk, Tomas Garrigue. *The Making of a State: Memories and Observations, 1914–1918*. New York: Frederick A. Stokes, 1927.

Matsch, Erwin, ed. *November 1918 auf dem Ballhausplatz: Erinnerungen Ludwig Freiherrn von Lutzow des Letzten Chefs des österreichischen Auswäartigen Dienst, 1895–1920*. Munich: Hermann Böhlau Nachfolger, 1982.

May, Arthur J. *The Hapsburg Monarchy, 1867–1914*. Cambridge: Harvard University Press, 1960.

————. *The Passing of the Habsburg Monarchy, 1914–1918*, 2 volumes. Philadelphia: University of Pennsylvania Press, 1966.

McCagg, William O. *A History of Habsburg Jews, 1670–1918*. Bloomington: Indiana University Press, 1989.

McGrath, William J. *Freud's Discovery of Psychoanalysis: The Politics of Hysteria*. Ithaca: Cornell University Press, 1986.

————. *Dionysian Art and Populist Politics in Austria*. New Haven: Yale University Press, 1974.

Meckling, Ingebord. *Die Aussenpolitik des Grafen Czernin*. Vienna: Verlag für Geschichte und Politik, 1969.

Mikoletzky, H.L. *Kaiser Franz I und der Ursprung der habsburgisch-lothringischen Familienenvermögens.* Vienna: Österreich-Archiv, 1961.

Molisch, Paul. *Geschichte der Deutschnationalen Bewegung in Österreich von ihren Anfängen bis zum Zerfall der Monarchie.* Jena: Gustav Fischer, 1926.

Mommsen, Hans. *Die Sozialdemokratie und die Nationalitätenfrage in Habsburger Vielvolkerstaat.* Vienna: Europa Verlag, 1963.

Musil, Robert. *The Man Without Qualities.* New York: Capricorn, 1965.

Nahowski, Anna. *Anna Nahowski und Kaiser Franz Joseph: Aufzeichnungen.* Ed. Friedrich Saathen. Vienna: Böhlau, 1980.

Naumann, Friedrich. *Mittel-Europa.* Berlin: Ulstein, 1915.

Nostitz-Rieneck, Georg. *Briefe Kaiser Franz Josephs an Kaiserin Elisabeth,* 2 volumes. Vienna: Herold, 1966.

Palmer, Alan. *Twilight of the Habsburgs: The Life and Times of Emperor Francis Joseph.* New York: Grove Press, 1995.

Pauley, Bruce. *The Habsburg Legacy, 1867–1939.* New York: Holt, Rinehart and Winston, 1972.

————. *Hitler and the Forgotten Nazis: A History of Austrian National Socialism.* Chapel Hill: University of North Carolina Press, 1981.

————. *From Prejudice to Persecution: A History of Austrian Anti-Semitism.* Chapel Hill: University of North Carolina Press, 1992.

Petermann, Reinhard. *Wien im Zeitalter Kaiser Franz Josephs I.* Vienna: Verlag R. Lechner, 1913.

Plaschka, Richard Georg, and Mack, Karlheinz, eds. *Die Auflösung des Habsburgerreiches: Zusammenbruch und Neuorientierung im Donäraum.* Munich: R. Oldenbourg, 1970.

Polatschek, Max. *Franz Ferdinand: Europas verlorene Hoffung.* Vienna Amalthea Verlag, 1989.

Polzer-Hoditz und Wolframitz, Arthur. *The Emperor Karl.* Boston: Houghton Miffin, 1922.

Popovici, Aurel C. *Die Vereinigten Staaten von Gross-Österreich.* Leipzig: B. Elischer Nachfolger, 1906.

————. *Die Rumanienfrage in Transylvanien und in Ungarn: Antwort der Rumanien Studeten der Transylvanien und Ungarn.* Antwerp: Jos. Theunis, 1892.

Pulzer, Peter G.J. *The Rise of Political Anti-Semitism in Germany and Austria.* New York: Wiley, 1964.

Redlich, Josef. *Kaiser Franz Joseph von Österreich.* Berlin: Ullstein, 1929.

Renner, Karl. *Osterreichs Erneuerung.* Vienna: I. Brand, 1916.

————. *Die Nation als Reichsidee.* Vienna: Ignaz Brand, 1914.

————. *Grundlagen und Entwicklungsziele der österreichisch-ungarischen Monarchie.* Vienna: Franz Deuticke, 1906.

Robertson, Ritchie, and Timms, Edward, eds. *The Habsburg Legacy: National Identity in Historical Perspective.* Edinburgh: Edinburgh University Press, 1994.

Rocker, Rudolf. *Nationalism and Culture.* Los Angeles: Rocker Publications Committee, 1937.

Roth, Joseph. *Radetzky March.* Berlin: Gustav Kiepenheuer Verlag, 1932.

Rothenberg, Gunther. *The Army of Francis Joseph.* West Lafayette, IN: Purdue University Press, 1976.

Rutkowski, Ernst, ed. *Briefe und Dokumente zur Geschichte der österreichisch-ungarischen Monarchie,* Teil I and II, *"Der Verfassungstreue Grossgrundbesitz, 1880–1898."* Munich: R. Oldenbourg, 1983.

Schneider, Josef, ed., *Kaiser Franz Joseph I und seine Hof: Erinnerungen und Schilderungen aus den nachgelassen en Papieren eines persönlichen Ratgebers.* Vienna: Leonhardt, 1919.

Schnitzler, Arthur. *Weg ins Freie.* Berlin: Fischer Verlag, 1920.

————. *My Youth in Vienna,* trans. Cathrine Hutter. New York: Holt, Rinehart and Winston, 1970.

————. *The Road into the Open,* trans. Roger Bayers. Berkeley: University of California Press, 1992.

————. *The Road to the Open,* trans. Horace Samuel. New York: Alfred A. Knopf, 1923.

Schnürer, Franz. *Briefe Kaiser Franz Joseph I an seine Mutter: 1838–1872.* Munich: R. Oldenbourg, 1938.

Schoenfeld, Jochim. *Shtetl Memories: Jewish Life in Galicia under the Austro-Hungarian Empire and in the Reborn Poland, 1898–1939.* Hoboken, NJ: Ktav Publishing House, 1985.

Schöffer, Peter. *Der Wahlrechtskampf der österreichischen Sozialdemokratie: 1888/89–1887.* Wiesbaden: Franz Steiner Verlag, 1986.

Schorske, Carl E. *Fin-de-Siècle Vienna: Politics and Culture.* New York: Alfred A. Knopf, 1981.

Schuschnigg, Kurt. *The Brutal Takeover: The Austrian Ex-Chancellor's Account of the Anschluss of Austria by Hitler.* New York: Atheneum, 1971.

Schwarzenberg, Adolph. *Prince Felix zu Schwarzenberg, Prime Minister of Austria, 1848–1852.* New York: Columbia University Press, 1946.

Seipel, Ignaz. *Staat und Nation.* Vienna: Braümuller, 1916.

Seton-Watson, Robert W. *Masaryk in England.* Cambridge: Cambridge University Press, 1943.

Seton-Watson, Hugh, and Christopher Seton-Watson. *The Making of a New Europe: R.W. Seton-Watson and the Last Years of Austria-Hungary.* Seattle: University of Washington Press, 1981.

Shanafelt, Gary. *The Secret Enemy: Austria-Hungary and the German Alliance, 1914–1918.* Boulder, CO: East European Monographs. 1985.

Shedel, James. *Art and Society: The New Art Movement in Vienna, 1897–1914.* Palo Alto, CA: Society for the Promotion of Science and Scholarship. 1981.

Sked, Alan. *The Decline and Fall of the Habsburg Empire, 1815–1918.* London: Longman, 1989.

Sondhaus, Lawrence. *The Naval Policy of Austria-Hungary, 1867–1918: Navalism, Industrial Development, and the Politics of Dualism.* West Lafayette, IN: Purdue University Press, 1994.

Spiel, Hilde. *Wien: Spektrum einer Stadt.* Munich: Biederstein, 1971.

Springer, Rudolf (Karl Renner). *Grundlagen und Entwicklungsziele österreichischen-ungarischen Monarchie.* Vienna: Franz Deuticke, 1906.

Srbik, Heinrich, *Quellen zur deutschen Politik Österreichs 1859–1866,* 5 volumes. Osnabrück: Biblio Verlag,1967.

Stern, Fritz. *The Politics of Cultural Despair: A Study in the Rise of the Germanic Ideology.* Berkeley: University of California Press, 1961.

Strong, David. *Austria (October 1918–March 1919): Transition from Empire to Republic.* New York: Columbia University Press.

Swistun, Hermann, and Baltazzi-Scharschmid, Heinrich, *Die Familien Baltazzi-Vetsera im kaiserlichen Wien.* Vienna: Hermann Böhlau, 1980.

Taylor, A.J.P. *The Struggle for Mastery in Europe, 1848–1918.* Oxford: Clarendon Press, 1957.

Tezner, Friedrich. *Die Wandlungen der österreichischen-ungarischen Reichsidee.* Vienna: Manz, 1905.

Thomson, S.H. *Czechoslovakia in European History.* Princeton: Princeton University Press, 1943.

Trost, Ernst. *Franz Joseph I von Gottes Gnaden Kaiser von Österreich apostolischer König von Ungarn.* Vienna: Fritz Molden, 1980.

Vasari, E. *Zita: Kaiserin und Königin.* Vienna: Herold, 1976.

Vivian, Herbert. *The Life of Kaiser Karl of Austria.* London: Grayson and Grayson, 1932.

Von Klemperer, Klemens. *Ignaz Seipel: Christian Statesman in a Time of Crisis.* Princeton: Princeton University Press, 1972.

Waissenberger, Robert ed. *Wien 1870–1930: Traum und Wirklichkeit.* Vienna: Residenz Verlag, 1984.

Watt, Richard M. *The Kings Depart: The Tragedy of Germany: Versailles and the German Revolution.* New York: Simon and Schuster, 1968.

Weininger, Otto. *Geschlecht und Charakter: Eine prinzipielle Untersuchung.* Vienna: Wilhelm Braümuller, 1908.

Werkmann von Hohensalzburg, Karl Martin. *The Tragedy of Charles of Habsburg.* London: P. Allen, 1924.

Whiteside, Andrew Gladding. *Austrian National Socialism Before 1918.* The Hague: Nijhoff, 1962.

———. *The Socialism of Fools: Georg Ritter von Schönerer and Austrian Pan-Germanism.* Berkeley: University of California Press, 1975.

Wiessensteiner, Friedrich. *Franz Ferdinand: Der Verhinderte Herrscher, Zum 70. Jahrestag von Sarajevo:* Vienna: Österreichischer Bundesverlag, 1983.

Wiskemann, Elizabeth. *Czechs and Germans.* New York: Oxford University Press, 1938.

Wistrich, Robert. *Socialism and the Jews: The Dilemmas of Assimilation in Germany and Austria-Hungary.* Rutherford, NJ: Fairleigh Dickinson University Press, 1982.

Zohn, Harry. *Half Truths and One-And-A-Half Truths.* Montreal: Engendra Press, 1976.

———. *In These Great Times: A Karl Kraus Reader.* Montreal: Engendra Press, 1976.

Zweig, Stefan. *The World of Yesterday: An Autobiography by Stefan Zweig.* Lincoln: University of Nebraska Press, 1965.

———. *Die Welt von Gestern, Errinnerungen eines Europaers.* Berlin: Fischer, 1968.

Multi-Author Works Consulted

Akadémiai Kiadó. *Die Nationale Frage in der Österreich-ungarnischen Monarchie.* Budapest: Verlag der ungarischen Akademie der Wissenschaften, 1966.

Lemberg, Hans; Litsch, Karel; Plaschka, Richard Georg; Ranki, Gyorgy; eds. *Bildungsgeschichte, Bevoelkerungsgeschichte, Gesellschaftsgeschichte in den Boehmischen Ländern und in Europa: Festschrift für Jan Havranek zum 60 Geburtstag.* Vienna: Verlag für Geschichte und Politik, 1988.

Engel-Janosi, Friedrich. *Probleme der Franzisko-Josephinischen Zeit, 1848–1916.* Vienna: Verlag für Geschichte und Politik, 1967.

Pfabigan, Alfred, ed. *Ornament und Askese im Zeitgeist des Wien Jahrhundertwende.* Vienna: Brandstätter, 1985.

Schloss Grafenegg. *Das Zeitalter Kaiser Franz Josephs: Von der Revolution zur Grunderzeit,* 2 volumes. Vienna: NÖ Landesmuseums, 1984.

———. *Das Zeitalter Kaiser Franz Josephs: 2 Teil. Glanz und Elend,* Katalog und Beiträge. Vienna. NÖ Landesmuseums, 1987.

Schloss Luberegg. *Kaiser Franz und seine Zeit: Von der Franz Revolution bis zum Wiener Kongress.* Marbach/Donau: J.& H. Sandler, 1991.

Virginia Humanities Conference. *The Treaty of Versailles and the Shaping of the Modern World.* Staunton, VA: 1989.

Wandruszka, Adam, and Urbanitsch, Peter, eds. *Das Hasburger-Monarchie: 1848–1918.* Three volumes. Vienna: Verlag des österreichischen Akadamie der wissenschaften, 1980.

Wagner-Rieger, Renate, ed. *Die Wiener Ringstrasse: Bild einer Epoche; die Erweiterung der inneren Stadt Wien unter Kaiser Franz Joseph.* 10 volumes. Vienna: H. Böhlau Nachf., 1969–.

Index

About the Author

George V. Strong teaches modern and recent European history at the College of William and Mary in Williamsburg, Virginia. He received his Ph.D. in history at the University of North Carolina at Chapel Hill. He is the author of many articles and reviews dealing with German and in particular, Habsburg history. He is an active member of the German Studies Association and often a participant in the Bradley University Berlin Seminar, which has enabled the author to both renew his interest in the past of central and south-central Europe as well as maintain a grasp on the unfolding contemporary events that so dramatically have been reshaping the region since 1990.